FINANCIAL
TERRORISM

FINANCIAL TERRORISM

Hijacking America Under the Threat of Bankruptcy

John F. McManus

The John Birch Society
Appleton, Wisconsin

First Printing .... November 1993

Published by
The John Birch Society
Post Office Box 8040
Appleton, Wisconsin 54913
(414) 749–3780

Printed in the United States of America
Library of Congress Catalog Card Number: 93–080358
ISBN: 1–881919–02–1

The preservation of the sacred fire of liberty, and the destiny of the republican model of government, are justly considered as deeply, perhaps as finally staked, on the experiment entrusted to the hands of the American people.

— George Washington
First Inaugural Address
April 30, 1789

Liberty cannot be preserved without a general knowledge among the people, who have a right ... and a desire to know; but besides this, they have a right, an indisputable, unalienable, indefeasible, divine right to that most dreaded and envied kind of knowledge, I mean of the characters and conduct of their rulers.

— John Adams
A Dissertation on the Canon and Feudal Law
1765

I know no safe depository of the ultimate powers of the society but the people themselves; and if we think them not enlightened enough to exercise their control with a wholesome discretion, the remedy is not to take it from them, but to inform their discretion.

— Thomas Jefferson
Letter to William Charles Jarvis
September 28, 1820

To my wife Mary with deep gratitude
for so many years of love and support;
to our wonderful sons and daughters;
and to my inestimable colleagues for
their encouragement and assistance.

Contents

CONTENTS

Introduction

If you want a picture of the future, imagine a boot stamping on a human face forever.

— George Orwell
Nineteen Eighty-Four [1]

Debt, deficits, taxation, regulation, and all the other hallmarks of economic slavery are already ravaging this nation. If the designs of those who are plunging America into economic catastrophe aren't blocked — and soon — America's future will resemble what novelist George Orwell had one of his characters forecast in his prophetic *Nineteen Eighty-Four*.

Orwell's famous book has given our language several expressions in common use today. Many Americans who have no idea where these terms came from can be heard referring to "Big Brother," "memory hole," "thought police," and "newspeak." They owe a debt to George Orwell and the novel he wrote that described a future existence under totalitarian dictators. That such expressions would be as well used and well understood today is not surprising, since America is heading toward the conditions Orwell was trying to prevent.

This same George Orwell (1903-1950) once stated in "Why I Write," an article he penned just before he died: "Every line of serious work I have written since 1936 has been written, directly or indirectly, against totalitarianism." [2] Educated at Eton, he authored over a dozen books, the most famous of which are *Animal Farm* (1946) and *Nineteen Eighty-Four* (1949). These two works are his most important warnings about the sinister designs of the socialists with whom he mingled during most of his adult life.

---

1. George Orwell, *Nineteen Eighty-Four* (New York, NY: Harcourt Brace Jovanovich, 1949).
2. C.M. Woodhouse's introduction to *Animal Farm*, (New York, NY: Signet Classics, The New American Library, 1946).

1

The "New World Order"

George Orwell never used the phrase George Bush made famous during 1990-1991. But the great English author's many warnings about totalitarians can well be applied to what it has long signified. Anyone who failed to hear any of President Bush's calls for a "new world order" during and after his campaign against Iraq had to have been fast asleep. He used the phrase repeatedly in public utterances from mid-1990 to mid-1991.[3] And he just as repeatedly included with it his hopes for a revitalization of the United Nations, the international organization intended by its creators to become a world government.[4]

Therefore, we know from the former President himself that his understanding of a "new world order" included a determined commitment to the United Nations. But it is curious in the extreme to know that even his closest advisers regularly admitted that the President never fully explained what he meant by the phrase. They even peddled the idea that Mr. Bush's national security adviser, Brent Scowcroft, dreamed up the phrase while he and the President were boating in the Atlantic off Kennebunkport in August 1990.[5]

Dreamed up by Brent Scowcroft in August 1990? Balderdash! Anyone making such a claim is hiding something. The phrase has been used for decades by individuals who were promoting world

---

3. Examples: 1. September 11, 1990: "Out of these troubled times, our fifth objective — a new world order — can emerge.... We are in sight of a United Nations that performs as envisioned by its founders." 2. January 9, 1991: "[The Gulf crisis] has to do with a new world order. And that world order is only going to be enhanced if this newly activated peacekeeping function of the United Nations proves to be effective." 3. January 16, 1991: "When we are successful, and we will be, we have a real chance at this new world order, an order in which a credible United Nations can use its peacekeeping role to fulfill the promise and vision of the UN's founders."

4. For the world government designs of the UN, see G. Edward Griffin, *The Fearful Master* (Appleton, WI: Western Islands, 1964); Robert W. Lee, *The United Nations Conspiracy* (Western Islands, 1981); William F. Jasper, *Global Tyranny ... Step By Step* (Western Islands, 1992).

5. Doyle McManus, "A New World Order: Bush's Vision Still Fuzzy," *Milwaukee Journal*, February 24, 1991.

government and its economic companion, totalitarian socialism.[6]

For more than 20 years, members of the John Birch Society (JBS) have also been referring to the "new world order," not to enthuse about it or adopt it as a slogan as George Bush did, but to show that it has long been a battle cry of the enemies of freedom.

JBS members came to know of the existence and significance of the phrase because Society founder Robert Welch had frequently pointed to its use by the agents of a powerfully entrenched conspiracy. In the September 1972 JBS *Bulletin*, for example, Welch wrote:

> The plan is to establish — very soon — the first stages of a "new world order" ... for which a self-perpetuating inner circle of Conspirators has been working and scheming relentlessly during some six generations.

Then, in the October 1974 JBS *Bulletin*, the same Robert Welch declared that the plans of the conspirators "include the conversion of the United States into a socialist nation ... and [its] merger ... into a new world order." In his view, and in the view of other clear-headed students of history, the "new world order" meant political dominance over the planet via the United Nations and economic subjugation of all mankind via socialism.[7]

---

6. Samuel Zane Batten, *The New World Order* (Philadelphia, PA: American Baptist Publication Society, 1919); Frederick Charles Hicks, *The New World Order* (Garden City, NY: Doubleday, Page and Company, 1920); H.G. Wells, *The New World Order* (New York, NY: A. A. Knopf, 1940.); Dennis L. Cuddy, Ph.D., *The New World Order, A Critique and a Chronology* (Milford, PA: America's Future, 1992). See also, among scores of examples, Nelson Rockefeller's Washington, DC speech delivered on July 25, 1968; Richard Nixon's February 25, 1972 toast to Chou En-lai in Peking; Henry Steele Commager's sovereignty-compromising "Declaration of Interdependence" in 1975; Fidel Castro's speech at United Nations headquarters on October 11, 1979; and Mikhail Gorbachev's speech at Stanford University on June 4, 1990 (two months before the purported creation of the term by Brent Scowcroft during the boat ride).

7. Socialism, under any of its forms (communism, socialism, fascism, naziism),

Economic Control: Part of the Plan

The purpose of this book is to sound an alarm to Americans that a dreaded "new world order" is being built around them. We don't intend to dwell on the ominously growing political and military power being acquired by the United Nations. Our colleague, William F. Jasper, has done exactly that with his magnificent book, *Global Tyranny ... Step By Step.*[8]

Instead, we will focus only on the steps being taken to build economic control over this nation as a certain route toward completing the enslavement of the American people. In a nutshell, this is the "new world order." While we will concentrate most heavily on our own government's destructive economic policies, we will also unmask plans of the new world order's apostles to cede the control they are amassing to the UN — as soon as they dare.

Both President Clinton and a supine Congress are continuing the drive toward George Bush's goal of a "reinvigorated United Nations."[9] In doing so, they are simultaneously following the lead of several past administrations and Congresses by arranging for the economic impoverishment and bureaucratic regimentation of the American people.

As we will further detail in these pages, national policies built around debt, deficits, inflation, taxation and regulation add up to war being waged on the American people by our own government. Has it all been planned? Consider:

In 1912, the man who one year later became the chief advisor and constant companion of President Woodrow Wilson, Edward

---

is simply economic control of the people by government. Achieved via taxation, regulations, controls, bureaucracy, and Big Brother omnipresence, it does not always include outright ownership of property. Under the form of socialism known as fascism, for instance, government exercises control over but does not own the means of production. Ultimately, any form of socialism amounts to totalitarian slavery for those who are unfortunate enough to become its victims.

8. William F. Jasper, *Global Tyranny ... Step By Step*, op. cit.

9. Mr. Bush stated this goal explicitly in a published interview appearing in *U.S. News & World Report*, January 7, 1991.)

Mandell House, released his book *Philip Dru: Administrator*.[10] In this fictionalized account of the kind of world House envisioned, he stated that he wished to establish "Socialism as dreamed of by Karl Marx...." As steps toward his goal, the book called for passage of a graduated income tax and the creation of a central bank that would provide "a flexible [inflatable non-metallic] currency." The graduated income tax and the central bank are two of the ten planks of the *Communist Manifesto* given to the world in 1848 by Karl Marx and Frederick Engels. America has been saddled with each since 1913.

Charles Seymour's *The Intimate Papers of Colonel House*[11] notes that this man was the "unseen guardian angel" behind the passage of the act creating the Federal Reserve. House's Marxian goal for America could not be achieved without either the Fed or the income tax, both of which came to life in 1913. Once initiated, the two mechanisms began speeding America toward the totalitarian socialism favored by Marx, House, and contemporary builders of the new world order.

During the period 1919-1921, House led the group that founded the Council on Foreign Relations (CFR) from which was eventually spawned the Trilateral Commission (TC). Along with other elitist power centers, these two organizations have been working covertly yet diligently to implement House's goals. Yet few in America are aware of the conspiratorial scheming behind our nation's continuing drift away from independence and the free enterprise system. Some who have been provided copious evidence about the monster plot have shrugged it off as if it were mere fantasy.

The diabolical conspiracy behind the ongoing destruction of our nation must be exposed and cast aside. If it is not, then the "self-perpetuating inner circle of Conspirators," to use Robert Welch's words, will indeed merge our nation with the rest of mankind in

---

10. Edward Mandell House, *Philip Dru: Administrator* (New York, NY: Huebsch, 1912).
11. Charles Seymour, *The Intimate Papers of Colonel House* (Boston, MA: Houghton Miflin, 1926).

a centrally managed economic system under a totalitarian world government. And Americans — along with the rest of the human race — will be their slaves.

These Problems Are Not Mistakes

We are acutely aware that numerous books, a never-ending stream of organizations, and a considerable number of political leaders and opinion molders have denounced the U.S. government's fiscal irresponsibility. They have warned about apocalyptic debt, looming bankruptcy, crippling regulation, etc. Unfortunately, virtually all would have the public believe that each problem — or the sum of all of them — results from the *mistaken* policies of well-intentioned leaders.

But if behind-the-scenes Insiders of a conspiracy are diligently working to have America commit fiscal suicide, such a conclusion is naive at best and supportive of the plot at worst. Believing that the many steps of a deliberate plan constitute a never-ending parade of witless mistakes and pathetic luck poses no threat to the conspirators and, intentionally or otherwise, actually serves to blunt the motivations of citizens who might otherwise resist. Propagating such a view throws a blanket of obfuscation over deliberate wrongdoing. And such a blanket is silently yet joyously welcomed by the plotters.

Conspirators aren't blunderers who make mistakes; they are calculating evil-doers. They seize power and wealth and then provide rewards to self-promoters who follow their lead and carry out their plans. Many ambitious and amoral individuals who care little about their nation or their fellow man are only too eager to accept the conspiracy's plums.

To be combatted effectively, a conspiracy must be exposed. When it is, the legions of self-promoters will cease doing its evil work.

This book, therefore, will not offer excuses for what we believe is abject treachery. Unlike other analyses of America's rapid descent into a fiscal abyss, we will present evidence of a well-advanced plot, not another apologia for haphazard ineptitude.

On the Road to Suicide

In 1838, a country lawyer from Springfield, Illinois named Abraham Lincoln looked at his country and concluded that it could never be destroyed except from within. Here is how he put it:

> At what point shall we expect the approach of danger? By what means shall we fortify against it? Shall we expect some transatlantic military giant to step the ocean and crush us with a single blow?
>
> All the armies of Europe, Asia and Africa combined ... could not by force take a drink from the Ohio, or make a track on the Blue Ridge in a trial of a thousand years.
>
> At what point then is the approach of danger to be expected? I answer, if it ever reach us, it must spring up amongst us. It cannot come from abroad. If destruction be our lot, we must ourselves be its author and finisher. As a nation of freemen, we must live through all times, or die by suicide.

Even before Lincoln's warning, President Andrew Jackson sounded a similar alarm. To Americans in his day, he declared:

> From the earliest ages of history to the present day there have never been thirteen millions of people associated in one political body who enjoyed so much freedom and happiness as the people of these United States. You have no longer any cause to fear dangers from abroad.... It is from within, among yourselves — from cupidity, from corruption, from disappointed ambition and inordinate thirst for power — that factions will be formed and liberty endangered....[12]

Closer to our own times, James Forrestal (1892-1949), our nation's first Secretary of Defense, concluded that random incompetence was assuredly not the root cause of America's suicidal

---

12. *The Meaning of Jacksonian Democracy*, edited by Edwin C. Rozwenc (Boston, MA: Heath, 1963), cited by William P. Hoar, *Architects of Conspiracy* (Appleton, WI: Western Islands, 1984), p. 28.

policies. He issued the following tart assessment of those responsible for a steady stream of foreign policy defeats:

> Consistency has never been a mark of stupidity. If they were
> merely stupid, they would make a mistake in our favor at least once
> in a while.

As growing debt, deficits, taxation, and controls strangle our
nation and our people, more Americans — even without an
awareness of extensive evidence to back up their assessment —
are arriving at a Forrestal-like conclusion about current national
leaders. The actions of those who have placed our nation in jeopardy are both consistent — and consistently harmful. We are not
being victimized by mistakes; our nation is slowly and deliberately being "suicided."[13]

The book you are about to read details the severity of America's
fiscal problems and their underlying cause. It also shows what
can be done to rescue our nation and ourselves. Toward its conclusion, there are assessments of several programs offered by others supposedly to solve America's woes. Practically all of them,
sad to say, are either absurdities, wishful-thinking nonsense, or
even deliberately contrived tangents designed to steer concerned
Americans into inconsequential busywork.

In all of what follows, our main purpose is to show that America
can survive. There is hope for the future. We can get out of the
mess that has been created by venal politicians and downright
conspirators. We can pass on to our children and our children's
children the marvelous legacy of freedom earned for us so long
ago by brave and far-seeing individuals. But the route to survival

---

13. Evidence to support the conclusion that a conspiracy is deliberately destroying this nation has been summarized in several carefully documented books
published by Western Islands, Appleton, WI 54913: *The Invisible Government*
by Dan Smoot; *Conspiracy Against God and Man* by Rev. Clarence Kelly; *Architects of Conspiracy* by William P. Hoar; *The Shadows of Power* by James
Perloff; *The Insiders* by this author; and *Global Tyranny ... Step By Step* by
William F. Jasper. There are also scores of valuable works supplying additional evidence available from other publishing houses.

must begin with an awareness that America is gripped by a conspiracy that is steadily tightening its grip.

America's founders knew enough about history and human nature to build a nation based solidly on the belief that government is hardly ever the solution and is usually the problem. That kind of sound thinking must again become dominant. If it doesn't, the "new world order" complete with Gestapo-like police in UN blue helmets, terror on a massive scale, and a United States reduced to poverty will become our hellish reality.

If the warning we are issuing isn't heeded, the American people will surely find themselves in bondage. And children of the future who ask their parents why such a fate wasn't prevented will receive little more than guilt-ridden and totally deficient responses.

Famed novelist George Orwell feared that the future would resemble "a boot stamping on a human face — forever."

Though he regularly touted the "new world order," George Bush studiously avoided telling the public what it has always meant.

John Birch Society founder Robert Welch warned repeatedly about the "new world order."

Brent Scowcroft was wrongly credited for dreaming up the phrase "new world order."

Goal Of Rockfeller—
'A New World Order'

WASHINGTON (AP) — New York Gov. Nelson A. Rockefeller says as president he would work toward international creation of "a new world order"...

...contender said he would begin a dialogue with Red China, if elected, to "improve the possibilities of accommodations" with that country as well as the...he would...race and...

...said this country and the Soviets must cooperate to prevent small wars in areas such as the Middle East from mushrooming into big ones.

Despite a long Communist record of broken commitments and the fact that Communist ideology remains hostile, he said, "we must also face the fact that the imperatives of the modern age impose the necessity for peace.

"We have no need to be mesmerized by our perils," Rockefeller said. "The possibility to build the new order we all seek is limited only by our imagination and dedication."

But he said there is no way to know when a "basic accommodation" would become possible.

...national Platform Association, an organization of professional lecturers.

Sen. Eugene J. McCarthy, a Democratic presidential aspirant, indicated meanwhile he will drop hopes of meeting with North Vietnamese diplomats in Paris to learn first hand the prospects for settlement of the Vietnam war.

McCarthy said in view of the Honolulu communique issued Sunday by President Johnson and South Vt rPsdneadmietn and South Vietnam President Nguyen Van Thieu, "the chances of my doing any good are significantly reduced."

He said the communique indicating this country will not further reduce its military action...

Nelson Rockefeller wanted a "new world order" in 1969 and worked for it during his entire life.

The Post-Register

East Idaho
★ Final ★

EAST IDAHO'S HOME PAPER — 99 YEARS OF SERVICE

Idaho Falls, Idaho, Friday, Oct. 12, 1979

Fidel Castro demands 'new world order'

By JOHN BAUSMAN
Associated Press Writer

UNITED NATIONS (AP) — Cuban President Fidel Castro, finger waving in the air and angry fist...

Demands 'new world order'

UNITED NATIONS — Cuban President Fidel Castro gestures Friday as he addresses the United Nations General Assembly.

Cuban dictator Fidel Castro called for a "new world order" in 1979. Doing so while speaking at UN headquarters was not by accident.

UPI/BETTMANN

11

With his 1992 book, *Global Tyranny ... Step by Step*, William F. Jasper detailed the threat to freedom posed by the UN.

Years before he became President, Abraham Lincoln insisted that America would live for all time, or "die by suicide."

Former Soviet leader Mikhail Gorbachev urged building a "new world order" in June 1990.

CHAPTER 1

A Glimpse of the Future

The voice of protest, of warning, of appeal is never more needed than when the clamor of fife and drum, echoed by the press and too often by the pulpit, is bidding all men fall in step and obey in silence the tyrannous word of command. Then, more than ever, it is the duty of the good citizen not to be silent.

— Charles Eliot Norton[1]

Even those who are working steadily to shape it don't know for sure what the future holds. What is inescapably true, however, is that our nation can't continue very much longer down the debt-laden road we are travelling. The piper will be paid! The day of reckoning will arrive! Where debt can force an individual into servitude, it can also force a nation to give up its independence.

So we issue a warning via the following scenario, a look into the future we wish were totally inapplicable to the United States. Another scenario built around the kind of hyperinflation that devastated Germany in 1923-24 (see Chapter 7) could credibly be painted by someone else. Indeed, additional calamities might just as readily befall us because of the red ink America's leaders have amassed. The only certainty is that monumental troubles lie ahead unless there is a sharp turnabout. Yet, though they provide plenty of talk, our leaders give no evidence of any intention to reverse course.

It is still true, however, that none of the final, horrible consequences of debt have to be endured by the American people. If

---

1. Charles Eliot Norton, *True Patriotism* (1898), cited in *Familiar Quotations, Fifteenth Edition* (Boston, MA: Little, Brown and Company), p. 598.

the people take their nation back from those whose policies have put America into such a huge debt hole, we can climb out of it and start to build once again. To be sure, there will be pain along the way. But it will quickly be forgotten as the rewards for having taken decisive action are reaped.

Patriotism, according to author and educator Charles Eliot Norton, means to speak out, especially when others continue to fall in line and remain silent. It's time for Americans worthy of the name to break out of lockstep acceptance of national policies speeding all toward national and personal disaster. We hope that the alarm we are sounding helps to keep America free.

*　　*　　*

America May Well Face ...

It's a few years after the Clinton Administration moved into Washington. In spite of a great deal of rhetoric and political showmanship, the national debt has continued to rise precipitously. Where an annual increase of $50 billion in red ink was considered an absolute horror only 20 years ago, this President launched his Administration congratulating himself for efforts that would produce annual deficits of "only" $200 or $300 billion for each of the next four years.

When realists outside official circles looked at the initial presidential deficit projections, they contended that the new Clinton estimates would also fall short — meaning that annual deficits would likely be in the $500 billion range each year. They were correct.

Larger deficits, of course, have forced increased amounts of borrowing. Now, the practice of diverting funds collected in the name of various federal programs — federal employee pensions, social security, highway construction and maintenance, etc. — no longer relieves any of the deficit pressure because expenditures in these programs now equal taxes collected in their names. As a result, government has added huge additional tax levies and has greatly increased borrowing — from the public, from foreigners, and from anywhere money could be obtained. More borrowing has led to rising interest rates.

More taxes cut into take-home pay for Sally and Pete Hart. Sally now works full-time to help pay the bills for their family of six. She recalls that her own parents raised and educated four children on her father's salary alone, and knows that those days are gone.

The Administration starts exercising another option. With the cooperation of an ever-eager Federal Reserve, government increases its practice of "monetizing" some of the debt, a fancy term for financing it with freshly printed paper money. Following this route cuts dramatically into the value of the dollar, and more economic horrors begin piling up for every American.

A letter from the local bank arrives at the Hart household. The adjustable interest rate on their mortgage has been raised, "due to conditions beyond our control" says the bank official. Sally gets a sick feeling in her stomach wondering if this rise in interest rates will be followed by others.

A Sick America Get Sicker

Several years into Bill Clinton's first term, large government bond issues gobble up much of the nation's borrowing pool. Tight money caused by massive government borrowing forces interest rates up and adds to the nation's economic doldrums. With less money available for private borrowing, the housing and construction industries go into their worst tailspins in history, and so does the automobile industry.

Because of the severe economic slowdown, the government collects less tax revenue, meaning that the deficit turns out to be remarkably larger than even the pessimists predicted. It also means people are being thrown out of work and on to the unemployment lines — where still more revenue is needed by government to meet the claims of the unemployed.

When the company president called for a meeting with the residential construction department, Pete Hart expected its purpose might be to congratulate department personnel for their work on the almost-completed housing subdivision. But Pete, a senior draftsman, was shocked to learn that his entire branch of the company was being closed down. "There just isn't enough work to keep everyone on the payroll," said the boss. "I'm sorry," he added, "and I'll certainly give each of you a fine recommendation for future employment." Pete was stunned. When he got home that evening and told Sally, she cried.

With the way the nation is being managed, the annual cost for interest on the national debt approaches the total of all receipts from the federal income tax. Rejecting the option of cutting taxes and abolishing federal programs, the government raises the income tax, creating even worse business conditions. Corporate, excise, and social security taxes are also boosted. But all of the tax increases fail to cover the loss in revenues caused by the accelerating business slump.

Monetizing a portion of the debt (inflation is its real name) cuts sharply into the value of the dollar. Restless and angry people, unable to maintain their standard of living as the value of the dollar evaporates and they lose their jobs and pensions, threaten riots. Everywhere, the people are demanding that the government, "do something!" Wage and price controls are suggested.

From coast to coast, banks holding record numbers of foreclosures are forced into bankruptcy, business firms are laying off workers or closing altogether, and worried Americans are stocking up on food.

The Hart family digs into savings. Pete has reluctantly accepted unemployment compensation, a mere fraction of what he had been earning. His job prospects grow bleaker as layoffs at other construction companies and other firms are reported. When the college tuition bills for 20-year-old Brian

and 18-year-old Margaret arrive, the money the Harts had ex-
pected to use isn't there. And they can't refinance their home
because they're already having trouble meeting the payments.
Pete reaches his son and daughter by telephone and tells them
that there's no money for the next semester and that they
should not plan to return in the fall. Sally looks at Billy and
Sue, both still in high school, and senses their awareness that
their going off to college in a few years is no longer a realistic
possibility.

The Breaking Point

As the day of final reckoning nears, the government suggests a
"means test" for social security recipients. A similar test is suggested for bondholders who might seek to cash in their government bonds. The government hires expensive public relations
firms to inform the people that it's their patriotic duty to refuse
social security payments and even to reinvest the amount due on
their bonds. The appeal is directed especially at those who don't
qualify as "needy," a term that isn't defined.

The public is being softened up for partial and then total repudiation of solemn government promises. Government officials and
liberal economists — mostly Council on Foreign Relations and
Trilateral Commission members[2] — begin floating trial balloons
about who is or isn't "needy."

As the people become more desperate, many rue the day they
trusted government with any of their money. When social security recipients and bondholders decline to abide by the "suggested" means tests, the tests become mandatory for U.S. citizens.
Everyone who wants payment is forced to undergo an audit of
personal finances by a government official. The travel industry,
greatly dependent on senior citizens and well-to-do vacationers,
follows many other industries into steep decline.

Still, government debt continues to mount, and our leaders pay

---

2. See Appendix for a capsulized history of the Council on Foreign Relations,
   the Trilateral Commission, the Bilderberger movement, and the Rhodes
   Scholar program.

off more creditors by monetizing more debt. They offer more bonds, and then more bonds. After all, hasn't a U.S. Treasury bond always been "the safest investment in the entire world"?

Sally Hart returns from a trip to the supermarket in tears. "The price of everything is higher each time I go shopping," she tells Pete, who has spent another unsuccessful day hunting for work. "I don't know how long we can last on what I earn as a secretary." Pete's last unemployment check will come at the end of the month. He has tried every way imaginable to find work in his field — to no avail. Now home from college, Brian and Margaret are also looking for work.

The people become acutely aware that American currency is losing value rapidly. Merchants start asking to be paid in gold or silver coins, jewelry, or other items of value. Businesses are failing left and right, and the government has seized control of several shaky major corporations.

Government officials urge the people to stay calm. Cabinet officials and senior members of Congress appear on television to reassure everyone that "U.S. currency is backed by the industrial might of the nation." But it begins to dawn on many Americans that, if this is true, the issuer of the currency must either own or have a claim on the nation's industries.

Foreign investors, leery of means testing even though it is not yet mandatory for them, and angry over getting caught with rapidly depreciating U.S currency, have completely abandoned the U.S. bond markets. Already high interest rates rise even higher. To obtain desperately needed revenue, the government turns to the American people.

But the people now realize that their own government has neither the ability nor the intention of redeeming its bonds. They hold back and spend what funds they have for tangible goods, or for gold or silver coins whose price in dollars has skyrocketed.

What was unthinkable only a few years ago has now come to pass: The United States government can't sell any more of its bonds to private individuals or institutions and can't raise revenue. The morning newspaper carries a headline: *U.S. Can't Borrow; Nation Nears Bankruptcy!*

Pete Hart reads the headline over his morning cup of coffee. His own troubles suddenly seem smaller when he thinks about his children's future. He decides to shield the bad news from Sally as she rushes to get to work. Brian has found a minimum-wage job and Margaret has hopes of finding one too. "If these two can help with family expenses for a while," he thinks, "things may work out." So far, by cutting expenses drastically, the Harts have been able to survive. But, Pete wonders, if the nation is forced into bankruptcy, what then?

The UN to the Rescue

Ah, but friends in high places come to the aid of a reeling United States. The United Nations has a plan. It can rescue the U.S. government, not by propping up the dollar but by substituting in its place an entirely new United Nations issue of currency. This UN currency, let's call its unit the "bancor," has long been on the drawing boards.

A Security Council resolution introduced by the U.S. ambassador to the world body calls for the immediate replacement of the dollar by the UN bancor. It passes overwhelmingly.

In Congress, legislation sails through both Houses approving the UN plan and calling on all U.S. citizens to turn in their dollars and convert their bank accounts to bancors at a UN-set ratio. Older Americans grimly recall the law passed during the Roosevelt Administration requiring everyone to turn in their gold for paper dollars. Younger citizens who remember hearing their grandparents discuss those terribly frightening days, or who studied the history of the 1933-34 monetary revolution, sense that another revolution is underway. But young and old alike know this one is more serious. President Clinton signs the new measures.

With UN and U.S. approval completed, the American people

are informed about the "improved monetary system" via a tele-vised presidential address. The President, as has been his prac-tice, paints a thoroughly misleading picture of what has actually occurred and fails to detail where the consequences of the UN takeover are leading the nation.

He doesn't tell the people that the UN has been given power over our nation's economic life. He doesn't admit that America is no longer sovereign. He assures everyone that all will be well, and that they'll rapidly get used to using bancors instead of dollars. He claims that the new arrangement will facilitate international trade and improve the U.S. job picture. He even informs the people that they should be grateful to the UN for helping our na-tion "turn the corner" after some very difficult times.

Brian comes home from his low-paying job and announces that he plans to apply for a government position in the morn-ing. "They're hiring people to enforce bans on gun ownership," he says. "And the pay's good. So what if it's in bancors." He urges Margaret and Pete to apply also. Pete urges caution but decides to investigate the possibilities. Margaret accompanies Brian and submits her application for a manager trainee po-sition.

Into the New World Order

The reality of the recent developments, however, is that our nation has now been forced into the "new world order." This, of course, was the actual goal of a succession of elected and ap-pointed leaders who propelled the nation toward astronomical in-debtedness in the first place.

As the full impact of these "emergency" measures becomes un-derstood across the land, Americans everywhere say to each other but especially to themselves, "If I had only known, if I had only listened to the few who warned that this was coming, there is no amount of work and sacrifice and effort I would have given — if I had only understood in time."

Rioting breaks out in many of the nation's cities. To quell the disturbances, UN troops who were recently moved into the former U.S. Army base at Fort Dix, New Jersey, are dispatched to various trouble spots. Other UN forces from Asian nations arrive in great numbers. Citing a precedent set when UN troops sought to disarm Somalia's citizen population in 1993, they proceed swiftly to carry out their first assignment: Disarm the American people.

UN forces close down gun shops, seize all lists of licensed gun owners, and start collecting the weapons of a distraught but powerless people. An edict appears stating that all citizens must have a UN-issued card confirming that they do not possess any weapons. Another proclamation outlaws any criticism of the United Nations. A further UN-issued card must now be shown to purchase food.

Without a UN card, no citizen can obtain or spend bancors, which have been declared the only legal tender. Another decree states that any citizen caught using gold or silver coins, or any merchant found accepting them in payment for goods, will be considered an enemy of the people and will face severe punishment.

Now government trainees, Brian and Margaret Hart are on the payroll. Brian finishes at the top of his class and is assigned to a unit under the command of a UN official from Zambia. Margaret is given an administrative job in the state capital. They receive blue UN armbands and are told that they are part of the "United Nations Stabilization Corps." Brian's first assignment: Report to a UN commander in another state and begin to enforce UN mandates over the American people.

Pete knows there's something very wrong, but Brian thinks only of the opportunity for advancement and eventually returning to college. He won't listen to Pete's concerns. Having received all his education at government schools, he has no appreciation of any fundamental difference between the American system and the new UN system. Neither does Margaret. Brian urges his dad to take a government job himself. Later that evening, Pete tells Sally that unless he applies for and receives what he knows is a UN job, they won't be able to hold on to their home.

The UN announces that all U.S. military units have been placed under its command and all police forces have been absorbed into the newly created, UN-directed federal bureau of police.

The President no longer appears on television. In fact, he no longer appears anywhere in public.

Government buildings start flying the UN flag. UN-appointed bureaucrats, seen everywhere, arrive to take control of major corporations. The independence of the United States and the freedom of the American people have disappeared.

Television news programs carry reports about pockets of resistance to UN dictates in the Dakotas and Rocky Mountain states. Similar resistance has already been crushed in the South and West. Heavily armed UN units are shown moving across the nation. Hundreds of thousands of blue-helmeted troops from Africa and Asia pour into the United States.

With Sally's reluctant concurrence, Pete Hart does not apply for the UN job. A few months later, when they can't make any more payments, the bank holding their mortgage forecloses on the Hart home. As they are packing amid tears for their move into a government-owned housing project, a uniformed UN official arrives with a telegram. Addressed to them, it states, "We regret to inform you that Brian Hart died in the service of the United Nations during Operation Serenity, the important UN program designed to pacify the United States."

In the space of a little more than three years, the Harts lost most of their income, their home, their nation, and their son. Had the United States never started down the road to big government and monstrous debt, none of this would have happened. Pete remembers the warnings a co-worker gave him five years ago, the warnings he and others ignored. It didn't seem possible that everything could fall apart the way it did. But it did!

*   *   *

As stated previously, the future is never completely predictable. However, evidence supporting the hypothetical scenario we have presented is provided in the pages ahead. Unless the course of our nation changes dramatically, what you have read may well come to pass.

The remainder of this book does not deal in speculation. It constitutes, as Charles Eliot Norton put it, a "voice of protest, of warning, of appeal."

We protest the actions and policies of the leaders of the government of the United States. We warn our fellow Americans that, indeed, it not only can happen here, it is happening here. And we appeal to the common sense and innate goodness of all to become aware, to resist, and to join with many others already enlisted in the fight to rescue our nation from the grip of internal enemies. America must be recaptured and returned to its rightful owners, the people of this great land.

CHAPTER 2

The Plan: From Debt to the New World Order

[T]he powers of financial capitalism had another far-reaching aim, nothing less than to create a world system of financial control in private hands able to dominate the political system of each country and the economy of the world as a whole. This system was to be controlled in a feudalist fashion by the central banks of the world acting in concert, by secret agreements arrived at in frequent private meetings and conferences.

— Dr. Carroll Quigley
Tragedy and Hope, 1966[1]

The American people don't want a new world monetary system. They especially don't want one if it includes propelling our nation into a world government. But powerful influences have been arranging for such an eventuality for over a century.

The currently unfolding plan calls for steamrolling the people of the United States into welcoming these developments in response to mountainous U.S. debt. Not surprisingly, the individuals whose policies have brought about the debt are among the same persons who have openly recommended the creation of a single world monetary system.

In his 1,348-page book cited above, former Georgetown University professor Carroll Quigley described in detail the creation of a "secret society" by Cecil J. Rhodes and his companions in late 19th Century England. Quigley knew a great deal about this

---

1. Carroll Quigley, *Tragedy and Hope* (New York, NY: Macmillan Company, 1966), p. 324.

group, he stated, because "I have studied it for twenty years and was permitted for two years in the early 1960s to examine its papers and secret records."[2]

As Professor Quigley noted, the goal of these would-be imperialists included the establishment of "a world system of financial control in private hands." Once achieved, this world system would constitute the vital stepping stone enabling these few "to dominate the political system of each country and the economy of the world as a whole."[3]

An ambitious undertaking to be sure. One that, if completed, would lead to control of virtually all mankind by a powerful and well-connected few. Quigley thought the idea had great merit and, therefore, never termed it a conspiracy. He preferred the term "network" while fully admitting that it was secret. But doesn't a secret plan calling for a very few to dominate the political and economic life of the many deserve to be labelled a conspiracy? By definition, a conspiracy is a secret plot entered into by two or more to accomplish an evil end. What Quigley described fits every element of the definition.

The secret network detailed by the Georgetown professor became the Royal Institute of International Affairs in England and the Council on Foreign Relations in America. He stated, "In 1919 they founded the Royal Institute of International Affairs (Chatham House).... Similar Institutes of International Affairs were established in the chief British dominions and in the United States (where it is known as the Council on Foreign Relations) in the period 1919-1927."[4]

CFR Members Form Trilateral Commission

In the early 1970s, Zbigniew Brzezinski held a post as a professor at Columbia University in New York City. Already a member of the Eastern Establishment by virtue of his membership in the

---

2. Ibid., p. 950.
3. Ibid., p. 324.
4. Ibid., p. 132.

world-government-promoting CFR, Brzezinski's 334-page book, *Between Two Ages: America's Role in the Technetronic Era*,[5] was released to bookstores in 1970 and lavishly touted in Establishment periodicals.

In this book, Brzezinski heaped praise on Marxism for being "a victory of reason over belief,"[6] contended that America's shortcomings had unmasked its "obsolescence,"[7] delighted in the prospect of "deliberate management of the American future,"[8] and called for a "community of nations" to be built "piecemeal ... through a variety of indirect ties and already developing limitations on national sovereignty."[9]

Toward the end of his work, the Columbia professor proposed the formal creation of his suggested "community of the developed nations" among the United States, Western Europe and Japan. He hoped to see the expansion of this community to "more advanced countries," and then in what he termed phase two, the further inclusion of "more advanced communist countries."[10]

Before he finished, Brzezinski lamented that although "the objective of shaping a community of the developed nations is less ambitious than the goal of world government," it is "more attainable."[11] Clearly, while he saw the "shaping of a community of nations" as an achievable goal, he ultimately longed for the creation of a centralized "world government" with dominion over all mankind. And why shouldn't he if his adopted United States of America, was — in his view — becoming obsolete?

The Brzezinski plan for the world — soon to be adopted by the Trilateral Commission as its own — was contained in this 1970 book. Forget national sovereignty! Forget the U.S. Constitution! Forget the Declaration of Independence! Remember only the need

---

5. Zbigniew Brzezinski, *Between Two Ages* (New York, NY: Viking Press, 1970).
6. Ibid., p. 72.
7. Ibid., p. 198.
8. Ibid., p. 260.
9. Ibid., p. 296.
10. Ibid., pp. 296-297.
11. Ibid., p. 308.

for a world government!

Early in 1972, as revealed by researcher and author Holly Sklar in *Trilateralism*,[12] an exposé of the Trilateral Commission (TC), CFR Chairman [David] Rockefeller proposed the creation of what he was then calling an "International Commission for Peace and Prosperity" in speeches before Chase Manhattan International Financial Forums in Western Europe and Canada. But the most enthusiastic and most crucial response came in the spring when Rockefeller and Brzezinski presented the idea of a trilateral grouping at the annual Bilderberg meeting.[13, 14]

Sklar further reports that, during July 23rd-24th, 1972, 17 prominent leaders from the United States, Western Europe, and Japan met at Rockefeller's Pocantico Hills estate in Tarrytown, New York to lay formal plans for the TC.[15]

In July 1973, according to Sklar, "The Commission was officially inaugurated after a series of regional meetings and extensive consultations."[16] Of the 60 original U.S. members and officers, 37 were CFR members at the time and several more

---

12. Holly Sklar, *Trilateralism* (Boston, MA: South End Press, 1980).
13. Ibid., p.78.
14. See Appendix for a capsulized history of the Bilderberg movement.
15. The 17 planners of the Trilateral Commission included seven Americans: Rockefeller; Brzezinski; George Franklin, a Rockefeller in-law who had just stepped down as executive director of the CFR and would later be named North American secretary for the TC; C. Fred Bergsten of the Brookings Institution; McGeorge Bundy, president of the Ford Foundation; Bayless Manning, then President of the CFR; and Henry Owen, also of the Brookings Institution.

  Western Europeans at this planning session included Karl Costens, Christian Democratic leader in West Germany's Bundestag; Guido Colonna di Paliano, president of La Rinascente and former commissioner of the European Community; Francois Duchene of the University of Sussex; René Foch, of the Partie des Republicans Independents; and Max Kohnstamm, director of the European Community Institute for University Studies who would be named TC's European chairman.

  And Japanese participants included Kiichi Miyazawa, member of Japan's Diet, former Minister of Foreign Affairs, and future Prime Minister; Kinhide Mushakoji, Sophia University, Tokyo; Saburo Okita, president of Overseas Economic Cooperation Fund; and Tadashi Yamamoto, president of the Japan Center for International Exchange. See Sklar, op. cit., pp. 78-79.
16. Ibid., p. 79.

would later be welcomed into the TC's big brother organization.[17] Both organizations promote internationalism.

In Their Own Words

Council on Foreign Relations and Trilateral Commission stalwarts have frequently indicated their intention to create a world monetary system. After each quotation given below, the author's membership in either CFR or TC is noted.

> [There must be] some dilution of sovereignty, to the immediate disadvantage of those nations which now possess the preponderance of power ... the establishment of a common money, might be vested in a body created by and responsible to the principal trading and investing peoples. This would deprive our government of exclusive control over a national money....
> — John Foster Dulles (CFR Founder), 1939[18]

> In the economic-technological field, some international cooperation has already been achieved, but further progress will require greater American sacrifices. More intensive efforts to shape a new world monetary structure will have to be undertaken, with some consequent risk to the present relatively favorable American position.
> — Zbigniew Brzezinski (CFR and TC), 1970[19]

> There must be a thoroughgoing reform of the world monetary system.... For its part, I can assure you, the United States will continue to rise to its world responsibilities, joining with other nations to create and participate in a modern world economic order.
> — President Richard Nixon (CFR), 1972[20]

In short, the "house of world order" will have to be built from the

---

17. Trilateral Commission membership list published by TC, November 1, 1973; *Annual Report, 1974*, published by the Council on Foreign Relations.
18. John Foster Dulles, Speech to YMCA, October 28, 1939, quoted in *New York Times*, October 29, 1939.
19. Brzezinski, *Between Two Ages*, op. cit., p. 300.
20. Speech to the Boards of the IMF and World Bank, September 25, 1972.

bottom up rather than from the top down ... an end run around national sovereignty, eroding it piece by piece, will accomplish much more than the old-fashioned frontal assault.

The non-Communist nations are embarked on a long-term negotiation for the reform of *the international monetary system*, aimed at developing a new system of reserves and settlements to replace the dollar standard and at improving the balance-of-payments adjustment process. The accomplishment of these objectives will almost surely require a revitalization of the International Monetary Fund, which would have unprecedented powers to create new international reserves and to influence national decisions on exchange rates and on domestic fiscal policies (emphasis in original).

— Richard N. Gardner (CFR and TC), 1974[21]

[T]o restore a more equitable relationship between government authority and popular control, [there must be] centralized economic and social planning ... centralization of power within Congress ... a program to lower the job expectations of those who receive a college education....

— Samuel P. Huntington (CFR), Michael Crozier, and Joji Watanuki, 1975[22]

The public and leaders of most countries continue to live in a mental universe which no longer exists — a world of separate nations — and have great difficulty in thinking in terms of global perspectives and interdependence. The liberal promise of a separation between the political and economic realm is obsolete: issues related to economics are at the heart of modern politics.

— Richard N. Cooper (CFR and TC), Karl Kaiser (TC), and Masataka Kosaka (TC), 1977[23]

---

21. Richard N. Gardner, "The Hard Road To World Order," *Foreign Affairs*, April 1974.
22. Samuel P. Huntington, Michael Crozier, and Joji Watanuki, *The Crisis of Democracy* (New York, NY: Trilateral Commission, 1975).
23. Richard N. Cooper, Karl Kaiser, and Masataka Kosaka, *Toward a Renovated International System* (New York, NY: Trilateral Commission, 1977).

The standard of living of the average American has to decline.... I don't think you can escape that.

— Paul A. Volcker (CFR and TC)
Federal Reserve Chairman, 1979[24]

Much of the discomfort relates to the large and burdensome external debt that has accumulated around the world.... The key point is that monetary control — the issuance of currency and of reserve credit — would be in the hands of a new bank of issue, not in the hands of any national government.... But a single currency is possible only if there is in effect a single monetary policy, and a single authority issuing currency and directing monetary policy. How can independent states accomplish that? They need to turn over the determination of monetary policy to a supranational body....

— Richard N. Cooper (CFR and TC), 1984[25]

But the world economy is in trouble unless there is some central steering mechanism.

— C. Fred Bergsten (CFR and TC), 1989[26]

Greater symmetry among the major economies has strengthened the case for closer economic policy coordination. Common objective indicators of economic well-being have already been developed by the G-7 nations [United States, England, France, Germany, Italy, Japan, and Canada]. These should now be used to guide and *enforce* economic coordination.... The time may even have come to establish a permanent secretariat.... (Emphasis added.)

— C. Michael Aho (CFR)
and Bruce Stokes (CFR), 1990[27]

---

24. Testimony before the Joint Economic Committee of the U.S. Congress, October 17, 1979.
25. Richard N. Cooper, "A Monetary System for the Future," *Foreign Affairs,* Fall 1984.
26. *Christian Science Monitor*, April 9, 1989.
27. C. Michael Aho and Bruce Stokes, "The Year the Economy Turned," *Foreign Affairs: America and the World 1990/91.*

The G-7 offers a forum for consultation and the capacity for effective world management that other institutions cannot provide.... While attention focuses on resurgent nationalisms ... two ideas are rising to challenge the established concept of the sovereign state. The first is cooperative intervention.... The other challenge to the tradition of sovereign decision making is supranationalism, the pooling of resources and authority on a permanent, regulated basis, as exemplified by the European Community.

— Flora Lewis (CFR), *New York Times* senior columnist,
1991[28]

... this strategy and structure recognizes that economic ties will determine the strength or weakness of many international linkages in this new era, including security relations. At best, economic interdependence can become a new glue.

— Robert B. Zoellick (CFR), 1993[29]

All of the quotations appearing above were written or stated by individuals who approve of world financial control in the hands of a powerful few. Financial control is to be followed by political control — world government. Carroll Quigley's statement with which we began this chapter then took on enormous significance on July 16, 1992 when Bill Clinton threw a verbal bouquet to his former Georgetown University professor while accepting the Democratic Party's nomination for the office of president.

In that acceptance speech, then-Governor Clinton said: "As a

---

28. Flora Lewis, "The 'G-7½' Directorates," *Foreign Policy*, Winter 1991-92.
29. Robert B. Zoellick, "Blueprint for a New Age," *International Economic Insights*, September/October 1993. The publisher of *International Economic Insights* is C. Fred Bergsten. Board members of its parent organization, the Washington-based Institute for International Economics, include Bergsten, Richard N. Cooper, CFR chairman Peter G. Peterson, former CFR chairman and TC founder David Rockefeller, TC North American chairman and CFR director Paul A. Volcker, Federal Reserve chairman and CFR member Alan Greenspan, former secretary of state and CFR member George P. Shultz, former prime minister of Mexico Miguel de la Madrid, former prime minister of France Raymond Barre, and TC Japanese chairman Akio Morita.

teenager, I heard John Kennedy's summons to citizenship. And then, as a student, I heard that call clarified by a professor I had named Carroll Quigley...."

Bill Clinton Welcomed by Insiders

Mr. Clinton graduated from Georgetown University in 1968. He studied under Professor Quigley after *Tragedy and Hope* had been published. It is highly likely that the future President was influenced by the book; there is no doubt he was influenced by its author.

Early in his book, Quigley supplied details about the establishment of the Rhodes Scholar program by the "secret" planners. Its purpose was to train individuals to carry out their conspiratorial plan to rule the world. Never condemning any aspect of the plot, however, Quigley thought it wonderful and stated:

> I know of the operations of this network because I have studied it for twenty years and was permitted for two years in the early 1960s to examine its papers and secret records. I have no aversion to it or to most of its aims and have, for much of my life, been close to it and to many of its instruments. I have objected, both in the past and recently, to a few of its policies ... but in general my chief difference of opinion is that it wishes to remain unknown, and I believe its role in history is significant enough to be known. [30]

It can hardly be overemphasized that President Bill Clinton is an admitted disciple of Carroll Quigley, studied in England as a Rhodes Scholar, accepted membership in the Council on Foreign Relations and its Trilateral Commission little brother, and is now the President of the United States. [31] He is an intelligent man who cannot be unaware of the intentions of his confreres, many of whom he has inserted into high positions in our nation's government.

---

30. Quigley, op. cit., p. 950.
31. For a capsulized history of the Rhodes Scholar Program, see Appendix.

Nor should George Bush's membership in the CFR and Trilateral Commission be glossed over.[32] In addition, it is vitally important to understand that hundreds of others who are members of the CFR have received appointment to high government positions during each of the past dozen administrations. Then, once the Trilateral Commission was formed in 1973, many its members — the majority of whom were already CFR members — also moved into cabinet and sub-cabinet positions.

The two groups have always worked for the same goal, a new world order built on the twin pillars of totalitarian socialism and world government. Always proceeding with patient gradualism, members gather regularly in the U.S. and abroad at conferences sponsored by the CFR, the TC, the Bilderberg movement, and other groups led by like-minded individuals. Based on the claim of a need for candor amongst the participants, the proceedings of each are deemed confidential and are not released to the public.

Many Opponents Speak Out

The Herculean efforts of many Americans to expose and rout these plotters have not yet succeeded in breaking the back of their conspiracy. But the forces resisting the plans of the Rhodes-originated "secret society" continue to gather strength and influence. They have been supported in their essential work by the written and spoken words of many, including such published statements as the following:

Today, the C.F.R. remains active in working toward its final goal

---

32. *Annual Reports* published by the CFR show that George Bush accepted membership in 1971, and a place on its Board of Directors in 1977. The membership list published by the TC on June 1, 1977 was the first to list George Bush as a TC member. In 1979, as he was making plans for a run for the Republican presidential nomination in 1980, he resigned from both organizations in order to present himself as a man apart from the eastern Establishment. But he has subsequently spoken at their gatherings while remaining in close contact with their members. It may well have been George Bush's influence that led President Ronald Reagan to host 200 persons at the April 2, 1984 meeting of the TC at the White House. See Robert Lewis, "Rightists Gag as Trilateral Panel Visits White House," *San Francisco Examiner*, April 3, 1984.

of a government over all the world — a government which the Insiders and their allies will control. The goal of the C.F.R. is simply to abolish the United States with its Constitutional guarantees of liberty. And they don't even try to hide it. Study No. 7, published by the C.F.R. on November 25, 1959, openly advocates "building a new international order."

— Gary Allen, 1971[33]

[The CFR goal is] the submergence of U.S. sovereignty and national independence into an all-powerful one-world government ... this lust to surrender the sovereignty and independence of the United States is pervasive throughout most of the membership.

— Admiral Chester Ward, USN (Ret.)
a 20-year veteran of membership in the CFR, 1975[34]

The Trilateral Commission's most immediate concern is the creation of a new world monetary system to replace gold and the dollar as the international exchange with a new currency.

— Jeremiah Novak, 1977[35]

In my view, the Trilateral Commission represents a skillful, coordinated effort to seize control and consolidate the four centers of power: political, monetary, intellectual and ecclesiastical.... What the Trilateralists truly intend is the creation of a worldwide economic power superior to the political governments of the nation-states involved.... As managers and creators of the system they will rule the future.

— Barry Goldwater, 1979[36]

What "history teaches us" — to use a phrase favored by tri-

---

33. Gary Allen, *None Dare Call It Conspiracy* (Seal Beach, CA: Concord Press, 1971).
34. Phyllis Schlafly and Chester Ward, *Kissinger On the Couch* (New Rochelle, NY: Arlington House, 1975).
35. *Atlantic* Magazine, July 1977.
36. Barry Goldwater, *With No Apologies* (New York, NY: William Morrow and Company, 1979).

lateralists — is that ruling elites are deadly serious about seeing that any renovation of the international system is in their interest. They will use a variety of carrot and stick tactics to maintain political and economic control — domestically and internationally. Control techniques will be more vicious or less, depending on a combination of factors involving the state of the economy and, more importantly, the state of popular opposition. The more threatening and persistent the moves to counter their plans and build alternative models, the more violent will be their tactics of repression.

— Holly Sklar, 1980[37]

Private organizations such as the Council on Foreign Relations, the Royal Institute of International Affairs, the Trilateral Commission, the Dartmouth Conference, the Aspen Institute for Humanistic Studies, the Atlantic Institute, and the Bilderberg Group serve to disseminate and to coordinate the plans for this so-called new world order in powerful business, financial, academic, and official circles.

— Sen. Jesse Helms (R-NC), Speech to the Senate, 1987.[38]

One Administration After Another

One of the first TC members chosen in the United States was Jimmy Carter. With the behind-the-scenes backing of his new associates, Carter was catapulted to the Democratic nomination in 1976 and on to the White House, where he promptly selected for vital posts more than a dozen fellow Trilateralists including Walter Mondale (Vice President), Cyrus Vance (Secretary of State), Harold Brown (Secretary of Defense), W. Michael Blumenthal (Secretary of the Treasury), Warren Christopher (Deputy Secretary of State), Zbigniew Brzezinski (National Security Advisor), and Richard N. Cooper (Undersecretary of State).[39] He also

---

37. Holly Sklar, op. cit., p. 47.
38. *Congressional Record*, December 15, 1987, pp. S18145-S18150.
39. In his 1975 campaign booklet entitled *Why Not the Best*, Jimmy Carter would state of the Trilateral Commission, "Membership on this Commission has provided me with a splendid learning opportunity, and many of the members have helped me in my study of foreign affairs." Jimmy Carter, *Why Not the Best?* (Nashville, TN: Boardman Press, 1975).

named Trilateralist Paul Volcker to be the Chairman of the Federal Reserve.

All of these men happened also to hold memberships in the larger and even more prestigious CFR.[40] Our nation's slide towards world government, especially via the route of debt, began to accelerate.

In 1977, fresh from his short tour as CIA director during the Ford Administration, George Bush, then a member of the CFR's Board of Directors, also signed on with the Trilateralists. And when Ronald Reagan chose him for a running mate at the Republican convention in the summer of 1980, the word "betrayal" was commonly uttered by delegates on the floor of the Detroit convention hall.

George Bush wasn't the only Trilateralist to hold a high government post during the Reagan Administration. Caspar Weinberger (Secretary of Defense), William Brock (Secretary of Labor), and Paul Volcker (renamed Federal Reserve Chairman during the Reagan Administration) were the most prominent. America's rush to fiscal madness, most notably through annual deficits exceeding $200 billion, moved into high gear.

When George Bush himself succeeded to the presidency, the number of Trilateralists serving our nation's government increased from what it had been during the Reagan years. He selected Richard Darman (Director of the Office of Management and Budget), Brent Scowcroft (National Security Advisor), Lawrence Eagleburger (Assistant Secretary of State), and Alan Greenspan (Federal Reserve Chairman). The Bush Administration then broke previous records for the number of CFR members serving at any one time when the total reached 387. And it actually outperformed its predecessor in running up astronomical deficits. America continued to commit fiscal hara-kiri.

While TC/CFR veteran George Bush was serving as the President of the United States, the young Governor of Arkansas, Bill Clinton, was invited into membership in both the Trilateral Com-

---

40. CFR *Annual Report* 1976.

mission and the Council on Foreign Relations. When he announced his candidacy for the highest office in the land, those who had no inkling of his critically important Establishment connections thought Mr. Clinton's candidacy to be laughable. They aren't laughing any more.

As President, just as did his predecessors, Mr. Clinton has turned to the membership rosters of the Trilateral Commission and Council on Foreign Relations for his staff. Appointees who belong to both of these organizations include Carter-retread Warren Christopher (Secretary of State), Alice Rivlin (Deputy Director of the Office of Management and Budget), Bruce Babbitt (Secretary of the Interior), Donna Shalala (Secretary of Health and Human Services), Henry Cisneros, (Secretary of Housing and Urban Development), and the trio of Winston Lord, Peter Tarnoff and Strobe Talbott (each of whom was given an important post at the State Department).[41]

Mr. Clinton seems sure to break previous records for the numbers of TC and CFR members he places in office. There is every reason to believe that he will work extremely hard to achieve the goals of those who are working for the new world order.

The Trilateral Plan

If we look back at what the Trilateral Commission seeks, as stated not only by one of its founders but also by several of its members, supporters, and critics, it becomes obvious that the Commission's strategy is to create a world monetary system — leading to a world government — in response to economic disruption. The disruption the Trilateralists and their CFR partners intend to capitalize on here in the United States is national indebtedness, the subject of our next chapter.

Yet, it can't be stressed too strongly that the debt they intend to address is the product of policies developed by elected and appointed officials who are their TC and CFR colleagues. Here we

---

41. Lord and Tarnoff have both served as President of the Council on Foreign Relations. Talbott was Bill Clinton's roommate during their years as Rhodes Scholars.

have a classic tactic of conspirators: Create a problem and follow it with a conspiracy-serving solution.

While this book will focus on the economic destruction of our nation, we don't in any way discount the subversion proceeding in political and diplomatic fields. CFR and TC members who now dominate the media, military, corporate world, government, and several other categories of national life are working in all of these arenas. They intend, literally, to convert our nation into a mere province in a one-world system run by them. If they succeed, the independence of our nation and the freedom enjoyed by Americans for over 200 years will disappear.

Proposals for a world currency, or for the United Nations to exercise monetary authority over all nations through the International Monetary Fund or some other UN-directed multi-national agency, are responses of debt-creators to the debt they and their global-minded associates helped to create.

Also, the building of economic union among nations (via such pacts as the North American Free Trade Agreement, the European Community, and other planned mergers) is an additional step toward world government.[42] Economic union generally precedes political union. Once established, an economic union substantially eases the transition to world government. Gathering several already-existing unions of nations into one centrally directed governing body is, for the conspirators, a much more practical approach than attempting to subjugate more than 150 independent nations, one at a time.

TC founder Brzezinski actually stated this portion of the overall plan in his 1970 *Between Two Ages* wherein he called for the

---

42. In "NAFTA: Clinton's Defining Task," *Washington Post*, July 20, 1993, written to drum up support for the agreement, Henry Kissinger stated: "It will represent the most creative step toward a new world order taken by any group of countries since the end of the Cold War, and the first step toward the even larger vision of a free trade zone for the entire Western Hemisphere." David Rockefeller added his support for NAFTA by stating in a signed article: "Grasping the moment means, first of all, winning the support of the American people, the administration and Congress for NAFTA...." — "A Hemisphere in the Balance," *Wall Street Journal*, October 1, 1993.

temporarily "attainable" goal of a "community of nations" in place of the desired long-range goal of "world government." But he has never abandoned that long-range goal and, as we have noted, his plan became the Trilateral plan. In the Fall 1991 issue of the CFR's *Foreign Affairs*, Brzezinski called for a "truly new world order," one that would be based on "an incipient global security structure, derived from widening and increasingly self-reliant regional cooperation, backed by selective and proportionate American commitments."[43]

None of the economic plans of the new world order's Insiders would have a ghost of a chance of realization if the American people possessed some basic economic awareness. If, for instance, the public knew how inflation robs and destroys, the planners could not have eroded the value of the dollar. If the people had a grasp of the enormity of the national debt and what it costs them, they would demand that government cease spending the nation and themselves into the poorhouse.

If Americans further understood how carefully the Constitution was written to guard against the introduction of unbacked paper money, they wouldn't keep electing individuals who ignore those safeguards and continue to speed our nation toward economic suicide. If many more Americans had even an inkling of the conspiratorial foundation of the Federal Reserve and the vast power it possesses over the economic life of this nation, they would speedily demand its abolition.

Politicians have generally been loathe to increase debt significantly because they have to offer themselves to the people for re-election. But financing debt can also be accomplished via inflation, the debt creator's dream. In order to use inflation for their schemes, they first must destroy sound money and then rely on the public's lack of understanding about the inflation mechanism, the Federal Reserve system, and the phoniness of claims calling for various debt-spending programs. All of these topics will be examined in detail in subsequent chapters.

---

43. Zbigniew Brzezinski, "Selective Global Commitment," *Foreign Affairs*, Fall 1991, p. 20.

Finally, if the conspiracy behind all of the nation-destroying economic and political treachery were exposed, the U.S. government would begin to act in the best interests of the people of this land — something it hasn't been doing for several generations.

And, lest anyone think that all we intend to do is present problems, we will offer real and workable solutions for saving our nation and ourselves from the designs of those who really intend to usher this nation into what Carroll Quigley termed "a world system of financial control in private hands able to dominate the political system of each country and the economy of the world as a whole."

In short, they intend total power for themselves and slavery for the American people. We offer a hard look at our nation's debt, the conspiracy's route to power, in the next chapter.

Carroll Quigley was President Clinton's mentor at Georgetown University.

Zbigniew Brzezinski's 1970 book *Between Two Ages* provided the idea for the Trilateral Commission.

David Rockefeller served for many years as chairman of the CFR.

Richard N. Gardner called for "eroding" our nation's sovereignty "piece by piece."

C. Fred Bergsten has worked for more than 20 years to create a world monetary system.

Former Japanese Prime Minister Kiichi Miyazawa helped to plan the Trilateral Commission.

Former Federal Reserve Chairman Paul Volcker said that the "standard of living of the average American has to decline."

President Richard Nixon called for "a modern world economic order" in a 1972 speech to IMF and World Bank leaders.

43

While accepting the Democratic Party's nomination for President, Bill Clinton praised Carroll Quigley, author of *Tragedy and Hope*.

Gary Allen's prolific pen supplied valuable evidence about the plans of a conspiracy to rule the world.

When Ronald Reagan selected CFR and TC veteran George Bush as his running mate, Republican stalwarts cried "betrayal."

In *With No Apologies*, Barry Goldwater condemned the Trilateral Commission's plans to "rule the future."

A CFR founder, John Foster Dulles called for "dilution of sovereignty" and international control of money.

Walter Mondale held membership in both CFR and TC when chosen by Jimmy Carter to be his running mate.

Jimmy Carter's early membership in the Trilateral Commission eased his way into the Presidency.

Cyrus Vance (CFR and TC) served in high-level positions in both Democratic and Republican Administrations.

Warren Christopher served as vice chairman of the CFR, and then as Secretary of State in the Clinton Administration.

Caspar Weinberger (CFR and TC) served as Secretary of Defense in the Bush Administration.

AP/ WORLD WIDE PHOTO

Once president of the CFR, Winston Lord is now a high official in the Clinton State Department.

CHAPTER 3

A Nation Ravaged by Debt

The power to tax involves the power to destroy.
— Supreme Court Chief Justice
John Marshall, 1819[1]

When more of the people's sustenance is exacted through the form of taxation than is necessary to meet the just obligations of government and the expenses of its economical administration, such exaction becomes ruthless extortion and a violation of the fundamental principles of a free government.
— President Grover Cleveland, 1886[2]

During World War II, the U.S. government found it necessary to borrow. Hardly any Americans opposed the plan because large amounts of money were needed to build a two-front military force. We had been attacked by Japan, and Germany had declared war on us. We had to fight back. It would be expensive.

Figures supplied by the U.S. government show that our entire national debt before entering the war (1940) totalled $50.7 billion. Wars do cost money, however, and some historians have shown that some of history's more sinister characters have steered nations into bloody conflicts as a way of forcing them to borrow.[3]

Not only does heavy borrowing reap large interest benefits for lenders, it can lead to a loss of a nation's ability to act in its own

---

1. *McCulloch v. Maryland*, 4 Wheaton 316,407; 1819.
2. Second Annual Message, December 1886.
3. Count Egon Caesar Corti, *The Rise of the House of Rothschild* (originally published by Cosmopolitan Book Corporation, 1928); newer edition (Appleton, WI: Western Islands, 1972).

self-interest. Heavy indebtedness can, in fact, cost a nation its sovereignty and its people their freedom. No one should delude himself into thinking that our leaders are unaware of these consequences of horrendous debt.

The Lost Opportunity

The United States borrowed hundreds of billions of dollars during the 1941-1945 war years. By 1945, our national debt had grown fivefold to $260.1 billion. But victory was ours and anyone who felt that amassing such a debt was unwarranted kept his thoughts to himself.

What should our nation have done about this huge obligation? Because these were more sensible days, many national leaders felt obliged to pay it off. After all, those from whom the money had been borrowed had a right to repayment, and the taxpayers who were being forced to pay interest on the debt had a right to be relieved of that burden.

So, steps were taken to reduce the debt. Some national leaders, however, were more interested in internationalism, socialism, and do-goodism with other people's money. They supported schemes to send huge amounts of America's treasure overseas via an array of foreign aid programs they insisted would revitalize war-torn nations. The same programs, of course, would weaken America and destroy the opportunity to get out of debt. Foreign aid is a major reason why America's World War II indebtedness was never retired.

When Americans allowed their government to institute completely unconstitutional foreign aid programs, the door was opened for the creation of many more costly and equally unconstitutional domestic programs.[4]

The foreign aid idea actually fit exactly into Joseph Stalin's designs for the post-war world. In his *Marxism and the National and Colonial Question*, the Soviet dictator advocated forcing the

---

4. For a survey of the abuse of the Constitution through the enactment of a multiplicity of federal programs, see "America's Vanishing Liberty," by this author in the May 17, 1993 issue of *The New American*.

advanced countries of the world to pour prolonged financial aid into the underdeveloped countries.[5] Stalin, who was far from alone in championing American giveaway programs, had numerous motives for advocating them, the chief of which were that they would consume our nation's wealth and would raise the economic level of smaller nations, facilitating their eventual absorption into the one-world tyranny he envisioned.

The Soviet dictator's call for foreign aid likely helped to energize enthusiasm for the idea amongst the likes of then-Assistant Secretary of the Treasury Harry Dexter White, one of the architects of foreign aid, who was later shown in sworn testimony to be a secret Soviet agent (see Chapter 4).

Debt From Foreign Aid

Foreign aid continues to be a substantial cause of our nation's growing indebtedness. Yet there is no authority whatsoever in the Constitution for the federal government to tax Americans and give their money to foreign governments — which is exactly what these aid programs accomplish.

In 1982, a constituent sent North Carolina Senator Jesse Helms a question he couldn't answer. Helms was asked: How much, including interest on the money borrowed by the U.S. government to finance the programs, has foreign aid cost American taxpayers?

The senator discovered that he wasn't alone; no one else in the federal government could answer the question either. So he set his staff to work searching through official documents, making needed inquiries, and adding up figures — for the period 1946 to 1981. With the help of the Library of Congress, they came up with the staggering figure of $2.3 trillion. At the time, the entire national debt of the United States totalled only $1.06 trillion, less than half of what the giveaway programs had already cost the American people.

It is important to realize that the term foreign aid includes a

---

5. Joseph Stalin, *Marxism and the National and Colonial Question* (New York, NY: International Publishers, 1942).

great deal more than the single "foreign aid" appropriation periodically approved by Congress. All foreign aid includes amounts spent for foreign economic assistance, foreign military aid, and numerous other forms of grants and loans, plus the interest required to borrow the money to be given away.

Senator Helms then informed his colleagues of the $2.3 trillion total.[6] But the figure he presented is more than a decade old and growing. With our federal government compiling annual deficits in excess of $300 billion, Congress and the President still manage to support more foreign aid giveaways.

If a fourth grader were told that the nation was heavily in debt and going in deeper every year, he'd recommend terminating all giveaway programs. He'd conclude that continuing such a policy would bring great harm to our nation. But America's leaders don't follow such a sensible course; they are pursuing an agenda markedly different from what would be followed by the average fourth grader, or the average American.

On June 25, 1992, the House voted 297 to 124 to appropriate $13.8 billion for direct foreign aid for fiscal 1993. By a vote of 87 to 12 on October 1, 1992, the Senate approved its version calling for $14.1 billion for fiscal 1993 foreign aid. Minor differences were ironed out in a conference vote. The parade of foreign aid giveaways is uninterrupted — even in the face of $300 billion deficits. And the nation's elected representatives continue to tell constituents that they are doing all in their power to hold down spending, balance the budget, ease tax burdens, etc.

On June 11, 1993, the House of Representatives approved (309 to 111) another foreign aid appropriation totalling $13 billion. The Senate was expected to do likewise. As noted previously, the single foreign aid appropriation is only a portion of all foreign aid.

Not only do federal officials regularly send funds to the four corners of the earth, they just as regularly boost the authorized limit on national indebtedness. On April 2, 1993, the House voted (237 to 177) to raise the allowable federal debt ceiling to a whopping

---

6. *Congressional Record*, May 18, 1982, pp. S5402-S5406.

$4.37 trillion. The Senate approved the same measure with a non-recorded voice vote, a rather cowardly way to take an unpopular stand. Once in possession of the new authorization to go deeper in debt, more foreign aid was one of the first items on the congressional agenda. There aren't too many certainties in this life, but one absolute certainty is that once in possession of authority to go further in debt, Congress will use it.

President Clinton's highly publicized August 1993 "deficit reduction package" (merely a reduction in a previously issued deficit projection) contained the largest single tax increase in the nation's history. But it also included a $755 billion boost in the debt ceiling. Both Houses of Congress barely approved the Clinton package, but approve it they did. There is now talk about abolishing congressional authorization for such increases and having increases in the debt ceiling occur automatically.

The nation needs real debt reduction, not phony deficit reduction. There is a need to reduce the total debt and its staggering interest burden, not just annual deficits that are added to that debt. And the evidence is strong that Mr. Clinton's "package" won't even cut into the annual deficits that are destroying America's economic vitality.

Where's the outrage? Where's the anger? If there isn't any to speak of, it's because very few Americans have any idea about what our leaders are doing. Yet, the people of this nation are seeing their wallets emptied and their future destroyed. This book is written to supply desperately needed information. We hope it also produces enough indignation in Americans to reverse this criminal behavior.

The Debt Spiral Takes Off

By 1950, even with the beginning of massive transfers of funds overseas through a variety of aid programs, the national debt actually dropped slightly, from $260.1 billion in 1945 to $256.9 billion in 1950. (It would have gone down a great deal more had there been no foreign aid.) Critics rightly pointed to the slow pace of cutting back on the debt, but others took comfort in knowing

Table 3-1
Annual Deficits: 1950 – 1993

End of Fiscal Year	Federal Debt	Published Deficit
1950	$256.9 billion	–
1955	$274.4	–
1960	$290.5	–
1965	$322.3	–
1970	$380.9	–
1971	$408.2	$23.0
1972	$435.9	$23.4
1973	$466.3	$14.9
1974	$483.9	$6.1
1975	$541.9	$53.2
1976	$628.9	$73.7
1977	$706.4	$68.4*
1978	$776.6	$59.2
1979	$828.9	$40.2
1980	$908.5	$73.8
1981	$994.3	$79.0
1982	$1,136.8	$128.0
1983	$1,371.2	$207.8
1984	$1,564.1	$185.4
1985	$1,817.0	$212.3
1986	$2,120.1	$221.2
1987	$2,345.6	$149.8
1988	$2,600.8	$155.2
1989	$2,867.5	$153.5
1990	$3,206.3	$220.5
1991	$3,599.0	$268.7
1992	$4,002.7	$310.7
1993	$4,396.7 (est.)	$305.2 (est.)

* 1977 figures cover 15 months because the end of the fiscal year was moved from June 30th to September 30th.

Source: *1993 & 1994 Budgets of the United States Government*[7]

that the nation was at least heading in the right direction.

There have actually been a few occasions over the next 40-plus years when government's annual receipts exceeded expenditures and the national debt didn't rise. But the rare surpluses were small and the far more frequent deficits grew larger and larger. As Table 3-1 shows, the accumulated national debt during each five-year period from 1950 until 1970 rose only slightly. Then it really started to balloon when spending for a variety of social programs began to bleed the taxpayers in the same manner that foreign aid programs had done.

The greatest annual deficit during the 1960s ($25.1 billion in 1968) occurred during the height of the Vietnam War when increased military expenditures were deemed necessary. But government receipts for 1969 slightly exceeded outflow resulting in a $3.2 billion surplus. *There have been no surpluses since 1969!*

These figures show that the spendthrift and debt-building policies of government actually rose to staggering heights during the years when Americans were regularly being told how fortunate we were to have skinflint leadership in the White House. There are some who still believe that the administrations led by Ronald Reagan (1981-1989) and George Bush (1989-1993) cut programs and savaged the poor. They didn't.[8]

When Ronald Reagan took office in 1981, the national debt had not yet reached $1 trillion. It was tripled during his eight years in office. It soared beyond the $4 trillion level before George Bush's four years were up. And, at a minimum, it is programmed

---

7. The *1993 Budget* contained an historical table of federal debt per year beginning in 1940. This annual feature was curiously missing from the *1994 Budget* issued by the Clinton Administration.

8. On February 18, 1981, in one of his first speeches to the nation as President, Mr. Reagan stated: "It is important to realize that we are reducing the rate of increase in taxing and spending. We are not attempting to cut either spending or taxing to a level below that which we presently have." After attacking Jimmy Carter over government spending totals, Mr. Reagan not only didn't work to cut spending, he submitted budgets calling for increases in overall spending which led to deficits that were double and triple those he had criticized.

Figure 3-1
National Debt: 1950 – 1993

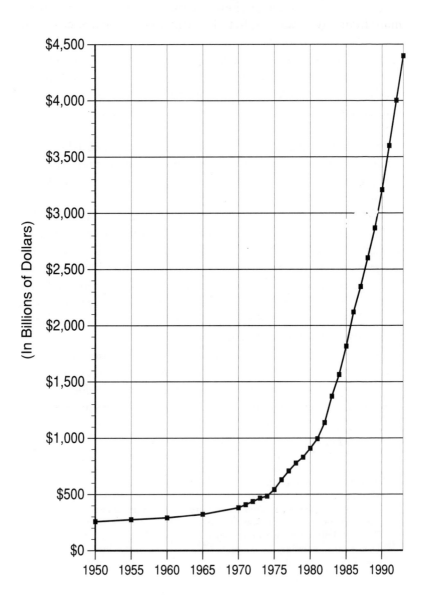

to soar beyond the $5 trillion level during Bill Clinton's first term.[9]

During the 1980s, the United States went from being owed more than any nation on earth to owing more than any other. No more can we scoff at the debt problems of Mexico, Brazil, and Argentina; we're in worse shape.

Occasionally, we hear the term "big spender" applied to some political figure. Forget it. Or at least add to it. These officials are not only big spenders, they're big borrowers and big taxers who are steering this nation toward fiscal disaster. They keep insisting that they're "holding the line," "producing a bare-bones budget," and "doing their level best to balance the budget." But the deficits keep getting worse and the day of reckoning continues to draw nearer.

Take a hard look at the graph in Figure 3-1. Its trend shows that the national debt is growing like a cancer. At the rate it's increasing, the amount of interest it commands will consume all of the nation's income tax receipts ($476.0 billion in 1992) in only a few more years. Then what? More taxes? More borrowing? Repudiation? UN rescue?

Figures Don't Even Add Up

The federal government's *1993 Budget*, a massive 1,713 pages plus a 448-page Supplement, lists the amount of debt incurred each year. Add any particular year's deficit to the previous year's debt total and you should have the new total for the national debt. But nothing is that easy when dealing with the princes of obfuscation at the federal level.

In Table 3-1, note the total debt figure for the end of 1987 ($2,345.6 billion) and add to it the published 1988 deficit ($155.2 billion). You should now have a new debt total of $2,500.8 billion at the end of 1988. Yet, the federal government reported that the new debt total at the end of 1988 was $2,600.8. Did someone simply make a mistake in arithmetic?

---

9. *1994 Budget*, p. 33.

Look at the next year and add the 1989 deficit ($153.5 billion) to the 1988 total debt ($2,600.8 billion). You should have a new debt total of $2,754.3 at the end of 1989. But the government reports that the new debt total at the end of fiscal 1989 is $2,867.5 billion. Again, the figures don't add up. The numbers given for the deficit at the end of each year don't even come close to what the government itself says is the actual increase in debt.

Maybe you're getting tired of figures and don't want any more. Did you ever stop to think this may be precisely what the government hopes? But there can be no doubt about the pattern. We are indeed being led into an economic abyss while being given less-than-honest deficit figures. And here's a figure anyone can understand: *The federal government is adding to the national debt at the rate of approximately $1 million every minute, $1 billion every day.*

As to what's going on here, we asked some questions of the Office of Management and Budget. Why, we queried, doesn't the sum of the yearly deficit and the accumulated federal debt add up to a new total for federal debt? After being bounced around from one bureaucrat to the next, we finally got an answer: "This disparity is due to monies transferred from other venues such as the Social Security Trust Fund. These transfers are not part of the deficit because we owe it to ourselves."

In his *Human Action*, the great Austrian-born American economist Ludwig von Mises had this to say about owing it to ourselves:

> The most popular of these doctrines is crystallized in the phrase: A public debt is no burden because we owe it to ourselves. If this were true, then the wholesale obliteration of the public debt would be an innocuous operation, a mere act of bookkeeping and accountancy. The fact is that the public debt embodies claims of people who have in the past entrusted funds to the government against all those who are daily producing new wealth. It burdens the producing strata for the benefit of another part of the people.[10]

---

10. Ludwig von Mises, *Human Action* (New Haven, CT: Yale University Press, 1949), p. 229.

The federal bureaucrat quoted above admitted that the keepers of federal monies are using funds collected for social security and other supposedly untouchable purposes as general revenue. Yet, even though budget officials won't add these transferred amounts to the annual deficit figure, they must add them to the federal debt figure.

But the government's dishonesty regarding the amount of its red ink is even greater than we've already reported. It has huge obligations extending far into the future such as social security payments for everyone currently paying into the program, future highway construction and maintenance, pensions for federal officials, etc. There is no money in the treasury to meet these promises. When these obligations are added to the debt total, as they should be, the total national debt exceeds $15 trillion!

Today's children have a huge millstone around their necks even though they had no say in creating it. Those who are responsible for this enormous injustice have little or no regard for children, even their own.

Astronomical Interest Per Person

An admitted debt of approximately $4.4 trillion at the end of fiscal 1993 means the government has a monster interest bill. If your federal tax burden is climbing, your portion of the government's obligation to pay interest is part of the reason. If you've lost a job, can't get a raise, or been forced to work for lower wages, you can likely blame government borrowing and subsequent interest for consuming private capital that otherwise could have created industries and jobs.

The interest paid on government indebtedness for fiscal 1991 was $286.0 billion.[11] The interest paid on government indebtedness for fiscal 1992 was $292.3 billion.[12] The estimated interest for fiscal 1993 is $294.6 billion.[13]

Why don't Americans get angry about this? Maybe the absence

---

11. *1993 Budget*, p. A1-91.
12. *1994 Budget*, p. A-921.
13. Ibid.

of justifiable fury is traceable to the incomprehensible size of the amounts we're discussing. So, let's break it down to the cost per person. In other words, how much does each American pay for interest?

In round figures, there are 250 million Americans. The admitted government interest bill for a single year is roughly $290 billion. *In 1992, therefore, the average tab — just for interest on the national debt — was over $1,000 for every man, woman and child in this nation.*

But not every man, woman, and child pays taxes. In fact, approximately half the population does. So, at very least, the average figure has to be doubled to *over $2,000 for every taxpayer —* just for interest on accumulated national debt. Just imagine what it would mean to this nation if every American had that much more to spend, save, or invest. There wouldn't be a recession or depression; America would be experiencing a boom!

Let's realize also that tax revenue collected for interest payments doesn't retire any portion of the debt; it just temporarily satisfies lenders. It benefits only those who have loaned to government, or who want to see America commit suicide. Interest has even become larger than the Defense Department's shrinking budget — $289.6 billion in 1993.[14] Expenditures for interest are now second only to the enormous budget for the unconstitutional Department of Health and Human Services.

The Treadmill Speeds Up

Most of the money our government borrows comes from the savings of the American people. (Some comes from the savings of foreign investors.) Government's enormous borrowing shrinks the pool from which business owners and private citizens obtain loans, boosting interest rates higher than they normally would be. The combination of heavy taxation and heavy government borrowing, therefore, curtails national productivity.

But government debt also paves the way for government con-

---

14. Ibid., p. 135.

trol. Consider: Debt leads to taxation to pay interest. Taxation leads to more economic control of the people by the same government that ran up the debt in the first place. It's hardly extreme to conclude that escalating debt is part of a plan, such as a plan to establish a new world order.

If the costs associated with debt and borrowing aren't reduced, paying social security recipients or meeting other government obligations will become impossible. Then, government's choices will include raising taxes dramatically, borrowing additional hundreds of billions of dollars, repudiating obligations, relying on inflation to cover the debt, or throwing the nation at the mercy of the United Nations.

More taxes will increase the drain on economic vitality. Additional borrowing will spike interest rates for the public, increase the government's bill for interest payments, and reduce business investment. If the government repudiates its obligations, there could easily be civil unrest that will make previous riots look like Sunday school picnics. And throwing the nation at the mercy of the UN will mean the end of U.S. independence.

All of these alternatives invite disaster. Yet the debt continues to grow. Less government, less taxation, less control of the people, and more honesty from our leaders is what the nation needs.

Formerly, the day of reckoning could be postponed for decades with additional borrowing. But the kind of borrowing we're talking about will now postpone it only for a few years. Soon, a few months; then, a few weeks; then, a few days; then, — ??

The source of federal revenues and the allocation of expenditures are shown in the nearby charts copied from the *1994 Budget*.

As can be seen in the chart in Figure 3-2 labelled "Where It Goes...," the largest slice of federal expenditures is "Direct Benefit Payments For Individuals." This is the category of federal expenditures known as "Entitlements," the subject of Chapter 12.

As shown in the companion chart labelled "Where It Comes From...," borrowing is a sizeable source of federal funds. This portion of federal revenue has been steadily rising over many years. Eventually, the U.S. government will be such a gargantuan bor-

Figure 3-2
The Federal Government Dollar
Fiscal Year 1994 Estimate

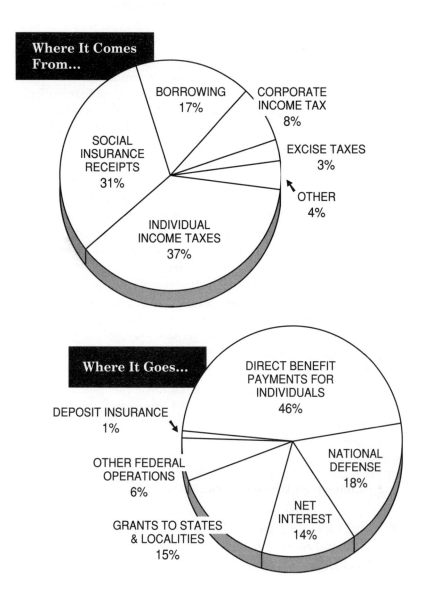

rower that lenders will label it a bad risk and refuse to lend it any more money.

Yes indeed, as John Marshall stated in 1819, "The power to tax involves the power to destroy." All by itself, taxation to pay interest on government debt could shut America down and usher in the enslavement of the American people. But taxation to pay interest is far from the only tax burden imposed on Americans.

When President Grover Cleveland warned in 1886 that escalating taxation could become "ruthless extortion and a violation of the fundamental principles of a free government," he was referring to what Americans endure today. If he could view the size and the cost of government today, he would be shocked and outraged. But he's long in his grave, meaning that any shock and outrage should come from you!

How to Throw Away the People's Wealth

The following examples of federal spending may convince you, as they have convinced many, that our leaders aren't even trying to hold down the cost of government. They are, instead, working diligently to find ways to throw the people's money away and saddle them with debt. All of these expenditures were included in legislation passed by Congress and signed by President Bush during fiscal 1992. None are properly the role of the federal government.

- $24 million for renovations to Chicago's State Street Mall.
- $6 million for a parking facility in Newark, New Jersey.
- $4 million for a rural economic development center for St. Norbert's College in Wisconsin.
- $325,000 to learn if Wheeling, West Virginia is a national historical site.
- $5 million for President Bush's Points of Light Foundation.
- $1 million for the New York Public Library.
- $1 million to renovate Tad Gormley Stadium in New Orleans.
- $2 million to study why truck drivers lose alertness at the wheel.
- $150,000 to interpret the Hatfield-McCoy feud.

- $49 million for a rock-and-roll museum.
- $5 million for Ted Turner's Goodwill Games.
- $15 million for a program at Dartmouth College to create 39 jobs ($324,000 per job).
- $25,000 for production of the "homoerotic" film *Poison*.
- $637,000 to the New York State Arts Council which funds a homosexual film company named "Women Make Movies, Inc."
- $12,000 for the San Francisco International Lesbian and Gay Film Festival.
- $1.7 million to study how to make "killer" bees less aggressive.
- $500,000 to study the effects of cigarette smoking on dogs.
- $107,000 to study the mating habits of the Japanese quail.
- $225,000 for an onion storage facility at the University of Georgia.
- $2.9 million to study new uses for wood.
- $603,000 for pickle research at North Carolina State University.
- $100,000 for barley malt research at the University of Wisconsin.
- $2 million for a bicycle and pedestrian path between Arlington and Cambridge, Massachusetts.
- $2.5 million for a bicycle path in Dade County, Florida.
- $1 million to learn why people don't use bicycles more often.
- $465,000 to McDonald's Corporation to promote Chicken McNuggets.
- $2.3 million to Ernest and Julio Gallo to promote Gallo Wines.
- $1.3 million to American Legend Mink Cooperative to promote furs.
- $7.6 million for Blue Diamond company to promote its nut products.
- $500,000 to the Georgia Department of Agriculture to market peanuts in Eastern Europe.
- $50,000 for Newman's Own company, owned by the millionaire movie star Paul Newman, to promote his products.

The American people don't want to be taxed for this. Or for foreign aid. Or for a long list of federal regulatory agencies destroying their jobs and livelihoods.

At its outset, our nation's federal government was given very few clearly specified powers, each of which was clearly stated in the Constitution. All other functions of government were to be left to the state and local governments where the people would be better able to guard against intrusions on their liberty. Even more, it was expected that the people would never allow government to involve itself in matters that were none of government's business. The American dream is fading from view. It's time to restore it!

The *1994 Budget* supplies spending totals for all government agencies and programs. A random selection of the cost of only a few of hundreds of unconstitutional programs follows:

African Elephant Conservation: $1,219,000. This expenditure appears in the budget for the Department of the Interior. If you thought this department of government concerned itself only with matters within the borders of the United States, you now know otherwise. Conserving African elephants should be financed by those who are interested in such a project. [15]

JFK Center for Performing Arts: $20,260,000. Here we have taxpayers subsidizing a beautiful theater and a steady stream of performers for the enjoyment of federal employees and DC-area residents. Other Americans must pay for their own theaters and performers. [16]

United States Institute of Peace: $10,912,000. Millions of dollars for grants, fellowships, publications, and conferences to teach the people about the value of international peace. Yet, wars are started by governments, not by people. It's the people who already know the value of peace who are sent by the governments to fight and die. [17]

---

15. Ibid., p. A-720.
16. Ibid., p. A-724.
17. Ibid., p. A-1162.

National Foundation on the Arts and Humanities: $174,764,000. Grants are supplied to artists, some of whose works are downright blasphemous, filthy, or pornographic. Artists should support themselves or find a private benefactor. They should not be subsidized by taxpayers.[18]

Volunteers in Service to America: $206,738,000. Pretty expensive "volunteers"! While those who volunteer their services are to be commended, the large bureaucratic costs associated with this program is borne by taxpayers.[19]

Commodity Credit Corporation: $25,562,367,000. A form of foreign aid that doesn't carry that name, Commodity Credit Corporation funds are given to foreign governments to enable them to purchase U.S. agricultural products. While some of the money is repaid, the cost of this multi-billion-dollar program is borne by taxpayers. If giving money to others to purchase agricultural products is proper (It isn't!), then there is no reason why money couldn't be given to others to purchase autos, television sets, air conditioners, etc.[20]

Equal Employment Opportunity Commission: $233,805,000. This commission enforces *unequal* employment opportunity for selected racial, ethnic, and gender classifications. Government should never set standards for employment; employers alone should make such decisions.[21]

National Fertilizer Research Center: $34,670,000. Aren't fertilizer companies, farmers, and private firms able to determine what constitutes good fertilizer? There are undoubtedly some who contend that fertilizer research would never be done, or never be done well, except by government. That's absurd! And taking $34 million from taxpayers for this purpose can never be justified.[22]

Why do Americans allow all of this? Simply because they don't know about it or don't know how to put a stop to it. Hence this book.

---

18. Ibid., p. A-1109.
19. Ibid., p. A-1033.
20. Ibid., p. A-376.
21. Ibid., p. A-1056.
22. Ibid., p. A-1151.

The Path to Liquidating the Nation

In his comprehensive *Human Action*, Ludwig von Mises offered the following opinion about public debt:

> The financial history of the last century shows a steady increase in the amount of public indebtedness. Nobody believes that the states will eternally drag the burden of these interest payments. It is obvious that sooner or later all these debts will be liquidated in some way or other, but certainly not by payment of interest and principal according to the terms of the contract.[23]

In 1949, when von Mises issued that assessment, the debt of the United States was a mere six percent of what it has become.[24] He was possibly intimating that there are other ways to liquidate the debt that can be far more devastating than a simple loss of wealth.

One way could well include the creation of a new world monetary system to supplant the dollar — the Trilateral Commission/Council on Foreign Relations/Cecil Rhodes plan. If the Insiders currently implementing that plan get their way, Americans can say farewell to personal freedom and national sovereignty.

It's time to demand an end to the debt spiral. It's time to realize that the agenda of those in power calls for the destruction of this nation's capability to remain free and independent.

It's also time to become aware of the parade of false alternatives offered as solutions to problems by the very people who created them. As shown in the next chapter, the missing alternative they never consider is economic freedom.

---

23. von Mises, op. cit., p. 228.
24. Some defenders of the practice of deficit spending point to the amount of the national debt as a percentage of the nation's gross domestic product (GDP) and claim that its explosive rise in recent years has merely paralleled the rise in the nation's GDP. But they conveniently ignore the huge burdens for interest on the debt and taxation in general borne by today's Americans, burdens the people were not forced to shoulder a generation ago.

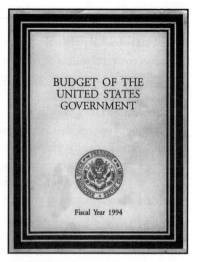

President Grover Cleveland warned that excessive taxation "becomes ruthless extortion."

The 1994 *Federal Budget* omitted the historical table of annual deficits.

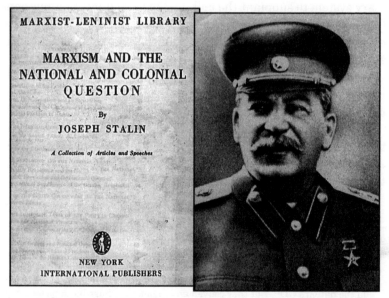

Joseph Stalin wanted the advanced nations of the world to pour foreign aid into the underdeveloped nations.

In 1982, Sen. Jesse Helms demonstrated that foreign aid had already cost the American people more than the accumulated national debt.

Ted Turner's "Goodwill Games" received $5 million in taxpayers' money.

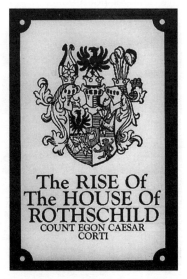

The House of Rothschild manipulated nations into wars and into debt.

The great Austrian economist Ludwig von Mises doubted that massive national indebtedness would ever be paid.

The annual cost of interest on the national debt averages more than $1,000 for each American, even these young people.

CHAPTER 4

Economic Freedom:
The Missing Alternative

There's small choice in rotten apples.
— William Shakespeare
The Taming of the Shrew

Commentary about the nation's economic problems in the daily press for June 1, 1993 differed little from what had been dispensed to the American people for many years. In typical fashion, the fare on this less-than-eventful day continued to keep Americans miserably confused about the economic future of their nation and themselves.

The lead article in that day's business section of the *New York Times* carried the headline, "The Federal Reserve Prepares for a Rate War." It was chock full of details about a "worried mood at the Fed" brought on by expectations of a coming battle with the Clinton Administration.

The major question: Should the Fed raise the nation's interest rates, thereby contracting the money supply and heading off an unexpected surge in the consumer price index (which government officials and the media equate with inflation); or should the Fed maintain low interest rates, thereby keeping the money spigots open and further stimulating job creation in particular and the nation's sluggish economy in general?

Talk about a choice of rotten apples!

Here's how *Times* Reporter Steven Greenhouse explained the looming battle between the Fed and the President:

The Federal Reserve's *raison d'être* is combatting inflation, and it

69

is deeply worried that prices have climbed at an annualized clip of 4 percent in recent months....

But President Clinton has a different mission: to create jobs and fix the nation's anemic growth rate.[1]

There are at least eight major "givens" in the thinking that buttresses this relatively short newspaper report. But each should have never been treated as a "given" in the first place. One after another, they confirm that the U.S. Constitution has been superseded, vast power has been placed in the Federal Reserve, a small group of individuals makes economic decisions affecting every single American, and the victims of this immense power grab have virtually no understanding of what is transpiring.

Here are the "givens," each of which is followed by our short comment:

1. The Federal Reserve should decide what the nation's interest rates should be. No it shouldn't! In a truly free country, the market will determine interest rates fairly and promptly. The Federal Reserve is the illegitimate and unconstitutional creation of individuals who seek to rule America. (See Chapter 10.)

2. Inflation is a rise in the Consumer Price Index. No! Inflation is an increase in the quantity of currency that results in the loss of its value and the rise in prices recorded by the Consumer Price Index. (See Chapter 6.)

3. The Federal Reserve should decide the volume of the nation's money supply. Whether there should be more or less currency should not be decided by any group or any individual. The Constitution established that gold and silver coinage was to be the nation's money, and it was left to the marketplace how much there should be. One of the main reasons for choosing gold as the nation's money is that it is a scarce commodity the supply of which cannot be inflated. (See Chapter 8.)

4. The Fed rightfully should make its decisions independently of the President and the Congress. Not only should

---

1. Steven Greenhouse, "The Federal Reserve Prepares For a Rate War," *New York Times*, June 1, 1993, p. D1.

the Fed be denied such power, it shouldn't have it even if it is shared with the President and Congress. Nor should either the President or Congress have the kind of power discussed in this article. Decisions regarding interest rates, etc., should be left to the marketplace.

5. The Federal Reserve exists to combat inflation. Not so! Without the Fed there would be little or no inflation. The Federal Reserve exists to create socialism in our nation. As is discussed later in this chapter, ten major steps are recommended in *The Communist Manifesto*[2] for the establishment of economic dictatorship in any nation. Step five in this economic guidebook for all socialists and communists reads: "Centralization of credit in the hands of the State, by means of a national bank with State capital and an exclusive monopoly." The Fed is the realization of that recommendation. It is using its illegitimate power both to steer our nation into tyranny and to expropriate the property of the American people.

6. The President's mission is to create jobs and fix the nation's anemic economy. What we have here is the assertion that the government, in the person of the President, should fix a problem with more of the same type of meddling that caused the problem in the first place. One excellent though indirect step a President could take to help create jobs would be to take the lead in reducing taxation, regulation, control, and bureaucracy. In a truly free society, job creation is no problem. But in the highly regulated and taxed environment suffocating America, job creation is increasingly difficult. Less government, not more, is the real answer to an anemic economy.

7. Pumping more money into the system will create jobs. This attitude essentially says that a government can spend the nation into prosperity. It can't be done. Jobs created by introducing more money into the system will not last. And numerous other problems associated with "pump-priming" will follow. Also, consider the absurdity of the attitude that government should take

---

2. Karl Marx and Frederick Engels, *The Communist Manifesto* (Appleton, WI: American Opinion Edition, 1974).

money from the people in order to create jobs for the people — as if the last thing on earth the people would do with their money is create jobs.

8. The Federal Reserve and the government — each acting alone or in concert with the other — can create prosperity. The Federal Reserve and the government produce nothing and, by their actions, are prosperity inhibitors. Prosperity (wealth) is productivity. Any nation whose people are free to take the raw materials of the earth and produce goods from them is prosperous. Whatever actions hinder wealth production, such as those mandated by the enormously restrictive network of federal regulatory agencies, will reduce prosperity.

A search for the real basis of our nation's deteriorating economic condition will lead to a dead end while these "givens" remain unchallenged. The great problem is that the American people are constantly supplied with the false premises detailed above — and more. But none of them is etched in stone. Each can and should be erased.

The Age of False Alternatives

Ours is an age when suggested alternatives for action are aimed at the American people almost daily. Unfortunately, practically all will cause more harm if implemented. They are like rotten apples from which to choose; whichever is selected is still rotten.

We have previously presented a classic example of the absence of a sound alternative. The nation is supposed to accept either of only two options to cure persistent economic doldrums: 1) Let the Fed's recommendations prevail; or 2) have the President and his advisors dispense the needed medicine. The way these options are regularly offered allows for no other possible solution to the nation's problems.

This tactic of forcing Americans into choosing from false and harmful alternatives is also being taught at the overwhelming majority of the nation's colleges and universities. Week after week, year after year, students studying economics, business and related subjects are programmed with the same false alternatives undergirded with an array of unsubstantiated premises.

There is no textbook containing the actual summary given below. But there are plenty of books and professors spewing out these incredibly flawed ideas. Here in a nutshell is what students are being taught:

> When the value of the dollar is high relative to other currencies, our domestic economy "slows down" because foreign goods become more attractive and consumers buy overseas. As a consequence, our nation experiences a trade deficit, and exporters are up in arms. The way to cure this problem is to lower the value of the dollar and expand the money supply by reducing interest rates.
>
> But when the value of the dollar sinks relative to the currencies of other nations, domestic goods become more attractive and the economy "heats up." The trade deficit becomes a surplus, and importers are up in arms. The cure for this development is to boost the value of the dollar and contract the amount of currency in circulation by raising interest rates.
>
> It is obvious that there is a need for great flexibility and enduring wisdom when the value of the dollar is established, interest rates are established, and the amount of currency is set. That is why the best available geniuses are appointed to decision-making posts at the Federal Reserve. And to keep their decisions from being influenced by political considerations, the members of the Fed's board who make these important determinations are appointed for 14-year terms by the President.
>
> While the President has the power to choose like-minded individuals for these sensitive posts, their 14-year terms guarantee that each will outlast him. Therefore, Fed leaders, who are encouraged but not required to consult with the President and Congress from time to time, are able to undertake moves that might not be popular with the reigning Administration. Aren't we fortunate in America to have such a marvelously conceived system managing the nation's economy?

Before any student, or anyone else for that matter, nods in agreement with what we have just presented (which is absolute nonsense from beginning to end), there is a need to consider a third alternative. It begins with the realization that no one should be given the awesome decision-making power to set interest rates, peg the value of the dollar, and decide how much currency should be in circulation. America's founding fathers didn't leave these matters in the hands of some economic guru or even a collection of them. Theirs was not the way of Karl Marx or some other hater of liberty.

The American system left the people with economic freedom, a government properly shackled by the Constitution, and would-be money managers held in check by a requirement that a valuable commodity such as gold or silver serve as money. The founders of the United States also wanted real competition in the banking industry, no irredeemable paper money, no inflation, and no manipulation from on high of interest rates or the value of the currency. Their study of history demonstrated that economic justice could be found, not in the decrees of an arrogant few, but in the marketplace where millions of individuals make economic decisions daily in their own best interests.

Karl Marx, on the other hand, wanted a monopolistic bank with all power over money placed in the hands of its leaders. His program called for granting authority to government-appointed "geniuses" to decide what is best for the nation and everyone in it. The hard truth is that America has been saddled with a Marxian program.

The Communist Manifesto

While it might come as a shock to many U.S. representatives and senators, numerous programs they champion for our nation can be found in the ten planks of *The Communist Manifesto* and cannot be found in the U.S. Constitution. In addition to its call for a central bank (the Federal Reserve), the *Manifesto* urges the following:

- **"Abolition of property in land...."** Using laws and regulations supposedly designed to protect the environment, the federal government has launched a concerted drive against owners of land. A multiplicity of regulations already deny land owners the right to use their land as they wish, thereby taking away the fundamental right of a property owner.

• **"A heavy progressive or graduated income tax."** That millstone was placed around the necks of the American people in 1913, the same year the Federal Reserve was created. Many elected officials stare in amazement at this date wondering how the federal government could possibly have functioned prior to 1913 without an income tax. It actually functioned quite well — and its size was scrawny as intended — with less onerous amounts of taxation derived from other sources.[3]

Income taxes unequivocally deny the principle of private property. They are based on the attitude that the state has first rights over a person's income and what it doesn't take amounts to a benevolent concession. With the power to alter the rate at which incomes are taxed and to set exemptions as it sees fit, government can theoretically take everything a person earns.

• **"Abolition of the rights of inheritance."** Numerous federal laws block Americans from giving their possessions to dependents or other desired inheritors. Inheritance taxes are based on the erroneous notion that much (or all) of what anyone accumulates belongs to government — another attack on the very existence of private property rights. But these taxes also constitute an attack on the family relationship and the ability of families to pass on their holdings to their own members.

• **"Free education for all children in public schools."** It surely follows that power seekers would want government to control the schools. The federal takeover of schools in America has occasioned the proliferation of government mandates about what

---

3. If there were no income tax, the federal government still possesses all of the taxing powers granted to it in Article I, Section 8 of the Constitution: "The Congress shall have power to lay and collect taxes, duties, imposts, and excises...." In other words, government could still collect excise taxes, customs duties, and several other taxes and fees.

may or may not be taught. The system is financed through compulsory taxation even of those who are childless or who pay to send their offspring to private schools. This is the Marxian plan exactly.

The *Manifesto* claimed that its message could "be summed up in the single sentence: abolition of private property." Responding to potential critics, Marx claimed, "... you reproach us for intending to do away with your property. Precisely so; that is just what we intend."

No one is free when he or she is unable to own property, keep the fruits of labors, and remain independent of government. Without property (an automobile, machinery, clothes, a home, etc.), a person is cut off from the means to accomplish personal goals. Abolishing property rights effectively establishes equality, the condition existing in prisons.

In keeping with its entire thrust, Marx and Engel's famous document also contains explicit attacks on the family, marriage, countries, nationalities, eternal truths, religion, morality, and more.

Look around this nation, and around the world, and you will see Marx's footprints everywhere. Yet no rational person wants to live as a slave to government. Americans should be asking how all of this could be happening if it is not being orchestrated by a diabolically driven conspiracy whose agents and dupes dominate government, the media, the schools, the military, and even the clergy.

The American people have been robbed of much of their economic freedom and are being rapidly steered into Marxian socialism. But even when the realization of what is happening begins to dawn, there is a real shortage of understanding about what to do to repair the immense damage.

If No Fed, Then What?

We are frequently asked to respond to the following question: If the Federal Reserve shouldn't manage the currency and the economy, who should? The simple answer: No one! Not the Fed, not the President, not the Congress, and not any combination of the greatest minds at the Fed, the White House, and the Congress. There cannot be any "management" of the economy in a truly free country.

A free market economy works well because of decisions made by millions of individuals about how best to use available resources. Individuals, not governments, know what is best for them. Managing the daily actions of millions of individuals cannot be accomplished without denying freedom and creating tyranny. (Acting in one's own self-interest does not mean acting without moral principle. A truly free individual sustains in his fellow men the same rights and freedoms he cherishes for himself).

What missing alternative should be instituted? It has the following elements: Abolish the Fed; have the U.S. Treasury issue currency fully redeemable in gold or silver; and allow free (competitive) banking. The nation's economic well-being should rise or fall as a result of the actions of a free people operating in the marketplace. Their individual decisions should be permitted to prevail instead of concentrating vast decision-making power in the Marxian Federal Reserve.

Even if Fed governors and Presidents were trying to serve the nation's best interests, they are no substitute for the marketplace where millions act individually. The good produced by the economic interactions and decisions of free individuals was recognized in clear terms by Adam Smith in his 1776 classic, *The Wealth of Nations*:

> As every individual, therefore, endeavors as much as he can both to employ his capital in support of domestic industry, and so to direct that industry that its produce may be of greatest value, every individual necessarily labors to render the annual revenue of society as great as he can. He generally, indeed, neither intends to promote the public interest nor knows how much he is promoting it ... he intends only his own security, and by directing that industry in such a manner as its produce may be of greatest value, he intends

only his own gain, and he is in this, as in many other cases, led by an invisible hand to promote an end which was not part of his intention....[4]

More Rotten Apples

Our nation is heavily in debt. If we don't soon stanch the flow of red ink, we face the threat of national bankruptcy and an array of devastating consequences.

But America is not alone in the sea of debt. As CFR and TC member Richard N. Cooper noted in his Fall 1984 *Foreign Affairs* article entitled "A Monetary System For the Future," there is a "large and burdensome external debt that has accumulated around the world."

So, how should this debt situation be addressed? Is there a need for new international arrangements beyond those created at the famous Bretton Woods conference of 1944? Professor Cooper answers:

> A new Bretton Woods conference is wholly premature. But it is not premature to begin thinking about how we would like international monetary arrangements to evolve in the remainder of this century. With this in mind, I suggest a radical alternative scheme for the next century: *the creation of a common currency for all of the industrial democracies, with a common monetary policy and a joint Bank of Issue to determine that monetary policy.* (Emphasis in original.)[5]

Here we have another set of false alternatives: 1) create a world currency and a new "Bank of Issue" to dispense it, thereby controlling the economic decisions of all industrialized nations (a world Federal Reserve); or 2) hold on to an outmoded Bretton Woods system. Both alternatives completely ignore economic freedom.

---

4. Adam Smith, *Wealth of Nations* (New York, NY: Penguin Books, 1970).
5. Richard N. Cooper, "A Monetary System for the Future," *Foreign Affairs*, Fall 1984, p. 166.

What's the Bretton Woods system? In July 1944, many of the world's prominent bankers and government planners met at Bretton Woods, New Hampshire at the invitation of President Franklin Roosevelt.[6] Their deliberations produced the UN's International Monetary Fund and the post-world War II monetary system which has been working for almost half a century to create a centrally controlled economic system for the planet. The IMF has also regularly created sufficient turmoil to topple governments and steer nations into the type of government-directed economic planning it favors.[7]

A good understanding of the thrust of the IMF can be gained through awareness of the individuals who guided it into existence. The April 20, 1971 issue of *The American Banker* reported:

> The main architects of the Fund were Harry Dexter White and John Maynard Keynes (later Lord Keynes) of the American and British Treasuries.... Keynes had written about a world central bank as early as 1930, while White had been instructed by the U.S. Treasury only a week after Pearl Harbor to start drafting plans for an international stabilization fund after the war.[8]

Unlike those authors whose articles appear in Establishment publications such as *The American Banker*, the late Gary Allen wanted his readers to know precisely who these "main architects" were. In his *Say "No!" To the New World Order*, he wrote:

> John Maynard Keynes was the darling of the British Fabian Society, the gang of socialist conspirators who had taken over and

---

6. This 1944 gathering, held a full year before the United Nations was actually founded, was formally known as the United Nations Monetary and Financial Conference. There was no doubt in the minds of these individuals that the UN would be formed.

7. Warren T. Brookes, "IMF Helped To Bring Marcos Down," *Boston Herald*, March 20, 1986. Also, Paul Craig Roberts, "IMF Is Working To Expand Its Power," *Houston Chronicle*, April 15, 1989.

8. Cited in Gary Allen, *Say "No!" To the New World Order* (Seal Beach, CA: Concord Press, 1987), p. 241.

wrecked Great Britain. An aggressive homosexual, Keynes also promulgated a queer brand of economics which, among other things, strongly encouraged unrestrained government spending and deliberate budget deficits as a cure for inflation-caused recessions....

Harry Dexter White was a bird of an even more crimson hue. While all the standard histories of the IMF fail to mention it, [he] was at once a member of the Council on Foreign Relations and a dedicated Soviet agent. White had moved into various positions of importance in the U.S. Treasury Department where he carefully laid out plans for a new monetary order....

On November 6, 1953, Attorney General Herbert Brownell revealed that Harry Dexter White's "spying activities for the Soviet Government were reported in detail by the FBI to the White House ... in December of 1945. In the face of this information, and incredible though it may seem, President Truman went ahead and nominated White, who was then Assistant Secretary of the Treasury, for the even more important position of executive director for the United States in the International Monetary Fund...."

While agreeing with Keynes that a centrally managed world fiat currency was the ultimate goal, White was more cautious. He knew the dangers of going too fast, recalling how the Senate had kept the United States out of the internationalist trap known as the League of Nations in the aftermath of World War I. The wily communist was concerned that the Senate would scuttle so obvious a move toward One World government.[9]

Yet, according to Professor Cooper, there are only two ways out of the debt mess: 1) stick with the Bretton Woods system; or 2) create a new Federal Reserve-type system for the world. Translated, the choice is loss of economic freedom through an existing mechanism established jointly by a socialist from England and a communist from the United States, or the loss of economic freedom through a new scheme dreamed up by leading CFR/TC Insiders. Some choice!

---

9. Gary Allen, op. cit., p. 241 et seq.

In his "A Monetary System For the Future," Cooper sought to throw a bone to anyone concerned about the rights of sovereign nations. He wrote: "Individual countries would be free to determine their fiscal actions, but those would be constrained by the need to borrow in the international capital market."[10] This means that nations would be free to act, except that their actions would have to jell with the dictates of the new Bank of Issue to which they would of necessity be joined.

In other words, nations would be free as long as they followed orders! George Orwell's Newspeak has been reborn. According to Cooper, freedom and constraint have the same meaning.

As far back as 1972, the CFR published a similar proposal authored by one of its members, also a Trilateral Commission founding planner, C. Fred Bergsten. His 95-page booklet entitled "Reforming the Dollar: An International Monetary Policy For the United States" amounted to a call for overhauling the entire international financial system.[11]

Of primary importance, wrote Bergsten, the reformed system "must be managed internationally." He proposed that international financial reserves should be based on Special Drawing Rights issued by the UN's International Monetary Fund. (Special Drawing Rights are frequently called "paper gold." But they are, in fact, paper paper.)

Still pushing his internationalism almost 20 years later, Bergsten, now a holder of both TC and CFR memberships, lamented in an interview appearing in the August 9, 1989 *Christian Science Monitor* that the world's economy had not yet arrived at "management by committee." He claimed that "the world economy is in trouble unless there is some central steering mechanism."

Here we have two prominent internationalists decrying both the world's mounting debt and the independent fiscal activity of the nations. They offer as alternatives either a Federal Reserve

---

10. Richard N. Cooper, op. cit., p. 166.
11. C. Fred Bergsten, *Reforming the Dollar: An International Monetary Policy For the United States* (New York, NY: Council on Foreign Relations, 1972).

system for the world or management of the world economy by a central authority. Both accept debt as inevitable, and neither exhibits any confidence in true fiscal independence. And they are joined by numerous others offering similar proposals to address problems brought on by like-minded mega-managers.

Trilateral Mischief

At periodically held Trilateral Commission meetings, Bergsten, Cooper and other internationalists continue to promote the idea of creating a centralized system to manage the economy of the entire world. They boldly point to the need to propagandize the American people, counter nationalistic attitudes wherever they exist, and overcome a lack of enthusiasm about the supposed need for "interdependence."

The TC meeting held in Madrid in May 1986 produced a report co-authored by Bergsten entitled "Conditions For Partnership in International Economic Management." Among his conclusions can be found:

> Americans must be brought to understand the ultimate costs of unilateral policies for America itself.... [M]ore effective international regimes need to be erected to foster macroeconomic and monetary policy cooperation.

Another paper co-authored by Bergsten, entitled "Future of the International Economic Order," was distributed at the April 1989 TC meeting in Tokyo. It stated:

> The only viable way, it seems to me, to structure the international economic order for the future is to install collective leadership among the Trilateral partners — to view the three regions not as the dictators or the dominators, but as a steering committee, which must work out its own differences first in order to lead a stable and prosperous world economy.

Then, at the TC meeting in Paris in 1989, a paper co-authored by Richard N. Cooper, Shijuro Ogata, and Horst Schulmann entitled "International Financial Integration: The Policy Challenges" contained the following closing statement:

> The keys to better international coordination include the strength of political will of national leaders to overcome nationalistic sentiment and regional and sectoral interests and the depth of understanding by the general public of the implications of global interdependence. It is extremely important to build up informed public opinion in all Trilateral countries, including influential citizens who are not usually exposed to international debates — a task in which the Trilateral Commission also has an important role.

In keeping with Cooper's perceived need "to build up informed public opinion in all Trilateral countries," members of the Commission and its partner-in-internationalism, the Council on Foreign Relations, continue to use their considerable influence within the mass media to propagandize the American people. CFR and TC members can be found in leadership positions at the major radio/television networks, *Time*, *Newsweek*, *U.S. News & World Report*, *National Review*, *New York Times*, *Washington Post*, *Los Angeles Times*, *Wall Street Journal*, and elsewhere.

Who Attends TC Meetings?

Some of the Americans who have participated in recent meetings of the Trilateral Commission, as noted in literature published by the Commission, include:

Paris 1989: TC Founder and Johns Hopkins University Professor Zbigniew Brzezinski; E. Gerald Corrigan, president of the Federal Reserve Bank of New York; Speaker of the House of Representatives Thomas P. Foley.

Washington 1990: Harvard University Professor Joseph S. Nye Jr.; chairman of the President's Council of Economic Advisers Michael J. Boskin; former chairman of the President's Council of Economic Advisers Martin Feldstein.

Tokyo 1991: Former Under Secretary of State Joseph J. Sisco;

former *U.S. News & World Report* Editor-at-Large and newly appointed counselor to the President David Gergen.

Lisbon 1992: Former U.S. Secretary of State Henry Kissinger; former U.S. Ambassador to Russia Robert Strauss; Zbigniew Brzezinski; former *Time* Editor-at-Large and current Assistant Secretary of State Strobe Talbott; David Gergen; former Assistant Secretary of State Robert Hormats.

In general, the great missing alternative to the many proposals of these one-worlders is freedom: national solvency, personal liberty, limited government, undiluted independence, and constitutionally authorized gold or silver money.

Yet the world, especially the United States, is inundated with internationalist schemes produced by experts and government agencies. Independent action by any individual or nation is all but condemned outright. The constant cry is that the world and its people must be managed. But, of course, the managing will be done by the brilliant, powerful, arrogant and determined members of a conspiratorial cabal.

All the conspirators want is political and economic control of the planet: the new world order. Obviously, they and their plans must be stopped.

As we have repeatedly stated, these individuals intend to have the United States so overwhelmed with debt and propagandized with false alternatives that management of the U.S. economy by a world system becomes the only plausible alternative. Creating that debt burden is an essential step toward their goal.

Practically everyone in America has some appreciation of growing federal debt. As a result, successive occupants of the White House (and virtually all politicians) have repeatedly pledged to do something about it. But, as we show in our next chapter, tough talk has been easy. But performance to back it up has been neither easy nor hard; it's been absent.

The tenets of Karl Marx's *Communist Manifesto* are being implemented in the United States.

John Maynard Keynes correctly exposed inflation, then led the U.S. into the debt/deficit spiral.

Harry Dexter White was a member of the Communist Party when he fathered the International Monetary Fund.

David Gergen, now Bill Clinton's "counselor," is a veteran member of the CFR and TC, and a Bilderberg participant.

Newspapers whose leadership includes CFR members.

Magazines whose leadership includes CFR members.

CHAPTER 5

Rhetoric, Cover-ups, and Duplicity

Our national debt is approaching $1 trillion. A few weeks ago, I called such a figure — a trillion dollars — incomprehensible. I've been trying to think of a way to illustrate how big it really is. The best I could come up with is to say that a stack of $1,000 bills in your hand only four inches high would make you a millionaire. A trillion dollars would be a stack of $1,000 bills 67 miles high.

— President Ronald Reagan
State of the Union Address
February 18, 1981

To move steadily toward a balanced budget we must also lighten government's claim on our total economy.... In our fiscal year 1986 budget, overall government program spending will be frozen at the current level; it must not be one dime higher than fiscal year 1985.

— President Ronald Reagan
State of the Union Address
February 6, 1985

And we must make a very substantial cut in the federal budget deficit.... We will not have the luxury of taking the easy, spendthrift approach to solving problems — because higher spending and higher taxes put economic growth at risk.

— President George Bush
Budget Speech to Congress
February 9, 1989

The plan has three key elements: economic stimulus to create jobs now and lay the foundation for long-term economic growth; long-term public investments to increase the productivity of American workers and businesses; and fair, balanced, and equitable deficit reduction measures to stop government deficits from preempting the private investments needed to create jobs and raise living standards.

— President Bill Clinton
Budget Message
April 8, 1993

As can be seen in the above statements, each of these Presidents knew that debt is ravaging America. This reassuring rhetoric appeared soon after each of the past four inaugurations. But each of their administrations — with assistance from a procession of spendthrift Congresses — promptly proceeded to set new records in the red ink department. The American people are being waltzed with sweet sounding talk while their economic and political freedom is disappearing.

Projected Debt Always Too Low

Year after year, federal budgets contain optimistic projections of lower deficits for the immediate future. For instance, when Ronald Reagan took office in 1981, his budget officials predicted a deficit for 1982 of $27.5 billion.[1] But the deficit for that year turned out to be $142.5 billion.[2]

Four years later as Mr. Reagan began his second term, administration officials told the nation that the deficit for 1986 would be $179.9 billion.[3] But when all the figures were finally in, it was $303.1 billion.[4]

George Bush began his term in 1989. His budget officials fore-

---

1. *1982 Budget*, p. 613.
2. See Table 3-1. The deficit figure for 1982 is arrived at by computing the difference between the national debt figure supplied at the end of Fiscal 1981 and the one supplied at the end of Fiscal 1982.
3. *1986 Budget*, pp. 9-10.
4. See Table 3-1.

cast a deficit for 1990 of $161.3 billion.[5] The actual figure turned out to be $338.8 billion.[6]

Early in 1993, Clinton Administration officials predicted that deficits for the next four fiscal years (1994-1997) would be $264.1 billion, $246.7 billion, $211.7 billion, and $214.0 billion.[7]

Add these four figures and their total shows that the Clinton team is *planning* to add close to $1 trillion to the national debt during its first term. But, based on the pattern set over the past 12 years, deficits for the four Clinton years will likely be double the estimates given.

Unlike his two immediate predecessors, Mr. Clinton is quite obvious about his determination to increase government programs, spending, and deficits. As columnist Paul Craig Roberts has summarized, "Restoring the primacy of government is what Mr. Clinton is all about.... People who dare to gain independence from government are going to be made to pay.... His overriding goal is to reduce the private sector's claim on the income it produces."[8]

The fact that deficit projections are always low isn't the worst feature of our nation's plunge into poverty. The worst part of this sorry picture is that the deficits are planned. The hole our nation is in keeps getting deeper — by design!

Hiding the Awful Truth About Interest

The Fiscal 1994 Budget claims that "Net Interest" for Fiscal 1992 was $199.4 billion.[9] What is net interest? Does it differ from actual interest?

Congressional Quarterly tells us: "Net interest payments exclude the interest the government pays itself for securities it holds, such as those in the Social Security trust funds."[10] Pays itself? How? And with what?

As a way to hide the horrendous cost of interest, the slight-of-

---

5. *1990 Budget*, pp. 10-47.
6. See Table 3-1.
7. *1994 Budget*, p. 33.
8. Paul Craig Roberts, "Over the Clintonomics Edge," *Washington Times*, February 22, 1993.
9. *1994 Budget*, p. A-19.

hand experts at the federal level take funds they lead the public to believe are untouchable (funds for social security, highway building and maintenance, etc.) and use them to pay other federal obligations.

What is the actual interest for fiscal 1992? Buried in the back of the *1994 Budget*, amidst scores of tables and bureaucratic statistics, "Total Interest" on the debt for the single year of 1992 is reported to have been a whopping $292.3 billion.[11] This is a far cry from the $199.4 billion net interest reported in the very same document. Net interest is a term used by a dishonest accountant.

Another dishonest term in official use is "trust fund," such as the one supposedly holding social security deposits. In 1937, shortly after the social security system was established, a Supreme Court decision put to rest any notion that there ever was, or ever would be, any social security "trust fund." In a case dealing with the Social Security system, the Court ruled that "the proceeds of both [employee and employer] taxes are to be paid into the Treasury like any other internal revenue generally, *and are not earmarked in any way ...*" (emphasis added).[12]

Federal officials have always led Americans to believe that social security is a government insurance program. It is not! If any private insurance company operated as the social security system is being run, its officers would be indicted for fraud. And if any corporation were run in the manner the federal government is being run, its board of directors would fire the CEO and all of his top officers in a minute.

Debt Actually Much Larger

We don't want to become buried in figures. We'd sooner have you infuriated than bogged down in numbers. But there is another type of debt-related dishonesty that must be addressed. It is simply that, in addition to covering over the full truth about

---

10. *Congressional Quarterly*, Jan. 26, 1991, p. 234. *CQ* is an authoritative, relatively objective, privately run publication that reports on national affairs.
11. *1994 Budget*, p. A-921.
12. *Helvering v. Davis*, 301 U.S. 619, 635; 1937.

projected debt and actual interest, U.S. officials are not telling us the whole story about the size of the nation's debt. Consider the following assessment of the deficit given in *Barron's* on February 5, 1990:

> In fiscal 1989, the official deficit was $152 billion. But the Treasury tapped the markets for $139.1 billion of new debt and, as noted above, issued $126.2 billion of new debt to government trust funds. In addition, the budget shows that the Treasury drew down its cash balances by $3.4 billion, and created $9.4 billion by such measures as the float on checks and the profits on minting coins and selling gold.
>
> These figures produce a truer government deficit of $278.1 billion, but there's more: Government agencies borrowed $11.7 billion. The largest share was debt issued by the Federal Deposit Insurance Corp. ($2.25 billion) and the Federal Savings and Loan Insurance Corp. ($8.8 billion) as assistance to the purchasers of failing banks and thrifts.
>
> And more: Government sponsored enterprises, from Fannie Mae and Freddie Mac to Sallie Mae and Farmer Mac,[13] borrowed $132.2 billion from the public, while government agencies guaranteed another $43.1 billion of fresh private debt. (A new disclosure in the budget estimates the value of the federal subsidy granted by loan guarantees in fiscal 1991 at $9.4 billion, but the figure isn't available for earlier years.)
>
> So the grand total of new government debt incurred during fiscal 1989 was $456.1 billion, or almost exactly three times the acknowledged government deficit.[14]

This pattern has not been interrupted. The actual borrowing by government in any fiscal year can add up to three times the published figure. Over the past several years, it is likely even higher because of huge "off-budget" expenditures earmarked for

---

13. The Federal National Mortgage Association (Fannie Mae), Federal Home Loan Mortgage Corporation (Freddie Mac), Student Loan Mortgage Association (Sallie Mae), and Federal Agricultural Mortgage Corporation (Farmer Mac).

14. T.G.D., "How Big Is The Deficit — Really," *Barron's*, February 5, 1990.

programs which don't even appear in the published budget figures — such as the hundreds of billions of taxpayer dollars the Resolution Trust Corporation has spent to bail out banks and savings and loan institutions.

Who Owns the Debt?

Years ago, and even today as noted previously, apologists for deficit spending regularly insisted that no one need worry about the national debt "because we owe it to ourselves." When sensible Americans challenged that nonsense by demanding to be paid their share at once, it turned out that we didn't owe it to ourselves after all.

Actually, the federal debt is owed to anyone who holds a U.S. government bond. Contrary to widespread rumors, a relatively small portion of this debt is held by the Federal Reserve. As financial columnist Neland Nobel has noted, ownership of the U.S. national debt is held by private U.S. investors (55 percent), U.S. government agencies and trusts (25 percent), foreign investors (12 percent), and the Federal Reserve (7 percent). [15, 16]

More recently, a new claim holds that we needn't worry about government debt because it's backed up by the tremendous wealth and productivity of our nation. But if that claim has validity, then the government doing the borrowing is essentially holding a lien on the wealth of the people, the value of our nation's natural resources, and the productive might of the entire nation. Aren't those who make such a claim telegraphing their intention to have the government own everything?

Blaming Each Other

During the years 1981-1993, Republican Presidents made a practice of blaming Democrats who controlled Congress for the

---

15. Neland D. Nobel, "Who Owns the National Debt?" *The New American*, June 29, 1992.
16. As we have already seen, the federal government cannot retire — and never had any intention of retiring — its notes held by the Social Security administration. Transactions involving federal "trust funds" are merely bookkeeping gymnastics for the purpose of hiding the truth.

deficits. And it's true that Democrats controlled the House of Representatives during this entire period while the Republicans held a slim majority in the Senate from 1981 to 1987.

Predictably, Democrats have countered by insisting that America's economic woes were the fault of the Republican Presidents. Anyone concerned about the debt and deficit pattern was told by each faction to blame the other.

The truth, of course, is that both parties are to blame. One year before he left office, President George Bush proposed a budget for Fiscal 1993 of $1,503 billion. The House-passed version totalled $1,497.9 billion; the Senate-passed version was $1,500.5 billion; and the budget finally agreed to after conferences and negotiations was $1,500 billion.[17] The budget for fiscal 1992 was $1,475.4.

Note that both the House and Senate, each controlled by Democrats at the time, offered slightly lower budgets than the Republican President. So the Republican claim that Congress is the chief culprit for huge budgets and correspondingly huge deficits is nonsense.

During the 1992 election campaign, one of President Bush's main themes stressed that the Democratic Congress deserved the blame for deficits. But, as bad as Democratic spending habits truly are, the truth is that the President's were worse. The September 7, 1992 issue of *The New American* reported: "Ten of the 13 regular appropriations bills passed by the heavily Democratic House contain less spending than the amount requested by the Bush Administration. In all, the House cut $10 billion from the Bush Administration budget requests."[18]

In addition, President Bush's budget for 1993 called for a planned deficit of $331.8 billion. The House planned a deficit of $324.5 billion; the Senate wanted it to be $327.1 billion; and the final version projected a deficit of $326.6 billion.[19]

---

17. *1992 Congressional Quarterly Almanac*, p. 102.
18. Thomas R. Eddlem, "Blame Congress? No, Blame Bush," *The New American*, September 7, 1992.
19. Figures compiled by the Congressional Budget Office and the House and Senate Budget Committees, published in *1992 Congressional Quarterly Almanac*.

On the Democratic side, President Clinton's proposed budget for fiscal 1994 ($1,500.6 billion) also exceeded the House-passed version ($1,495.0), the Senate-passed version ($1,498.0), and the final version ($1,496.6).[20]

But we're diverting attention away from the critically important realization that it isn't so much Presidents, or Congresses, or Democrats, or Republicans who are destroying our nation with debt and deficits. The destruction stems from the work of a conspiracy made up of, or greatly aided by, some Democrats, some Republicans, and a lot of unelected members of "the Establishment."[21]

Consider: There were 284 Council on Foreign Relations members and 17 Trilateral Commission members holding high government posts during the Carter Administration.[22]

There were 313 CFR members and several key Trilateral Commission members holding high government posts during the Reagan Administration.[23]

There were 387 CFR members and several additional TC members holding high government posts during Bush Administration.[24]

As shown in the accompanying chart gleaned from the most recent CFR and TC membership rosters, many of the top Clinton administration appointees, even the President himself, have CFR and/or TC lineage.

Congress is currently led by Speaker of the House Thomas

---

20. *Congressional Quarterly*, April 3, 1993, p. 824.
21. In one of her syndicated columns published in 1961, Edith Kermit Roosevelt stated: "The word 'Establishment' is a general term for the power elite in international finance, business, the professions and government, largely from the northeast, who wield most of the power regardless of who is in the White House. Most people are unaware of the existence of this 'legitimate Mafia.' Yet the power of the Establishment makes itself felt from the professor who seeks a foundation grant, to the candidate for a Cabinet post or State Department job. It affects the nation's policies in almost every area."
22. 1978 *CFR Annual Report*; January 31, 1978 membership list issued by the Trilateral Commission.
23. 1988 *CFR Annual Report*; February 15, 1987 membership list issued by the Trilateral Commission.
24. 1992 *CFR Annual Report*; April 4, 1991 membership list issued by the Trilateral Commission.

Bill Clinton and Some of His Major Appointees

	CFR*	TC*
President		
Bill Clinton	✓	✓
Secretary of State		
Warren Christopher	✓	✓
Deputy Secretary of State		
Clifton R. Wharton	✓	
CIA Director		
R. James Woolsey	✓	
National Security Advisor		
W. Anthony Lake	✓	
Deputy National Security Advisor		
Samuel R. Berger	✓	
Secretary of Defense		
Les Aspin	✓	
Chairman, Foreign Intelligence Advisory Board		
William J. Crowe	✓	✓
U.S. Ambassador to the United Nations		
Madeleine Albright	✓	
Secretary of the Treasury		
Lloyd M. Bentsen	✓	
Deputy Secretary of the Treasury		
Roger C. Altman	✓	
Secretary of Health and Human Services		
Donna E. Shalala	✓	✓
Deputy Director, Office of Management and Budget		
Alice M. Rivlin	✓	✓
Secretary of Housing and Urban Development		
Henry G. Cisneros	✓	✓
Chairman, Council of Economic Advisors		
Laura D. Tyson	✓	
Secretary of the Interior		
Bruce Babbitt	✓	✓

* Present or Past Member

Foley (CFR and TC), House Majority Leader Richard Gephardt (CFR), and Senate Majority Leader George Mitchell (CFR). Dozens of other senators and representatives — some waving Republican banners and others sporting Democratic labels — are also CFR and TC members. The treachery is bi-partisan![25]

Yes, there are some fiscally responsible members of the House and Senate who are neither conspirators nor ball-carriers for the conspiracy. But they are too few in number to stop the fiscal madness plaguing our nation. There is a critical need to replace the big spenders and big borrowers with determined Americans who will adhere strictly to the Constitution.

Can America's rush to the new world order be stopped? Yes it can, and we cover the actual mechanics of the solution in Chapter 13.

An essential element in stopping the drive to create the new world order includes widespread awareness that our nation's leaders are merely talking about holding down the deficits. Actually, the deficits are planned. If federal officials truly wanted to stop the flow of red ink, they could do so. A mere majority in either House of Congress could force the balancing of the budget — without new taxes.

Stopping the debt and deficit spiral would throw a crippling monkey wrench into the plans of the conspiracy. So those bent on having America commit suicide not only keep adding more indebtedness, they make a practice of vilifying those who oppose their policies and expose their plans.

While the plans of the conspirators call for creating massive federal debt leading inexorably to a loss of sovereignty, they also call for steadily increasing control over the lives and fortunes of the American people.

---

25. Not every member of the CFR or TC is a committed conspirator. Many, in fact, are self-servers who will follow whatever direction they perceive will help them achieve personal fame and fortune. Should it become advantageous in their eyes to reverse course and reject the promptings of a conspiracy, most would do so immediately. Making such a reversal appealing is the job of every American.

One certain route to this kind of totalitarian control is inflation, the little understood and extremely devious technique employed by governments to steal the people's wealth and lead them into dependency. Putting an end to inflation would help to cripple the conspiratorial drive.

In the next few chapters, we examine inflation's thievery and destructiveness. And then, because inflation could not wreak its horrors without a monopolistic central bank and a woeful lack of awareness about the nature of money, we tackle those topics as well.

Immediately ahead: An explanation of inflation and its use by a conspiracy to steal, and then destroy.

Richard Gephardt (D-MO) is the House Majority Leader and a CFR member.

George Mitchell (D-ME) is the Senate Majority Leader and a CFR member.

Former Texas Senator Lloyd Bentsen, a CFR veteran, serves as Secretary of the Treasury.

Columnist Edith Kermit Roosevelt labelled the Establishment a "legitimate Mafia."

CHAPTER 6

Inflation: Stealing the People's Wealth

*By a continuous process of inflation, governments can con-
fiscate, secretly and unobserved, an important part of the
wealth of their citizens. By this method, they not only confiscate, but they confiscate arbitrarily; and while the process impoverishes many, it actually enriches some.... The process
engages all of the hidden forces of economic law on the side of
destruction, and does it in a manner that not one man in a
million can diagnose.*

— John Maynard Keynes
Economic Consequences of the Peace, 1920[1]

Throughout history, truth about the thieving nature of inflation has generally been kept from its victims. Yet the leaders of
our government and those who sit atop the Federal Reserve certainly know what they're doing as they confiscate the people's
wealth, destroy America's economic vitality, and lead the entire
nation into servitude. The harmful effects of inflation serve the
cause of those who seek to impose their new world order on mankind. But if inflation were understood by the people, creating such
a totalitarian world would be far more difficult, probably impossible.

John Maynard Keynes was a British socialist, a member of the
Fabian Society of London. Fourteen years after he wrote *Economic Consequences of the Peace*, he came to America at the invitation of President Franklin Roosevelt and led many U.S. officials

---

1. John Maynard Keynes, *Economic Consequences of the Peace* (New York, NY:
Harcourt, Brace and Howe, 1920), p. 235.

and academics to champion the absurd notion that a government can spend itself into prosperity. He is rightly called the father of deficit spending.[2]

Regardless of whatever else he did, he is worth quoting about inflation because what he said is absolutely correct. Consider: Using inflation, governments can silently confiscate the people's wealth; many individuals become impoverished; a few get rich; and hardly anyone is able to grasp what is happening. Obviously, inflation is powerful stuff!

But what is inflation? Several years ago, a reader of the *New York Times* tried to get an answer to this simple question from the newspaper's editorial page editor, Max Frankel. Shown nearby is the tart response he received, demonstrating that power not only corrupts, it breeds arrogance. All the *Times* official offered was, "Dear Sir: I guess if you don't know what inflation is you don't have to worry about it."

When Frankel sent his sassy reply, Jimmy Carter occupied the White House. That period was marked by daily worries in the *Times* and virtually all organs of the mass media about the twin scourges of inflation and high interest rates. But the *Times* and other major suppliers of the public's information rarely bothered to define inflation and, still today, very few Americans truly understand it. Frankel might have taken the time to send his response, but he refused to supply an accurate answer to the simple question because he and his peers were relying on keeping the public uninformed.

The *Times* reader who received Max Frankel's note also received a response from Leonard Silk, the newspaper's chief economic columnist. Silk displayed none of the arrogance sent by Frankel, but he fully subscribed to the popularly held erroneous definition when he offered that inflation was "a general and persistent rise in prices." It should come as no surprise to learn that both Frankel and Silk are veteran members of the Council on Foreign Relations, a premier promoter of the new world order.

---

2. For more about John Maynard Keynes, see Rose L. Martin, *Fabian Freeway* (Appleton, WI: Western Islands, 1966).

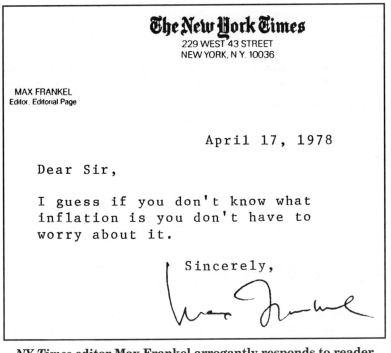

NY Times **editor Max Frankel arrogantly responds to reader**

A Correct Definition

Older dictionaries, though not all of them, give an accurate definition of this commonly misunderstood term. *Webster's New Twentieth Century Unabridged Dictionary of the English Language* (1957), for instance, offers the following:

> Inflation: an increase in the amount of currency in circulation, resulting in a relatively sharp and sudden fall in its value and rise in prices.[3]

Those few words supply the key to unlocking a problem that has troubled men throughout history. Note that it says the rise in prices is the *result* or the *effect* of inflation, not inflation itself.

---

3. *New Twentieth Century Unabridged Dictionary of the English Language* (Cleveland and New York: World Publishing Company, 1957), p. 939.

Note also that inflation is nothing more than an increase in the quantity of currency. Currency's amount is increased (inflated), not prices, not wages, not anything else but the sum total of money being circulated. Anyone who grasps this elementary point can begin to understand that inflation causes upward pressure on prices and wages.

The damage done by inflation isn't caused by the merchant who raises his prices or the working man who seeks higher wages. The crime of inflation is committed by whatever agency (or agencies) increase the amount of currency.

When the amount of currency is increased, the value of currency already in circulation is cheapened. All business is conducted in what amounts to an auction. If everyone at an auction is suddenly given additional dollars, the bids for goods will rise. Within the confines of the auction, the dollars have become less valuable while the value of the goods they purchase remains the same.

Money and wealth are not the same. If they were, a government printing press could solve everyone's financial problems by simply churning out crisp new bills to be passed along to everyone. But doing so does not increase the wealth of the nation.

In his excellent 1946 book, *Economics in One Lesson*, Henry Hazlitt defined inflation as "increased quantities of money (including bank credit)" and then demolished the commonly held and erroneous notion holding that money and wealth are synonymous. He wrote:

> The most obvious and yet the oldest and most stubborn error on which the appeal of inflation rests is that of confusing "money" with wealth.... Real wealth, of course, consists in what is produced and consumed: the food we eat, the clothes we wear, the house we live in. It is railway and roads and motor cars; ships and planes and factories; schools and churches and theaters; pianos, paintings and books.... Each man sees that if he personally had more money he could buy more things from others.... And to many the conclusion seems obvious that if the government merely issued more money

and distributed it to everybody, we should all be that much richer.[4]

As anyone who buys and sells knows — and that's all of us — the U.S. dollar won't buy as much as it formerly did. While prices regularly rise and fall due to a host of reasons, the major cause of steadily rising prices over the past few decades is that inflation has caused the value of the dollar to evaporate.

A loaf of bread that could be purchased in 1943 for less than 10 cents now commands $1.50 or more. Actually, this dramatic increase in price was not caused so much by any change in the value of bread, even though changes in production techniques or ingredients may affect its value slightly. The dramatic change in the amount of dollars needed to obtain bread today has resulted from the steady destruction of the value of money.

Stop and think about a young man who inherited $10,000 in crisp $100 bills in 1940. Such a windfall amounted to a veritable fortune at the time. But, for whatever his reason, he stuffed the bills in the bottom drawer of his dresser. We can disagree with his decision not to invest or spend his inheritance, but it was his money and he certainly had the right to do whatever he wanted with it.

Fifty-three years later, he digs out his $10,000 and finds its purchasing power is about five percent of what it was when he inherited it. He could have bought a very nice home for his $10,000 in 1943, and now he can barely make a down payment on one. Where did the value of his money go?

Or, consider that a man living in the 1920s could buy a decent suit of clothes for a one-ounce $20 gold piece. Today, a $20 gold piece "costs" roughly $400, the price of today's decent suit of clothes.

It would be ridiculous to say that $20 has become $400, even though that's what appears to have happened. What we should be saying is that it took only $20 to purchase an ounce of gold in 1930, and it takes approximately $400 to do so today. The great-

---

4. Henry Hazlitt, *Economics in One Lesson* (New York, NY: Crown Publishers, 1979), pp. 164-165.

est cause of this change is the deterioration in the value of the dollar.

Value Stolen

What happens to the value of money during a period of inflation? The answer is that it ends up in the possession of whoever does the inflating. The counterfeiter is the simplest example of an inflator at work. If he produces some good-looking bills, he can "spend" them and walk away with someone else's goods or services for the cost of paper, ink, and some time on a printing press. He has traded essentially worthless paper for valuable goods.

The previous owner of the goods or the provider of the services is left holding the counterfeit bills. If he fails to realize that they're counterfeit, he will pass them on in some other transaction. (He also may realize that they're bogus and still pass them on.) In virtually all cases, the fact that the bills are illegitimate will eventually be discovered and someone will be defrauded.

If the counterfeit currency is not discovered to be bogus and the counterfeiter continues to introduce quantities of it into the system, then all holders of currency are defrauded. Inflation, in a very real sense, steals from those who hold money. When practiced by governments, inflation is a hidden tax on holders of money.

The point we wish to make is the same one Keynes correctly observed: Inflation amounts to confiscation, and through the chain of events it triggers, some persons are enriched, many more are impoverished, the economic condition of the nation is upset, and booms and busts result.

A counterfeiter is an inflator, and counterfeiting is a fancy form of stealing. Although governments regularly practice this form of thievery, they spend great amounts of energy tracking down counterfeiters. They literally want no competition.

Ask yourself the following questions:
- Shouldn't there be prohibitions against this thieving process when government practices it?
- Can a fraudulent scheme perpetrated by a counterfeiter be

made acceptable merely through the passage of some law?
- Can a government law cancel an economic law?
- How can it be right for government or its creation, the Federal Reserve, to do what a counterfeiter is barred from doing?

Each of these questions deserves an answer. In order, we offer:
- Yes.
- No.
- Of course not.
- It can't.

The man who inherited $10,000 in 1940 but didn't try to spend it until 1993 was defrauded. And it doesn't really matter that the fraud was accomplished through procedures legally sanctioned by government and carried out by the Federal Reserve. His 1940 bonanza of $10,000 has been reduced in value to about $500 in today's purchasing power.

Not surprisingly, there is somewhere in the order of 20 times more "legal" currency in circulation today than there was in 1940. From nothing, the additional currency pumped into the system acquired value at the time it was issued through a hidden process that results in "confiscation," to use the very accurate term chosen by Keynes.

Because of inflation, the regular trip to the supermarket has become a source of real anguish as prices rise steadily. For many years, anyone who earns a five percent annual increase in pay is either standing still or going backwards.

Governments turn to inflation when taxpayers begin to balk at higher taxes to fund unwanted programs. They create new currency and finance their schemes with it. In effect, government sidesteps the people who would refuse open requests to fund certain programs. These unwanted programs are instituted anyway, and government pays for them with funds created by inflation. As former Congressman Ron Paul has stated, "Government will use all the power it is given, including the power to print unlimited quantities of paper money."[5]

---

5. Ron Paul, *Ten Myths About Paper Money* (Lake Jackson, TX: The Foundation for Rational Economics and Education, 1983), p. 24.

Another important feature of inflation is that it's a hidden tax. Properly and simply defined, taxation is the taking of the wealth of the people by government. Inflation fits that definition exactly, just as surely as does an income tax, a sales tax, or any other kind of tax. Therefore, anyone figuring his tax bill must add amounts taken not only via income tax, corporation tax, excise tax, and others, but also the hidden tax of inflation.

But how many are aware of the real impact of inflation? As John Maynard Keynes correctly maintained, "not one man in a million can diagnose" what is happening. Denying the people a proper definition of inflation helps to keep the grand scheme going.

So widespread has the misinformation about inflation become that virtually all newer dictionaries offer a misleading definition. Definitions completely aside, however, the action involving increasing the quantity of currency — call it what you wish — accomplishes all of the thieving effects noted by Keynes. The process enables government to gain economic control over the people while it cripples the vitality of the nation.

How the Federal Reserve Inflates

In our nation, the government-created Federal Reserve initiates and carries out the process of inflation when it purchases government bonds (Treasury bills, for instance). The Fed actually creates the currency it uses for such purchases, and it benefits in an extraordinary way when, as promised to any bondholder, it is paid the interest due. The Fed, now owning bonds, collects further when the bonds mature, or when they are sold.

Imagine yourself able to do the following: Create currency with a simple bookkeeping entry, purchase bonds with this newly created currency, and then collect interest on the bonds. What a remarkable privilege the Fed enjoys!

In the January 1993 *National Geographic* magazine, our nation's legally sanctioned inflationary process is explained with amazing clarity in an article entitled "The Power of Money." Its author, Assistant Editor Peter T. White, provides clear insight about the operations of the Fed and where it claims to get the authority to operate as it does. We pick up the article's text as White discusses a Fed purchase of $100 million worth of Treasury bills from a securities dealer. Where did the Fed get the money to buy these government bonds? White explains:

> We created it, a Fed official tells me. He means that anytime the central bank writes a check, so to speak, it creates money. "It's money that didn't exist before," he says.
>
> Is there any limit on that?
>
> "No limit. Only the good judgment and the conscience of the responsible Federal Reserve people."
>
> And where did they get this vast authority?
>
> "It was delegated to them in the Federal Reserve Act of 1913, based on the Constitution, Article I, Section 8. 'Congress shall have the power ... to coin money and regulate the value thereof....'"[6]

Here's an unnamed Federal Reserve official confirming that the Fed creates money simply by writing a check. His openness about the Fed's activity isn't terribly unusual. But what Fed officials won't be candid about are the destructive consequences of their actions.

Also, the Fed official claims authority to create money based on the Constitutional grant of power to Congress to *coin money*. But creating check-book money out of nothing, even if such an act is sanctioned by government, is a far cry from stamping precious metal into coins.

Inflation From Another Source

In this same *National Geographic* article, author White details how additional expansion of the currency supply takes place — again legally — through the banking system. Let us note at this point that if White sees anything wrong with the money-creation

---

6. Peter T. White, "The Power of Money," *National Geographic*, January 1993, p. 83.

process he's describing, he doesn't say so. The article continues:

> Now watch how the Fed-created money lets our commercial bank-
> ing system create even more. The Fed requires banks to put aside a
> portion of their depositors' funds as reserves. Say this ratio is put at
> 10 percent — then for every $1,000 in new deposits, a bank must
> keep at least $100 in reserves but can loan out the rest, namely
> $900. On the bank's books, this loan remains as an asset, earning
> interest until it is paid off. The customer who got the loan is likely
> to spend it right away, say for a used car. The car dealer deposits
> the $900 check in his bank, which then has an additional $900 in
> reserves and can in turn loan out 90 percent of that — $810. And so
> on and on, until the original $1,000 put into one bank may enable
> dozens of banks to issue a total of $9,000 in new loans. [7]

It is not our intention to be harshly critical of all local bankers
who operate under rules established by national leaders. It's the
system under which bankers operate that must be exposed. Yet,
the fact remains: The process described by author White in *National Geographic* constitutes inflation — even if he doesn't label
it as such. Laws have been passed to make all of this legal, and
these laws supply cogent proof of the axiom holding that legality
and justice are frequently poles apart.

The actions of the Fed and the banks, permitted and encouraged by government, have diluted the value of America's currency. The newly created currency — in most instances not
freshly printed Federal Reserve notes but checkbook-type entries
— does the job just as surely as when counterfeiters produce and
spend their privately printed $20 bills.

Checkbook entries are a form of currency, and there are other
forms in addition to familiar paper money. Which is why the accurate definition of inflation holds that it is an increase in the
quantity of "currency," not simply an increase in the quantity of
tangible "money."

---

7. Ibid.

Some Actual Inflation Figures

Each Friday under the title "Monetary Aggregates," major newspapers publish money supply figures given by the Federal Reserve. From these, we can get an idea of what the Fed and the banks are doing to the value of the dollar. In simple terms, we can know why the cost of groceries continues to climb.

The figures are given in three categories of the nation's money supply. M-1 includes cash in circulation, deposits in checking accounts, and non-bank traveler's checks.

M-2 is M-1 plus accounts such as savings deposits and money market mutual funds. And M-3 is M-2 plus less-liquid accounts such as certificates of deposit in minimum denominations of $100,000.

On May 14, 1993, the *Los Angeles Times* reported the figures under the headline "Money Supply Rises." Though figures are given for each category of money, it is less confusing to focus on M-3, which is the most inclusive of these categories. For the week ending May 3rd, the *Times* reported that M-3 rose from $4,139.2 billion to $4,149.8 billion. That's $10.6 billion in a single week.

On May 21, 1993, under the headline "Money Supply Surges," the *Los Angeles Times* reported that M-3 had risen to $4,171.8 billion, an increase of $22.0 billion for the week ending May 10th.

In the two weeks we have noted, therefore, the nation's money supply had grown by $32.6 billion. At this rate, the currency would be increased by about 20 percent in a single year. There are, of course, some weeks when the money supply doesn't rise, even goes down. Decisions regarding the amount — and therefore the value — of money are made by unelected Fed officials. (Chapter 10 contains additional discussion of the Federal Reserve.)

Fluctuations in the money supply don't result from additions or withdrawals of gold or silver in circulation. They occur because of increases and decreases in the amount of money substitutes (paper bills, checkbook entries, etc.). Increases always cut into the value of all existing paper money — yours, mine, your neighbor's, everyone's.

Bad Definitions Cover the Crime

The crime is the arbitrary and largely undetected confiscation of the property of anyone who has money, or who receives money as compensation for labor, etc. If the American people understood the crime of inflation, they would understand that removing the power to inflate would put an end to its deviously thieving effects.

Also, if inflation were widely understood, no one would blame businessmen, consumers, labor leaders and others for its effects because it would be known that no one but the issuer of the currency has caused the problem. Yet, by distorting inflation's definition and constantly equating it with its effect, those who are responsible for inflation are able to shift the blame for their crime to others.

This is disinformation on a massive scale, and it is aided by the steady introduction of erroneous definitions into newer dictionaries.

Earlier we gave a correct definition of inflation from a 1957 dictionary. Now, let's look at several examples of remarkably different definitions that leave the American people in the dark and enable the money managers at the Fed to use their awesome power to "confiscate." After quoting from these highly regarded reference works and statements, we add our assessment of the consequences of the misleading information each supplies.

• The 1987 *Random House Dictionary of the English Language, Unabridged* defines inflation as follows:

> ... a persistent, substantial rise in the general level of prices related to an increase in the volume of money and resulting in the loss of value of currency.[8]

Inflation is not a rise in prices "related to" an increase in the volume of currency. It *is* the increase in the volume of currency. Anyone seeking the truth about what is happening to the value

---

8. *Random House Dictionary of the English Language, Unabridged* (New York, NY: Random House, 1987), p. 979.

of his income, savings, or pension is not going to find it with this definition. He will likely become convinced that his adversary is anyone who sets a higher price on goods or services.

• Webster's 1991 *Ninth New Collegiate Dictionary* defines the term this way:

> ... an increase in the volume of money and credit relative to available goods resulting in a substantial and continuing rise in the general price level.[9]

Based on this commonly found definition, increasing the amount of currency is acceptable if producers increase production at the same pace. Prices won't go up in such circumstances, *but increased productivity should result in prices going down*. In addition, this definition leads to the belief that producers who didn't produce enough to keep pace with the money suppliers ought to be blamed for the rising prices. The truth is that inflation impacts the value of the currency and that this impact is unrelated to how much is or isn't produced. The volume, quality and availability of goods may affect the prices of goods, but inflation affects the price (value) of money.

• In 1975, the U.S. Department of Commerce, the U.S. Department of Labor, and the Advertising Council, jointly issued a booklet entitled "The American Economic System ... and Your Part In It." Using cute drawings of "Peanuts" comic strip characters, the booklet informed readers that holding down inflation was everyone's job. But here's the definition it offered:

> Inflation means a rise in the general level of prices.... When consumers, businesses and governments spend too heavily on available goods and services, this high demand can force prices up.[10]

---

9. *Webster's Ninth New Collegiate Dictionary* (Springfield, MA: Merriam-Webster Inc., 1991), p. 620.
10. *The American Economic System ... and Your Part In It*, prepared by the Advertising Council and the U.S. Department of Commerce in cooperation with the U.S. Department of Labor, p. 13.

There you have it: We're all guilty, even government. Everyone is buying too much and spending too much for it. Aren't we lucky to have our government point this out!

What an insult! What a misleading parcel of gibberish!

Note that this definition indicts government, not for increasing the quantity of currency but only for spending too heavily, the same bad habit consumers are supposedly practicing. Once again, there's no slightest inkling of what inflation really is. And, if the people don't know what it is, how can they combat it?

• In 1974, President Gerald Ford told the nation that it was every citizen's duty to help him fight inflation. He admonished the American people to clean up their dinner plates, plant a victory garden, balance the family budget, and recycle waste. [11]

These ideas may have merit but they have nothing to do with inflation. His ridiculous "Whip Inflation Now" campaign gave more legitimacy to the fraudulent definition of inflation and contributed greatly to the public's confusion about this critical matter.

Some Good Sense

The late Gary Allen, author of the best-selling 1971 paperback *None Dare Call It Conspiracy*, held that calling inflation the condition of rising prices "was like blaming wet streets for rain." Correct!

Journalist Mel Tappan once authored a question and answer column for a national magazine. During a particularly intense period of inflation, a reader suggested that he support the government's campaign to hold prices down as a way to combat its ravages. Tappan issued the following tart response: "Having the government urge us, as private citizens, to fight inflation is like having an airline pilot tell the passengers that the plane is going too fast and suggesting that they all stick their heads out the window and blow." [12]

In 1963, Professor Murray N. Rothbard produced an extremely

---

11. Philip Shabecoff, "Ford Urges Steps To Curb Inflation," *New York Times*, October 16, 1974.
12. *Guns & Ammo*, December 1978.

helpful booklet entitled *What Has Government Done to Our Money.*[13] In it, he defined inflation as "any increase in the economy's supply of money not consisting of an increase in the stock of money-metal." What he was telling readers is that slightly increasing the amount of coins made of gold or silver (both of which are in finite supply) does not confiscate the people's wealth as does increasing the amount of paper or bookkeeping-entry currency regularly practiced by government and the Fed.

Ludwig von Mises supplied the same definition we are touting in his monumental 1949 work *Human Action.* As a caution to future students of these matters, he added: "A metallic currency is not subject to government manipulation."[14] He also warned about the harm done by the ongoing "semantic revolution," especially as it affects a term like inflation:

> What many people today call inflation or deflation is no longer the great increase or decrease in the supply of money, but its inexorable consequences, the general tendency toward a rise or a fall in commodity prices and wage rates. This innovation is by no means harmless. It plays an important role in fomenting the popular tendencies towards inflationism.[15]

One of the most profound students of von Mises, Dr. Percy Greaves, stated in his 1973 book *Understanding the Dollar Crisis*:

> Inflation, as we shall use the term, is any increase in the quantity of money other than an increase resulting from a switch of the money commodity, gold, from non-monetary use to monetary uses. For example, the melting down of gold ornaments to increase the quantity of gold coins is not inflation. This is merely a market transaction.[16]

---

13. Murray N. Rothbard, *What Has Government Done to Our Money?* (Novato, CA: Libertarian Publishers, 1981).
14. von Mises, *Human Action*, op. cit., p. 780.
15. Ibid., p. 420.
16. Percy L. Greaves, *Understanding the Dollar Crisis* (Appleton, WI: Western Islands, 1973), p. 178.

Professor Hans Sennholz maintained in his 1979 book *Age of Inflation*: "Inflation is the creation of money by monetary authorities. In more popular usage, it is that creation of money that visibly raises goods' prices and lowers the purchasing power of money."[17]

Economist Dr. Clarence Carson wrote in his 1988 book *Basic Economics*:

> Inflation is simply an increase in the money supply. It is accomplished by debasing or devaluing it if it is paper currency. In 20th Century American political lingo, inflation has been made to mean a general rise in prices. The rise in prices, however, is the effect; the increase in the money supply — inflation — is the cause.[18]

In a glossary of terms placed at the end of his *Basic Economics*, Dr. Carson hinted at the motivation of those who have shut off the public's access to a proper definition:

> Inflation has historically meant an increase of the money supply. However, for the past 50 years, there has been a politically inspired effort to have inflation mean the general rise in prices that follows upon a monetary inflation. This change in terminology helps to obscure the cause of the rise in prices.[19]

Frederick Soddy spent a lifetime working in the field of chemistry. But he also had a keen interest in economics and eventually took the time to put his thoughts in a book. A fierce opponent of inflation, he once observed of the practice of creating money out of nothing that if "we reasoned that way in physics, we would have to assign the property of levity to weight."[20]

---

17. Hans F. Sennholz, *Age of Inflation* (Appleton, WI: Western Islands, 1979), p. 22.
18. Clarence B. Carson, Ph.D., *Basic Economics* (Wadley, AL: American Textbook Committee, 1988), pp. 95-96.
19. Ibid., p. 373.
20. Frederick Soddy, *Wealth, Virtual Wealth and Debt* (London: George Allen & Unwin, Ltd., 1926.)

And, as far back as 1817, economist David Ricardo correctly fingered inflation for what it really is. Positing that paper money should be redeemable in precious metal, he stated:

> Though it [paper money] has no intrinsic value, yet, by limiting its quantity, its value in exchange is as great as an equal denomination of coins, or bullion in that coin. Experience, however, shows that neither a state nor bank ever has had the unrestricted power of issuing paper money without abusing that power; in all states, therefore, the issue of paper money ought to be under some check and control; and none seems so proper for that purpose as that of subjecting the issuers of paper money to the obligation of paying their notes in either gold coin or bullion.[21]

Mistakes or Something Worse?

What we have offered above is neither mysterious nor so deeply hidden that those who take the time to search could not find it. It is all readily available to politicians, researchers, authors, government economists, newspaper reporters, television commentators, and anyone who will take advantage of what can be found in decent libraries.

Yet, misinformation about inflation dominates the thinking of the vast majority. Even some who know better join in the fraud being perpetrated. They submit to a kind of "definition correctness," a plague similar in many ways to the political correctness being forced on Americans. All the while, the value of the American people's money continues to deteriorate, their pensions and insurance policies become less valuable, and the future looks bleaker and bleaker.

Could all of this economic disruption be occurring despite the efforts of intelligent leaders to stop it? Hardly. But it certainly could be happening because intelligent leaders who have a hidden agenda for the nation want it to happen.

Americans are being victimized by political and economic forces

---

21. David Ricardo, *The Principles of Political Economy and Taxation* (New York, NY: Everyman's Library Edition, E.P. Dutton, 1911).

that are inexorably leading all to the poorhouse. The thieving policies of the past and present will always lead to the bad consequences we are witnessing. But these policies can be changed. It was Karl Marx who believed in economic determinism; Americans should know better. What some men have set in motion, other men can reverse.

Though few wish to consider it, there is a simple explanation for the massive obfuscation regarding the truth about inflation. It is that the chief leaders of this nation aren't even trying to correct the problem. This means that they know the truth and work to smother it, and that their goal is to confiscate the people's wealth, destroy the nation's economic vitality, and lead America into servitude.

Occasionally, some sound analysis, even some sensible policy suggestions, can be heard above the ongoing roar of cover-up. It seems as though a few are trying to set things right. But right now, there are obviously too few preaching economic reality, and it is even likely that some political leaders are practicing an art that has become highly fashionable in recent years: Say one thing but do another.

Inflation is indeed thievery. And its thieving nature cannot be unknown by our leaders. But if its victims are led to believe that inflation is merely rising prices, then the inflator is "off the hook." He can quietly continue his thievery while others are blamed for it.

Those who seek to impose their new world order, however, are not interested only in stealing from the people. They want control, both economic and political. Which is why our discussion of inflation has to be expanded to include an explanation of its even more destructive effects on society — and on government itself.

The destructive nature of inflation is analyzed in the next chapter.

Former Rep. Ron Paul has warned about giving government the power to print paper money.

Economist Murray Rothbard correctly defined inflation in several of his valuable books.

While serving as President, Gerald Ford said that cleaning up our dinner plates and recycling waste would combat inflation.

Dr. Clarence Carson pointed to rising prices as "the effect" of inflation in his *Basic Economics*.

Dr. Hans Sennholz spelled out the real nature of inflation in his book, *The Age of Inflation*.

Dr. Percy Greaves favored gold as money and combatted false definitions of inflation in his *Understanding the Dollar Crisis*.

Henry Hazlitt cautioned against confusing money with wealth and showed the absurdity of government simply distributing money.

CHAPTER 7

Inflation: A Destroyer of Nations

Inflation tends to reverse the rules of economic behavior: where once it was prudent to save money, it becomes expedient to spend it; where once it was good business to supply customers with durable goods, it becomes profitable to delay the sale for the rising prices; where once creditors were those who were better off generally, it now becomes good business to borrow money and repay it with currency that is less valuable than when the loan was made.

The solid citizen who is cautious and prudent can do well over the years by hard work, careful investments, and savings, when the money supply is stable. His prosperity may even be described as virtue rewarded. Inflation sets the stage for wealth to be gained in a different fashion: by borrowing, by holding on to goods for the inevitable higher prices, and by attending closely to the swift changes in the value of money. Of course, there are many losers in this gain: those who have saved for old age may find their life savings wiped out, and so on.

— Clarence Carson, Ph.D., 1988[1]

It [inflation] discourages all prudence and thrift. It encourages squandering, gambling, reckless waste of all kinds. It often makes it more profitable to speculate than to produce. It tears apart the whole fabric of stable economic relationships. Its inexcusable injustices drive men toward desperate rem-

---

1. Carson, *Basic Economics*, op. cit., p. 101.

*edies. It plants the seeds of fascism and communism. It leads
men to demand totalitarian controls. It ends invariably in bit-
ter disillusion and collapse.*

— Henry Hazlitt, 1946[2]

In the previous chapter, we emphasized the personal consequences of inflation. As we attempted to demonstrate, the process amounts to government-sanctioned stealing from the people
on a grand scale.

But the devastating consequences of inflation will also impact
the social fabric and very survivability of the nation. Dr. Clarence
Carson, the author of 14 books about economics and American
history, capably summarized some of inflation's harmful effects
on men's attitudes in the above quotation from his excellent *Basic Economics*.

Addressing these same consequences, Henry Hazlitt pointed
out in his *Economics In One Lesson* that inflation forces men from
virtue to vice. This alone can prove to be devastating to a nation.

But Hazlitt, a former economic editor of *Newsweek* and a lifelong crusader for economic sanity, additionally recognized that
inflation leads men "to demand totalitarian controls." If inflation
results in the fostering of vice instead of virtue and in creating a
demand among the people for a tyrant, its total effect is far more
destructive than mere thievery.

An Invitation to a Tyrant

Previously, we focussed on what John Maynard Keynes had
written about inflation's effect on the people's wealth. But Keynes
also noted that those who inflate could have far more destructive
motives. Here is a more complete passage from *The Economic
Consequences of the Peace*, written by the famous British socialist
in 1920:

Lenin is said to have declared that the best way to destroy the

---

2. Hazlitt, *Economics in One Lesson*, op. cit., p. 176.

Capitalist System was to debauch the currency. By a continuing process of inflation, governments can confiscate, secretly and unobserved, an important part of the wealth of their citizens. By this method they not only confiscate, but they confiscate arbitrarily; and, while the process impoverishes many, it actually enriches some. The sight of this arbitrary rearrangement of riches strikes not only at security, but at confidence in the equity of the existing distribution of wealth. Those to whom the system brings windfalls ... become "profiteers," who are the object of hatred of ... [those] whom the inflationism has impoverished.... As inflation proceeds ... the process of wealth-getting degenerates into a gamble and a lottery.

Lenin was certainly right. There is no subtler, no surer means of overturning the existing basis of society than to debauch the currency. The process engages all of the hidden forces of economic law on the side of destruction, and does it in a manner which not one man in a million is able to diagnose.... The governments of Europe ... are fast rendering impossible a continuance of the social and economic order of the 19th century. [3]

According to Keynes and Lenin, inflation can "destroy the Capitalist System," the term both used for the opposite of the government-controlled socialist system each wanted. Inflation, they maintained, is matchless as a subtle and sure "means of overturning the existing basis of society." Its effect makes "impossible a continuance of the social and economic order" of the past.

What Keynes and Lenin both claimed, though not as directly as did Hazlitt, is that inflation sets the stage for the rise of a tyrant. It obviously must be understood and combatted by anyone who would remain free.

Germany After World War I

Germany was soundly defeated in World War I. At the close of the war, the reparations forced on her by the Versailles Treaty prepared the way for an even more complete destruction of the

---

3. Keynes, *Economic Consequences of the Peace*, op. cit., p. 235.

nation. Keynes himself, prior to his rise to prominence in our nation, actually walked out of the treaty negotiations because of the harshness of the measures being planned for the German people.

Keynes noted that the German economy depended on overseas commerce, an assortment of industries built around coal and iron, and a transport and tariff system. But the treaty, he correctly noted, targeted the systematic destruction of all three. In *Economic Consequences of the Peace*, he insisted that "the Peace is outrageous and impossible and can bring nothing but misfortune behind it." Yet, the allies went ahead with their plans.

One section of the treaty contained draconian monetary demands. Germany's leaders turned to inflation to satisfy them. Those demands were met with paper currency whose value had been increasingly watered down.

Germany's leaders printed so much unbacked paper currency that it became virtually worthless. They then used it to satisfy the monetary obligations forced on them by the Versailles Treaty. Thus, through inflation, Germany was able effectively to default on an obligation it considered unjust.

But, as their currency was destroyed, the German people suffered incredible hardships. The subsequent widespread bitterness among the people created by the Versailles Treaty created the conditions enabling Adolph Hitler to come to power only a few years later.

Germany's horrifying experience with runaway inflation in the early 1920s contains a lesson that ought to be ingrained in the mind of every American. We recount it here for the clear warning it supplies. Those who insist, "It can't happen here," had better realize that it could indeed happen here — if that is the way our nation's money managers decide to take us.

In his *The Rise and Fall of the Third Reich*, William L. Shirer noted that the German mark began to lose value in 1921 when it "dropped to 75 to the dollar." He reported the German experience as follows:

The strangulation of Germany's economy hastened the final

plunge of the mark ... in January 1923, it fell to 18,000 to the dollar; by July 1 it had dropped to 160,000; by August 1 to a million. By November, when Hitler thought his hour had struck, it took four billion marks to buy a dollar, and thereafter the figure became trillions. German currency had become completely worthless. Purchasing power of salaries and wages was reduced to zero. The life savings of the middle classes and working classes were wiped out. But something even more important was destroyed: the faith of the people in the economic structure of German society. What good were the standards and practices of such a society, which encouraged savings and investment and solemnly promised a safe return from them and then defaulted?[4]

Table 7-1
Value of the Reichsmark

Date	$1.00 U.S. Converts To
Jan. 1922	189 RM
Apr. 1922	303 RM
Jul. 1922	1,815 RM
Jan. 1923	7,200 RM
Apr. 1923	210,000 RM
Jul. 1923	1,660,000 RM
Oct. 1923	3,120,000,000 RM
Jan. 1924	4,350,000,000,000 RM
Jul. 1924	4,180,000,000,000 RM
Oct. 1924	4,200,000,000,000 RM
Nov. 1924	Reichsmark revalued: 1 trillion RM = 1 new Mark

Shirer noted that "the government deliberately let the mark tumble in order to free the State of its public debts, to escape from paying reparations...." It was inflation with a vengeance. And while it essentially freed government of the Versailles-imposed

---

4. William L. Shirer, *The Rise and Fall of the Third Reich* (New York, NY: Simon and Schuster, 1960), p. 61.

demands, its effect on the people was catastrophic. But it also invited another kind of calamity for Germany. Shirer told of the devastation suffered by the people:

> All they knew was that a large bank account could not buy a straggly bunch of carrots, a half peck of potatoes, a few ounces of sugar, a pound of flour. They knew that as individuals they were bankrupt. And they knew hunger when it gnawed at them, as it did daily. In their misery and hopelessness, they made the Republic the scapegoat for all that had happened.
> Such times were heaven-sent for Adolph Hitler.[5]

Indeed they were "heaven-sent for Adolph Hitler." Or for any other potential tyrant who promised to undo the misery caused in great part by inflation. A few years later, Hitler came to power and Germany's march toward even greater calamities was underway.

Let us make one more point about the inflation that ravaged the German people in the early 1920s. Pictured nearby is a poor but legible copy of a 1925 letter sent by the Deutsche Bank in Berlin to a man named Attilo Eneiui living in Portland, Oregon. Mr. Eneiui had inquired about the status of his bank account containing one million marks. But inflation had destroyed the value of the mark, and Germany had created new Reichsmarks, each one of which was worth one trillion of the former marks. Of his one million marks, Mr. Eneiui was informed by the bank official:

> ... as this amount cannot be expressed in the smallest units of the new currency a conversion into Reichsmark is impossible. The balance on your account has in fact been wiped out....

Wiped out! That's pretty cold terminology and a pretty devastating personal setback. Could something as horrible as this happen in America? Why not? Everything is in place for a rapid

---

5. Ibid., p. 62.

DEUTSCHE BANK

AMERIKA-ABTEILUNG

CABLE ADDRESS:
DEUTSHBANK

BERLIN, December 30th, 1925

Mr. Attilio Eneiui

100 First Street

PORTLAND, Oregon

Dear Sir/Madam, In reply to your letter of the 26th ult. we beg to inform you of the following:

By reason of the new Bank Act and the new Mint Law of August 30th, 1924 the new Reichsmark currency has been established in Germany on October 11th, 1924. The Reichsmark is now legal tender in th country. In accordance with the Mint Law one Reichsmark of the new currency is equal to one billion (1,000.000.000.000) Marks of the former currency.

With the establishment of the new Reichsmark as legal tender, we as well as the other German Banks and Bankers had to introduce the Reichsmark in our bookkeeping system. On December 31st, 1923 your account showed a balance of Papermarks   1.000.000.-- ✓   in your favor and as this amount cannot be expressed in the smallest units of the new currency a conversion into Reichsmark is impossible. The balance on your account has in fact been wiped out by the depreciation of the Mark and by part of the charges for carrying the account since the last statement we sent to you. For these reasons we must, to our great regret, inform you that we were obliged to close your old Mark account on our books.

If at any future time you should wish us to transact for you any business in the new Reichsmark we shall be pleased to place our service at your disposal.

We Are, dear Sir/Madam,

Yours very truly

DEUTSCHE BANK

This man's account was "wiped out" in 1924

increase in U.S. currency. There is no precious metal backing for it; there is virtually no check on how much of it can be issued; and an acceleration of inflation here — brought on by the enormous and growing national debt — could result in a duplication of the horror that befell Germans in 1923-24.

Nevertheless, runaway inflation has not been America's experience. In our opinion, it has not occurred here because those who set our nation's monetary policies apparently don't want such a development. They prefer continuous erosion while building up our nation's indebtedness. With this steady erosion has come a conclusion on the part of most Americans that the nagging consequences of inflation — especially the steady loss of the dollar's purchasing power — are inevitable. In a very real way, the patient gradualism of the inflation producers is destroying the will to resist, and even the awareness that prevailing policies *can* be resisted.

Meanwhile, the social fabric of our nation continues to be torn apart. Vice is replacing virtue to a great extent, and a frustrated, confused, and unaware public is constantly being told that only government can solve its fiscal problems. If present trends continue, public clamor for a dictator — or a world government — looms in our future.

If the money destroyers aren't stopped, America's steadily depreciating dollar would not likely be converted to a new denomination of American currency. As noted in Chapter 4, those who have brought on debt and deficits would far more readily propose that our nation accept world currency controlled by the United Nations. And many Americans, increasingly angry and impoverished as were the German people in 1925, would welcome such a development.

But there is a fundamental difference between what happened in Germany and what is happening here in America. Where the German people — ravaged by inflation — never gave up their nation's independence to any world government, many of today's Americans would readily walk into such a trap.

Once again, our point in recounting the German experience is to issue a warning to Americans. If our government (or an agency it has created such as the Federal Reserve) has power to issue unbacked paper money, it can destroy the existing basis of society; it can destroy prudence and thrift; it can encourage wheeler-dealer speculation instead of real production; it can undermine the very foundations of a stable society; it can drive men to demand totalitarian controls; it can lead to tyranny.

Wage and Price Controls

History is full of government leaders who inflated the currency and then imposed wage and price controls as a supposed cure. As is so often the case, these leaders treated the symptoms, not the problem. Why? Simply because doing so helped them to become more powerful. If a government and those who are in charge of it have power to control wages and prices, they have power over everyone.

Far from solving any problem brought on by inflation, wage and price controls bring on additional woes. The quality and quantity of goods begin to decline; black markets are formed to skirt the controls; police power to combat the black markets proliferates; productivity declines; and jobs and business are lost.

If controls keep prices low, producers who must earn a profit to survive can be forced to cease operations. Inevitable shortages will occur, leading either to long lines of shoppers or rationing. Should the prices set by government approximate market prices, little harm is done (other than establishing the precedent that it is government's proper role to set wages and prices). But the longer government price controls remain in effect, especially during an inflationary period, the greater will be the divergence from prices set by the market, and the greater the disruption.

Price controls, more precisely, are people controls. A government that imposes them has assumed power to make decisions that people can and should be left alone to make for themselves.

Nearly two thousand years before Christ, Hammurabi established wage and price controls in the first Babylonian Empire. His move destroyed the freedom, creativity and industriousness of the people and set the stage for the destruction of the empire.[6]

After debasing silver coinage and substituting tin-plated copper coins in its place (a pre-paper-money type of inflation), the Emperor Diocletian turned to controls on wages and prices in 301 A.D. The penalty for violating his regressive laws was death. But his supposed remedy predictably led to shortages, less productivity, hoarding, and more misery.[7]

The same devastating consequences occurred after the imposition of wage and price controls during the reign of Louis XV of

---

6. Robert Welch, "What Is Money?", JBS *Bulletin* (Appleton, WI: The John Birch Society, April 1970), p. 18.

7. Ibid.

France, during the early days of our nation's independence, and at numerous other times and places throughout history.[8]

On August 15, 1971, at a time when inflation was lowering the value of the dollar by approximately four percent each year, President Nixon slapped wage and price controls on this nation. For three years, his multi-phased program caused predictable problems.[9]

Government agents armed with vast new powers fanned out to all corners of America seeking violators. The American people were being conditioned to accept economic control by government, the very essence of fascism. Three years later, when the poorly enforced Nixon program was scrapped, prices had still risen by more than ten percent despite all of the rules. And surveys showed that 97 percent of U.S. corporations were experiencing unusual difficulties getting supplies. Wage and price controls don't solve any problems; they are instead an additional problem.

During his 1968 campaign, Richard Nixon termed inflation "the cruelest tax of all," and actually quoted Fabian Socialist John Maynard Keynes about it being the best way "to destroy the capitalist system." He told a CBS radio audience that "the continuing process of dollar debauchery is today robbing our citizens of their wealth and aggrandizing the power in Washington."[10]

Once elected, Nixon completely reversed course, even turning his well-known campaign oratory upside down. And then in a televised interview broadcast on January 6, 1971, he shocked television newscaster Howard K. Smith with the admission that he

---

8. Ibid.
9. Gary Allen, "Nixon, vs. Nixon, A Special Capitol Report" (Costa Mesa, CA: Capitol Report, 1972), p. 10. Allen further reported that Nixon, elected in 1968 in a close race with Humphrey, stated on October 17, 1969, "Wage and price controls are bad for business, bad for the working man, and bad for economics." On June 17, 1970, he stated: "Now here is what I will not do. I will not take this nation down the road of wage and price controls, however politically expedient that may seem. Controls and rationing may seem like an easy way out, but they are really an easy way in — to more trouble.... Wage and price controls only postpone a day of reckoning. And in doing so, they rob every American of a very important part of his freedom."
10. Ibid., p. 9.

was "now a Keynesian in economics." Smith should have been shocked only by the President's frank admission because the President's policies were indeed following the Keynes outline. But he responded to the President: "That is a little like a Christian Crusader saying, 'All things considered, I think Mohammed was right.'"[11]

Keynes believed that a nation could spend its way out of depression by having government greatly expand the money supply. But history confirms that no government has ever spent itself into prosperity, and many governments have spent their nations into serfdom.

The Nixon policies of tax, spend, and inflate were followed by similar policies during the short-lived Gerald Ford Presidency (1974-1977). The Republican failures convinced many Americans that the Democrats couldn't be any worse. So the nation turned to Jimmy Carter, a carefully groomed member of the new Trilateral Commission.

Inflation rose dramatically during the Carter years (1977-1981), but wage and price controls — frequently discussed by the administration — were never imposed. The economic malaise endured by the nation during these years made the change to Republican rule a virtual certainty. Eight years with Ronald Reagan at the helm began and were immediately followed by four years of George Bush's leadership.

But after 12 years of Reagan and Bush Administrations, Republican leaders actually congratulated themselves for holding the rise in prices to approximately four percent — the same increase that stimulated the Nixon Administration to impose wage and price controls 20 years earlier.

After the double-digit Consumer Price Rise increases of the Carter years, the 12 Republican years that were marked by smaller increases may have looked good by comparison. But CPI figures should not be the only criterion. If inflation was the mechanism for treating deficits in the Carter years, borrowing did

11. Associated Press, "Nixon Says 'Keynesian' on Economy," *El Paso Times*, January 8, 1971.

most of this work in the Reagan-Bush years.[12] Explosive deficit totals were the Republican price, and America was still speeding toward economic crack-up. In addition, the pattern involving debt, borrowing, interest, and taxation to pay the interest is effectively being used by government to gain economic control of the people.

The American people have now been conditioned to expect the value of their dollars to fall steadily, even while being told that their leaders are doing everything humanly possible to correct the problem. It's as if we are victims of economic forces that no one can alter, a notion heartily endorsed by Karl Marx. With such an attitude deeply planted in the consciousness of most Americans, the potential for more and even runaway inflation has grown.

Not Just Thievery

In 1949, in his highly acclaimed book *Economics and the Public Welfare*, Benjamin J. Anderson penned the following bit of wisdom:

> There is no need in human life so great as that men should trust one another and should trust their government, should believe in promises, and should keep promises in order that future promises may be believed in and in order that confident cooperation may be possible. Good faith — personal, national, and international — is the first prerequisite of decent living, of the steady going on of industry, of government financial strength, and of international peace.[13]

Inflation destroys such trust and faith. It sets men against men, men against governments, and governments against governments.

Again, all of what we have presented about inflation isn't any

---

12. Since much of the U.S. debt during this period was purchased by overseas investors, the heavy borrowing to finance the Reagan-Bush-era deficits did not drive up domestic interest rates.

13. Cited by Greaves, *Understanding the Dollar Crisis*, op. cit., pp 181-182.

deep and dark mystery government leaders can't fathom. It can be known even by them. In our opinion, it is known but is carefully being kept from the American people.

Inflation is a tactic turned to by governments in debt, a hidden way of forcing the people to pay for programs they would not allow if direct taxation were demanded of them. It is also the tactic of those who would destroy in order to build tyranny on the ashes of their destruction. Once in power, and no longer encumbered by anything so restrictive as a nation's constitution, such conspirators always make slaves of the people who were their targets in the first place.

In America today, inflation is being used as a weapon by powerful forces who seek the creation of an all-powerful new world order run by them.

Yet, if the people understood what constitutes sound money, no one could employ inflation to steal their wealth and destroy their nation. Our next chapter takes a much-needed look at money, another topic which is understood by those would-be rulers and largely misunderstood by those who are being programmed for serfdom.

Adolph Hitler came to power in Germany on the heels of devastating inflation forced on that nation.

V.I. Lenin knew that inflation had the capacity to "overturn the existing basis of society."

William K. Shirer's *The Rise and Fall of the Third Reich* detailed the horror experienced in Germany because of inflation.

Television journalist Howard K. Smith was stunned when President Richard Nixon admitted to being "a Keynesian in economics."

CHAPTER 8

The Criminal Destruction of Sound Money

A most important truth now emerges from our discussion: money is a commodity. Learning this simple lesson is one of the world's most important tasks. So often have people talked about money as something much more or much less than this. Money is not an abstract unit of account, divorceable from a concrete good; it is not a useless token only good for exchanging; it is not a "claim on society"; it is not a guarantee of a fixed price level. It differs from other commodities in being demanded mainly as a medium of exchange.
— Murray N. Rothbard, Ph.D.[1]

While most governments and many individuals would have us believe otherwise, there is nothing magical or mystical about money. As Dr. Murray Rothbard has explained so well, it is simply whatever commodity serves as a medium of exchange.

The use of money permits indirect exchange, a huge improvement over the barter system where goods or services must be traded for other goods or services. Once money appears, goods or services can be traded for it, and commerce flourishes. In effect, a person buys money when he sells his goods or services; and he sells money when he buys goods or services.

Once money is universally accepted, it spurs commerce, allows for a wide diversification of labor, stimulates productivity, fills the need for a measure of value, and in general advances civilization. Sound money is not the result of advancing civilization; it is,

---

1. Rothbard, *What Has Government Done to Our Money?*, op. cit., p. 4.

rather, one of its causes. John Birch Society founder Robert Welch made this very point in his essay about money in 1970:

> When Tacitus said of the German aborigines nearly two thousand years ago, "we have taught them to accept money," he was boasting justifiably of this step towards bringing the benefits of civilization to some barbarian tribes. [2]

"Once it is universally accepted," is the key to understanding a great deal about money. Money that is universally accepted is sought after, widely used, and brings all of the benefits listed above. On the other hand, bad or bogus money is rejected.

History clearly indicates the qualities of good money. Looking back over the past should also keep us from falling victim to modern money manipulators. As George Santayana so wisely warned a few generations ago, "Those who cannot remember the past are condemned to repeat it." [3]

History's Lesson

Among the many commodities that have served mankind as a medium of exchange can be found cattle, seashells, tobacco and nails. Each possessed *value* to all parties concerned.

Experience with these commodities helped men to discover that money ought also possess such characteristics as *divisibility*, *transportability*, *durability*, and *relative scarcity*. With the availability of a kind of money possessing all of these qualities, the use of cattle, seashells, etc. was seen to be impractical.

What commodity satisfies all of the needed qualities of good money? What has value to all parties concerned, and is divisible, transportable, durable, and relatively scarce? The answer is gold. It is universally desired and therefore has worth to all parties. It is divisible and can be shaped into coins, ingots, bars, etc. It is readily transportable. Its durability is almost unmatched as it won't rust or rot and doesn't have to be fed. And in the few places

---

2. Welch, *What is Money?*, op. cit., p. 1.
3. George Santayana, *The Life of Reason*.

where it is found in the earth, it is difficult to extract and therefore relatively scarce.

Because it satisfies all of the requirements of good money, gold has been employed as money for at least 3,000 years of man's history. What's more, the use of gold as money has not been decided upon by a government, a professor, or some economic guru. Trial and error, plus the accumulated wisdom of mankind, have repeatedly shown gold to be the best commodity to serve as money. Silver also satisfies these requirements, though not as capably as does gold.

History also records the employment of several other commodities as money. The Romans used coins made of bronze, the Latin word for which is *aes*. Our own word *estimate* is derived from the Roman's use of bronze coins as a measure of value. At another point in history, salt was so widely used as a preservative that it was also used to pay workers. As a result, the word "salary" and the phrase "worth his salt" worked their way into our language.

The key feature to remember is money should be a commodity which is valued aside from its use as money.[4] Tobacco, bronze, salt, even sea shells are commodities possessing such value. A piece of paper carrying a notice requiring everyone to accept it as "legal tender for all debts public and private" is nothing of the kind. The paper money now in use in America and elsewhere has no value of itself, is certainly not scarce as long as paper and printing presses are available, and serves enticingly as an invitation to fraud.

Another point that must be made is that there is no need whatsoever for a central authority (such as a government or bank) to manage commodity money. The value and availability of gold does not have to be managed, nor does the value and availability of

---

4. We have refrained from using the word "intrinsic" to qualify the attribute of sound money known as value. While "intrinsic" will help many to understand that sound money has to have value in use, it must be remembered that even gold does not possess value at all times. It is, for instance, of little value to someone who is marooned, is dying of thirst or hunger, and has no water or food. Anyone in such a circumstance would much prefer something to eat and drink to tons of gold.

the other commodities that have served as money throughout history. A free market (which is to say, free people) manages money quite nicely.

There is, however, a great temptation to manage the value and availability of money substitutes such as paper notes. And with that management, a door is opened to defraud an unsuspecting public. At one point in his discussion of the history of money, Robert Welch concluded that there has never been honesty in the management of any nation's paper currency. What has happened to our nation's paper dollars adds credence to his conclusion.

Types of Money

History tells us that there are three basic types of money. As Dr. Edwin Vieira, Jr. has pointed out in his booklet entitled *The Federal Reserve System: A Fatal Parasite on the American Body Politic*,[5] these are:

1. Commodity money which we have already described above. Examples include gold, silver, etc.

2. Fiduciary money which is an essentially valueless substance serving as a substitute for commodity money. Bank or Treasury notes, token coinage, checking accounts, and other financial instruments may serve as money substitutes. A money substitute will be valued equivalent to the commodity money it represents if everyone has complete confidence that the substitute is fully and easily redeemable for the real thing. The special value of money substitutes which enables them to be accepted as money originates solely from their convertibility into commodity money.

Our word "fiduciary" is derived from the Latin word *fiducia*, meaning trust or confidence. The problem with fiduciary money is that its issuers have historically betrayed the trust and confidence of the public by converting fiduciary money to fiat money.

3. Fiat money is an essentially valueless substance — such as

---

5. Dr. Edwin Vieira, *The Federal Reserve System: A Fatal Parasite on the American Body Politic* (Manassas, VA: National Alliance For Constitutional Money, Undated), pp. 2-3.

a small piece of paper — which does not serve as a substitute for commodity money. Made legal tender by law or fiat, it is redeemable neither in a valuable commodity nor in fiduciary money. The word *fiat* comes from the Latin for "let it be done" and has come to mean "edict" or "decree." Fiat money, therefore, is money by government edict.

Both fiduciary and fiat money present an inherent invitation to a counterfeiter of either the official (government) or private (common criminal) variety. Where commodity money is used, however, there is little opportunity for this type of fraud. Money substitutes of any type always open the door to an increase in the quantity of currency (inflation), a major cause of America's economic problems.[6]

Money In the United States

Colonial America experimented with paper fiat money and paid a heavy price in lost credibility, economic slowdown, civil disruption, and personal hardship. In 1764, the British Parliament stepped in and outlawed irredeemable paper money in the colonies. Immediately, gold coins from Europe began circulating as money.[7] The stability thus provided led to widespread economic progress and good fortune. A valuable lesson had been learned by many.

Then came the Declaration of Independence and the War for Independence. In order to finance the war effort, the Continental

---

6. We are not contending that all transactions in America should include the transfer of physical commodity money. When all parties to a transaction are willing to use fiduciary instruments (redeemable paper currency, checkbook money, tokens, etc.), and as long as the holder of the money substitute is certain that it can be exchanged for commodity money at any time, there is no fraud. As von Mises has stated: "When an indirect exchange is transacted with the aid of money, it is not necessary for the money to change hands physically; a perfectly secure claim to an equivalent sum, payable on demand, may be transferred instead of the actual coins." Ludwig von Mises, *The Theory of Money and Credit* (Irvington-on-Hudson, NY: Foundation for Economic Education, 1971), p. 50.
7. Ron Paul and Lewis Lehrman, *The Case For Gold* (Washington, DC: Cato Institute, 1982), p. 22.

Congress turned to the issuance of paper fiat money. When many of the colonists refused to accept the "continentals," as the paper bills were called, the government did what governments throughout history have done in similar circumstances: It passed "legal tender laws" compelling the people via a variety of penalties to accept the paper money it had issued.

But those who knew the difference between valuable gold coins and worthless paper money continued to use the former and reject the latter. The people began to describe any worthless object as "not worth a continental," a phrase still occasionally heard today.

Though the war with Britain ended in triumph for America, the new nation was suffering the consequences of the flood of unbacked paper money. George Washington pointed to the disruptions caused by paper money and stated in 1787: "If any person had told me that there would have been such formidable rebellion as exists, I would have thought him fit for a madhouse."[8]

Widespread awareness of this root cause of America's internal problems dominated the 1787 deliberations in Philadelphia leading to the creation of an entirely new Constitution. One of the main points of agreement at the constitutional convention was the need to ban the issuance of valueless paper money. The delegates eventually decided to bar the federal government from issuing paper money.

The infant nation, buttressed by sound money, swiftly became a productive marvel earning the envy of the entire world. How then did we arrive at our present predicament where we have completely unbacked "bills of credit" issued by a privately run central bank called the Federal Reserve? Why is it that our nation is plagued by inflation, subjected to alternating booms and busts, and victimized by a worldwide loss of confidence in the stability of the dollar?

In great measure, the answer to these questions begins with the fact that the people ceased being vigilant. Then the Congress

---

8. Cited by G. Edward Griffin, "Survival Course on Money" (Westlake Village, CA: American Media, 1985).

assumed powers it has never legally been granted. And finally, Congress delivered those assumed powers into the private hands that now manage our currency through the Federal Reserve.

Moving Away from "Good as Gold"

A simple survey of the paper money used in America during the 20th century provides a compelling story of monstrous fraud.

1. Pictured below is a U.S. Treasury "gold certificate" issued in 1928. Printed with green and black ink except for a yellow or gold-colored seal, these were totally and readily redeemable in gold. Note the pledge it carried: "This certifies that there have been deposited in the Treasury of The United States of America Ten Dollars in Gold Coin Payable to the Bearer on Demand."

1928 U.S. Treasury note — redeemable in gold

Any holder of this form of fiduciary money could present it at the U.S. Treasury, or at any bank in the nation, and receive a ten-dollar gold piece (a half-ounce of gold) in return. This paper money was labelled "good as gold," and it truly was. But in 1933, Congress and President Roosevelt repudiated that solemn pledge — for American citizens but not for foreigners. Yet, Americans could still exchange their paper money for silver.

1934 U.S. Treasury note — redeemable in silver

2. Our next example in the evolution of U.S. currency is the "silver certificate" such as the one shown above issued in 1934. Its forthright pledge stated: "This certifies that there is on deposit in the Treasury of The United States of America Five Dollars in Silver Payable to the Bearer on Demand."

Any holder of this fiduciary money could exchange it at the U.S. Treasury or at any bank in America for silver coins. But in 1968, President Johnson and Congress repudiated that pledge, again for American citizens only but not for foreigners. Then in 1971, President Nixon severed all ties of fiduciary money to precious metal for foreigners as well. American paper money had now been completely converted into fiat currency.

Our first two samples of currency were U.S. Treasury notes. But soon after the creation of the Federal Reserve, this government-created agency began issuing its own currency. Its first notes circulated side-by-side with U.S. Treasury gold certificates. So they, too, had to be redeemable in gold. For many years, the public found no difference whatsoever between the value of U.S. Treasury notes and Federal Reserve notes. Hence, the people accepted the Federal Reserve and the power it had been given to issue currency.

1928 Federal Reserve note — redeemable in gold

3. Federal Reserve notes, such as the 1928 note pictured above, contained the following pledge printed in its upper left-hand corner: "Redeemable in Gold on demand at The United States Treasury or in Gold or Lawful Money at any Federal Reserve Bank." Any American citizen could obtain gold for this note — until 1933.

4. After 1933, Federal Reserve notes carried a new pledge. The 1934 Federal Reserve note shown on the following page was no longer redeemable in gold, nor was gold obtainable in exchange for any of the older gold certificates issued by the U.S. Treasury. It circulated side-by-side with silver certificates which were redeemable in silver and, because it could be exchanged for them, it too was redeemable in silver.

Beginning in 1968, not only was the pledge to redeem notes in silver repudiated, America's coins were no longer made of silver but of a copper-nickel sandwich. As inflation ate away the value of the dollar, the value of the silver content of the coins had become greater than the value of the coins as money. Whenever this has happened throughout history, the people made a practice of melting the coins for their silver content. So the government substituted far less valuable metal and, in effect, admitted that America's currency had lost value.

THIS NOTE IS LEGAL TENDER FOR ALL DEBTS, PUBLIC AND PRIVATE, AND IS REDEEMABLE IN LAWFUL MONEY AT THE UNITED STATES TREASURY, OR AT ANY FEDERAL RESERVE BANK.

1934 Federal Reserve note — redeemable in "lawful money"

Between 1933 and 1968, Federal Reserve notes issued concurrently with U.S. Treasury silver certificates carried the pledge: "This Note is Legal Tender for All Debts Public and Private and is Redeemable in Lawful Money at The United States Treasury or at any Federal Reserve Bank."

Soon after silver was no longer offered in exchange for either silver certificates or Federal Reserve notes, a perceptive citizen took a $50 note carrying this pledge to a local Fed-affiliated bank, presented it to the teller, and asked to exchange it for some "lawful money." The totally confused teller offered smaller denominations carrying the same pledge. The citizen responded: "No, the paper currency you are offering claims that it can be redeemed in lawful money. If it can be redeemed in lawful money, it can't be lawful money. I would like some lawful money."

This individual knew that "lawful money" in this nation meant gold or silver. When the bank teller and other bank officials who had been called to assist their befuddled teller would not provide gold or silver, the man reclaimed his $50 note and left with confirmation of the fact that American paper money was now totally fiat money.

5. Which brings us to the fifth of our pictorial samples of paper

142

THIS NOTE IS LEGAL TENDER
FOR ALL DEBTS, PUBLIC AND PRIVATE

1990 Federal Reserve note — redeemable in nothing

currency, a 1990 Federal Reserve note which states only: "This Note is Legal Tender for all Debts Public and Private." This is what all Americans use today. It is not issued by the U.S. Treasury and is not redeemable in precious metal.

Older Americans have seen our nation's currency deteriorate from the most honest fiduciary money the world has ever known to fiat money redeemable in nothing. Also, its value is being continually eroded by the monetary policies set by the privately run Federal Reserve, about which more will be stated in Chapter 10 of this book.

The Federal Reserve now possesses a monopoly on the issuance of this fiat money. No longer limited by the amount of gold or silver in the Treasury, or even in its own vault, the Fed has the power to create money for lenders — the government and banks which are part of the Federal Reserve System — who borrow and pay interest. And it also has power to withdraw vast amounts of money from circulation at will by calling in loans to member banks, creating a condition known as deflation. Hence the Fed has the power to expand the money supply and create a boom, or contract the money supply and create a bust.

The greatest fears of our founding fathers have been realized.

The Constitution they so carefully crafted in order to keep monetary treachery from our shores has been ignored.

As Tacitus knew two thousand years ago, sound money aids remarkably in the advancement of a civilization. Unsound money, on the other hand, does precisely the opposite.

Inflation, the predictable consequence of unsound money, has both thieving and destructive capabilities. Such potential has not escaped the attention of those who would steal the wealth of the people, destroy their nation, and usher them into the new world order.

But if the people had a solid understanding of what money is and is not, they would not tolerate such treachery.

Again, all of this information cannot be unknown to all of our nation's leaders, teachers, and mass information purveyors. Yet, the people are kept largely in the dark and their civilization continues to unravel. It is not by chance that our nation's money degenerated from the most honest paper money in history ("good as gold") to completely irredeemable paper money. Nor was it by chance that the Federal Reserve replaced the U.S. Treasury as the issuer of our money.

Determined individuals planned and accomplished this change as a major step in their conspiratorial plan to steer our nation into totalitarian control and world government.

Along the way, the Constitution and the many warnings of our founding fathers have been ignored or forgotten. We take a look at their warnings and what they stated in the Constitution about money in our next chapter. Returning to the Constitution's clear mandates cannot be accomplished until these principles become widely understood.

Delegates to the constitutional convention agreed not to give the new government the power to issue paper money.

George Washington recognized that the abuse of paper money had inspired "formidable rebellion" in the infant United States.

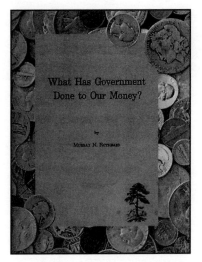

Murray Rothbard's booklet *What Has Government Done to Our Money?* taught the essential lesson that money is a commodity.

In 1933, Congress and President Roosevelt refused to allow Americans to redeem U.S. "gold certificates" in gold.

In 1968, Congress and President Johnson repudiated the silver pledge on U.S. Treasury notes for Americans.

In 1971, President Richard Nixon severed the last ties of fiduciary money to precious metal for foreigners as well.

The Federal Reserve now exercises a monopoly on the issuance of fiat (unbacked paper) money in the United States.

CHAPTER 9

The Constitution on Money

In questions of power, then, let no more be said of confidence in man, but bind him down from mischief by the chains of the Constitution.

— Thomas Jefferson[1]

In Chapter 6, we examined the January 1993 *National Geographic's* tellingly accurate account of the inflation-creating activities of both the Federal Reserve and the nation's banks. That article also made obvious the utter disdain with which the precise wording of the U.S. Constitution is held. When anyone claims that the grant of power to Congress to "coin money" sanctions the printing of irredeemable paper money by the Federal Reserve and the banking system, there is obviously little respect for the venerable document.

Much of the abuse of the Constitution stems from the widely held belief that the government can do anything not specifically forbidden in the document. But it is revolutionary indeed to attribute to the framers anything but the following basic assertion: *If power to engage in any activity is not specifically granted in the Constitution, no federal department or agency may assume it.* As we shall see, that is precisely the main point of the Tenth Amendment.

The Constitution — Literally

Regarding money, the Constitution has very little to say. But the following powers were granted to Congress in Article I, Section 8:

To coin money, regulate the value thereof, and of foreign coin, and

---

1. Quoted by Mortimer J. Adler et al., *The Annals of America* (Chicago, IL: Encyclopedia Britannica).

fix the standard of weights and measures.

To provide for the punishment of counterfeiting the securities and current coin of the United States.

There can be little dispute about what the founders intended with their listing of the power to "coin money." They meant taking precious metal and stamping it into coinage for use as a medium of exchange.

By "regulate the value thereof, and of foreign coin," they granted power to Congress to create what James Madison explained was "uniformity in the value" of both domestic and foreign coin.[2] The founders sought to prevent disputes about the value of domestic and foreign coinage among the states, and by the states with foreign nations, so they gave power to Congress to keep any such wrangling from occurring. Madison explained:

> Had every State a right to regulate the value of its coin, there might be as many different currencies as States, and thus the intercourse among them would be impeded; retrospective alterations in its value might be made, and thus the citizens of other States be injured, and animosities be kindled among the States themselves. The subjects of foreign powers might suffer from the same cause, and hence the Union would be discredited and embroiled by the indiscretion of a single member.[3]

The Constitution lists no grant of power to Congress to print paper money or emit "bills of credit," the term for paper money in common use at the time. And if no such power was granted, Congress has no authority to engage in the process — or to delegate it to any future central bank including the Federal Reserve.

As for the constitutional grant of power to punish counterfeiters of both "the securities and current coin of the United States," the founders intended that the same governmental unit possess-

---

2. Alexander Hamilton, James Madison and John Jay, *The Federalist Papers*, (New York, NY: Mentor Books, 1961 edition), Essay #42, pp. 264-271.

3. Ibid., Essay #44, p. 282.

ing power to insure uniformity in the value of the coin of the United States would also have the power to punish anyone who counterfeits it. Note that there was no power given to punish counterfeiters of U.S. paper money or bills of credit. The founders saw no reason to include punishment for counterfeiting something they refused to allow to exist.

While Article I, Section 8 granted specific powers to the federal government, Article I, Section 10 lists restrictions on state power. These restrictions were freely accepted by the delegates even though all were jealous guardians of state power and extremely wary of ceding any of their authority to the federal government. Yet they agreed to several prohibitions directed at the states including the following:

> No State shall ... coin money; emit bills of credit; make anything but gold or silver a tender in payment of debts....

We again turn to James Madison for an explanation of these constitutional bans:

> The extension of the prohibition to bills of credit must give pleasure to every citizen in proportion to his love of justice and his knowledge of the true springs of public prosperity. The loss which America has sustained since the peace, from the pestilent effects of paper money on the necessary confidence in the public councils, on the industry and morals of the people, and on the character of the republican government, constitutes an enormous debt....
>
> ... it may be observed that the same reasons which show the necessity of denying to the States the power of regulating coin prove with equal force that they should not be at liberty to substitute a paper medium in the place of coin.[4]

Over the years, proponents of paper money — issued either by the federal government or an agency to which it delegates such

---

4. Ibid., Essay #44, pp. 281-282.

authority (e.g., the Federal Reserve) — claim that prohibiting the states the power to issue "bills of credit" binds only the states and not the federal government.

In other words, monetary revisionists amongst us hold that the absence of any specific prohibition against federal power to print money (bills of credit) means that the federal government can print as much as it desires. Nothing could be more destructive of the intent of the founders and the constitutional system they established.

In a remarkably self-indicting September 15, 1993 letter to Congressman James C. Greenwood (R-PA), Federal Reserve Chairman Alan Greenspan (CFR and TC) ran roughshod over this fundamental constitutional precept. Greenwood had written to the Fed after being asked by a constituent where the Fed had acquired authority to "coin paper." Seeking to justify the completely illegal issuance of paper money by the Fed, Greenspan wrote:

> The Supreme Court of the United States has determined that the term "bills of credit" refers to a paper medium of exchange amounting to currency and that states cannot issue currency.... The Supreme Court also determined that Article I, section 10 [of the U.S. Constitution] applies only to the states and not to the Federal Government. Consequently, while no *state* government may "emit bills of credit" or make anything other than gold or silver coin a legal tender in payment of debts, the federal government is not limited in what it may designate as legal tender (emphasis in the original).[5]

We repeat: *If power to engage in any activity is not specifically granted in the Constitution, no federal department or agency may assume it.* Printing fiat money is certainly included. The whole truth is that the federal government was deliberately barred from printing paper money through the absence of any grant of power to do so. And the states were not only barred from printing paper

---

5. September 15, 1993 letter from Fed Chairman Alan Greenspan to Rep. James C. Greenwood; transmitted by Mr. Greenwood to Mr. A.C. Frattone of Hatboro, Pennsylvania on September 24, 1993.

money with an explicit prohibition, they were also forbidden to make anything but gold and silver a tender in payment of debt.

What this meant was that all governments in the United States were barred from printing paper money.[6] The founders were adamant about this matter because they had experienced devastating turmoil wrought by the issuance of paper money under the authority of the Continental Congress. "Continentals" were indeed "not worth a continental," meaning they were worthless.

Then, as yet another safeguard against the federal government assuming power — including the power to print money — the founders added the Tenth Amendment:

> The powers not delegated to the United States by the Constitution, nor prohibited by it to the States, are reserved to the States respectively, or to the people.

What could be more clear? Yet, what seems so eminently lucid has been muddied to such an extent that the Federal Reserve official quoted in the *National Geographic* article can state that the agency he represents was granted power to create paper money by the Constitution's grant of power to Congress to coin money. And Fed Chairman Alan Greenspan could claim the same privilege while completely ignoring the Tenth Amendment.

The Founders Speak

In his excellent *Basic Economics*, Dr. Clarence Carson presented the attitude of our nation's founders about paper money and the power to inflate. He wrote:

> The experience with paper money during the War for Indepen-

---

6. We are not calling for the sole use of precious metal by the American people. But we agree with the founders that neither governments nor agencies they create (e.g., the Fed) should print paper money. The people should always be free to conduct their business via the use of checks or notes as long as a creditor is willing to receive such money substitutes. In addition, truly free banking (see Chapter 11) would stimulate the use of valuable money substitutes.

dence left such an imprint on the minds of some of the men that they took care to leave no such opening for it when they drew up the Constitution in 1787. The matter came up for question whether or not the United States government should have the power to "emit bills of credit." The decision was that the government should not have the power to issue such paper money or make it legal tender, and no such power was granted.

Some who voted against such power had very strong views. Oliver Ellsworth of Connecticut, for example, declared that this was "a favorable moment to shut and bar the door against paper money. The mischiefs of the various experiments which had been made were now fresh in the public mind and had excited the disgust of all the respectable part of America ... the power [to issue unbacked paper money] may do harm, never good."

James Wilson of Pennsylvania thought that it "will have a most salutary influence on the credit of the United States to remove the possibility of paper money." It was stated of Pierce Butler of South Carolina that "[H]e was urgent for disarming the government of such power."[7]

In addition to Dr. Carson's assemblage of the strong attitudes of the founders about paper money, Ron Paul and Lewis Lehrman noted in *The Case For Gold* the even more emphatically negative sentiment of another constitutional convention delegate:

John Langdon of New Hampshire said that he would rather reject the whole Constitution than allow the federal government the power to issue paper money.[8]

Again, what could be more clear? The pertinent portions of the Constitution written and agreed to by these men have never been amended. Yet, the Federal Reserve Act, by which Congress both assumed and then delegated to a private agency it created the

---

7. Carson, *Basic Economics*, op. cit., p. 104.
8. Paul and Lehrman, *The Case for Gold*, op. cit., p. 168.

power to print unbacked paper currency, was passed by Congress in a rush to adjourn for Christmas on December 22, 1913.

Modern Interpretation Wrong

As we have noted, the modern interpretation of the Constitution claims that the federal government has power to do anything the Constitution does not explicitly prohibit. Over the years since 1789, the American people have allowed a continuous stream of moves by federal officials to skirt what Thomas Jefferson called "the chains of the Constitution," especially the shackles forbidding the issuance of paper currency.

In the past, the people were helped in their efforts to hold down federal assumption of powers by competent and honorable leaders who believed, as Jefferson did, that the government and those who held its posts should be restrained by "chains." But as the number who understood the Constitution's limits declined, so did the number of competent and honorable officeholders who abided by their solemn oath to uphold everything in the document.

In 1791, with the ink on the Constitution barely dry, Congress granted a federal charter to a central bank, the First Bank of the United States. Sold to Congress in part as a vehicle to retire war debts, its paper notes were to be fully redeemable in precious metal. As could be expected, it issued millions of dollars of irredeemable notes. Abolished in 1811, it was followed by the Second Bank in 1817 that not only reinstituted the practice of inflation for itself, but supported state and regional bank inflation as well.

As will be discussed in detail in Chapter 11, Andrew Jackson won election on a pledge that "the Federal Constitution must be obeyed." He meant exactly what he said, and he successfully waged war on inflation-minded banking interests throughout his eight years in office.

During the debate over the merits of the Second Bank, Daniel Webster offered the following very sound perspective:

> If we understand, by currency, the legal money of the country, and that which constitutes a lawful tender for debts, and is the stat-

153

ute of measure and value, then undoubtedly, nothing is included but gold and silver. Most unquestionably, there is no legal tender and there can be no legal tender in this country under the authority of this government or any other, but gold and silver, either the coinage of our mints or foreign coin at rates regulated by Congress. This is a constitutional principle, perfectly plain and of the very highest importance.

The states are expressly prohibited from making anything but gold and silver a tender in payment of debts, and although no such expressed prohibition is applied to Congress, yet as Congress has no power granted to it in this respect but to coin money and to regulate the value of foreign coins, it clearly has no power to substitute paper or anything else for coin as a tender in payment of debts in a discharge of contracts....

The legal tender, therefore, the constitutional standard of value, is established and cannot be overthrown. To overthrow it would shake the whole system.[9]

In 1832, a Select Committee on Coins of the House of Representatives issued a report to the full Congress stating that

... the enlightened founders of our Constitution obviously contemplated that our currency should be composed of gold and silver coin.... The obvious intent and meaning of these special grants and restrictions [in the Constitution] was to secure permanently to the people of the United States a gold or silver currency, and to delegate to Congress every necessary authority to accomplish or perpetuate that beneficial institution.[10]

Then in 1836, when the battle against the existence of the Second Bank had been won, Jackson's message to Congress reaffirmed what any honest student of the Constitution was perfectly willing to state:

---

9. Cited by Paul and Lehrman, op. cit., p. 169.
10. Ibid., p. 170.

It is apparent from the whole context of the Constitution, as well as the history of the times which gave birth to it, that it was the purpose of the Convention to establish a currency consisting of the precious metals. These ... were adopted ... by a permanent rule as to exclude the use of a mutable medium of exchange ... or the still more pernicious expedient of paper currency.[11]

Paper Currency Enters the System

As we have seen, the founders of this nation did all they could to keep the federal government from issuing paper money. Yet, in Article I, Section 8, the Constitution authorizes Congress to "borrow money on the credit of the United States," and to "provide for the punishment of counterfeiting the securities and current coin of the United States."

The combination of borrowing and issuing securities was the beginning of paper money. Edwin Vieira explains in his *Pieces of Eight* that the common practice employed during the early days of the nation saw the government issuing securities "to all public creditors willing to receive them as paper evidences of the indebtedness of the national government, and to declare those Securities a legal tender for the discharge of all public dues to the national government...."[12] Note that these "securities" were not declared legal tender for the discharge of *private* debts.

Vieira further explains that this carry-over from common law principles in England applied to certificates, notes, bills, and debentures signifying public indebtedness. Under these circumstances, these notes, etc. did not fall into the category of paper money or bills of credit forbidden by the Constitution.

Congress issued treasury notes during the War of 1812 and followed its issuance with legislation covering such matters as reimbursement, reasons for issuance (federal borrowing, payment

---

11. Andrew Jackson, "Eighth Annual Message," December 5, 1836; *A Compilation of the Messages and Papers of the Presidents* (Washington, DC: Bureau of National Literature, 1913), p. 1465.
12. Edwin Vieira, *Pieces of Eight*, (Fort Lee, New Jersey; Sound Dollar Committee; 1983), p. 123.

for supplies, etc.), transferability to another person, and use of the notes to pay taxes. Again, this procedure was not considered a violation of the constitutional prohibition against paper money.

However, with the issuance of Civil War "greenbacks" (claims against the U.S. Treasury) and the accompanying declaration that they were legal tender for debts public *and private*, the Constitution was circumvented. Also, the precedent for the government — and later the Federal Reserve — to issue paper money was established.

Vieira presents a fascinating account of the debate in Congress over the constitutionality of the act authorizing the greenbacks. He quotes a Representative Horton reminding his colleagues that "all the legislation of the Congress of the United States ... cannot make paper currency anything but what it is."[13] And a Representative Lovejoy added that "[t]he piece of paper you stamp as five dollars is not five dollars and it never will be unless it is convertible into a five dollar gold piece; and to profess that it is, is simply a delusion and a fallacy."[14]

Summarizing the outcome of these intensely crucial debates held in both houses of Congress, Vieira wrote:

> Overall, then, the legislative debates illustrate that the proponents of legal-tender paper currency could muster no sound constitutional argument or precedent in favor of the "greenbacks" — having, instead, to proffer the obviously anti-constitutional theory that Congress is a "sovereign" body with "inherent" powers far beyond those the Constitution enumerates in Article 1, Section 8, and subject to no limitation or restraint save the discretion of its members themselves. Nevertheless, Congress passed the legal-tender bill; and President Lincoln signed it into law.[15]

Vieira then showed how an initial Supreme Court decision holding that this law was unconstitutional (*Hepburn v. Griswold*,

---

13. Ibid., p. 176.
14. Ibid.
15. Ibid., p. 194.

1870) was quickly overturned by another Supreme Court ruling (*Knox v. Lee, 1871*). Paper money, issued by the federal government, had entered the system.

Americans Must Reawaken From Slumber

As the years have piled up, too many Americans have either forgotten, never heard, or completely discounted William Cullen Bryant's stern admonition:

> Not yet, O Freedom! close thy lids in
> slumber, for thine enemy never sleeps.

By 1944, many had already fallen asleep when Montgomery Ward Chairman Sewell Avery refused labor's demands on his company and faced an imminent strike. Federal agents insisted that a shutdown of his company would be harmful to the nation while at war. They stormed into the building and forcibly removed Avery from his office, depositing him on the sidewalk while the man was still seated in his office chair.

Attorney General Francis Biddle defended this actual takeover of the company with the claim that "the government of the United States can do anything not specifically prohibited by the Constitution."[16] That revolutionary attitude completely ignores the Tenth Amendment and the entire spirit of the Constitution. It is an unusually clear — but still wholly fraudulent — justification of illegal assumption of federal powers that are destroying this nation.

Biddle had sworn an oath to uphold the Constitution when he took office. So has every president, senator, representative, cabinet officer, and federal judge who ever served this nation. But too few citizens are aware of the wholesale violation of those oaths of office. By allowing *their* Constitution to be gravely ignored and contravened, the people effectively issue both a stunning indictment of themselves and a wide-open invitation for government to

---

16. Lloyd G. Herbstreith and Gordon Van B. King, *Action For Americans* (Los Angeles, CA: Operation America, 1965 Edition), p. 71.

confiscate their property and destroy their liberty. Allowing federal officials to proceed unchecked is asking for the destruction of the United States of America.

Attacks on the Constitution, including the incessant drive to open it up for radical change via a constitutional convention, become more understandable once the full meaning of the document is understood. Those who want a "new world order" greatly fear a restoration of the Constitution's limiting provisions. They want, instead, a wholesale revision or even an outright repeal of this "supreme law of the land."[17]

But returning to the true spirit and the intent of the Constitution is essential. If this nation is to endure, there is really no other way. Impossible, you say? When you get to Chapter 13, you will see how possible it is.

The founders of the United States certainly had no intention of allowing the federal or state governments to issue paper money. Never in their wildest dreams did they envisage creating a privately run central bank with vast powers to inflate and manipulate our nation's currency and credit. Yet, the Federal Reserve, the fulfillment of one of Karl Marx's dreams and the engine of the destruction of our nation's economic power, exists and hangs like a millstone around America's neck.

The Fed's powerful grip on our nation must be broken, but it obviously must be understood before action to have it abolished can succeed. Our next chapter analyzes the Fed.

---

17. Gary Benoit, "Bicentennial Plot," *The New American*, February 10, 1986; John F. McManus, *Keeping Faith With America* (Appleton, WI: The John Birch Society, 1987).

Thomas Jefferson's Declaration of Independence was followed by his urging that men should be held down "by the chains of the Constitution."

James Madison explained the meaning of the Constitution regarding money and other matters in *The Federalist Papers*.

Lewis Lehrman teamed up with Ron Paul to make *The Case for Gold*.

Fed Chairman Alan Greenspan turned the Constitution on its head.

160

CHAPTER 10

Karl Marx Would Have Loved the Fed

The proletariat will use its political supremacy to wrest, by degrees, all capital from the bourgeoisie.... Of course, in the beginning this cannot be effected except by means of despotic inroads on the rights of property.... These measures will of course be different in different countries. Nevertheless, in the most advanced countries the following will be pretty generally applicable:

... 5. Centralization of credit in the hands of the State, by means of a national bank with State capital and an exclusive monopoly.

— Karl Marx and Frederick Engels[1]

In 1913, the U.S. Congress created the privately run agency known as the Federal Reserve. A central bank with an exclusive monopoly, the Fed possesses vast powers, some of which it gained at its creation in 1913 and others of which it was given via additional congressional action in 1933 and 1935. The Fed is exactly what Karl Marx called for in the fifth plank of his *Communist Manifesto*, the document that has guided all communists and socialists for a century and a half.

Using its authority, the Fed can create money out of thin air. The money thus created has regularly been loaned to the U.S. government, which then pays interest on it. The American taxpayers are the real interest payers.

---

1. Karl Marx and Frederick Engels, *The Communist Manifesto*, 1848, op. cit., p. 25.

The Federal Reserve not only creates money, it sets rules whereby the nation's banks also create money. The process was explained by *National Geographic* magazine's Peter White and quoted in Chapter 6. As White showed, when the Fed's reserve requirement is 10 percent, a $1,000 deposit in one bank can readily be parlayed by other banks into as much as $9,000 in loans of newly created currency.

This legal power to create money often leaves a bank short of liquid cash to meet an unexpected flood of depositor demands. If such an eventuality occurs, its officers can apply to the Federal Reserve as the "lender of last resort" for currency to ride out the storm. What it receives from the Fed is also money created out of nothing.

Banks in the United States are always in the precarious position of facing a sudden rush of demands by depositors. They operate legally under what is called the "fractional reserve" system of banking. They keep only a portion of their deposits and lend out the rest. If the rules under which banks operate are changed — even slightly — many would find themselves in an untenable position. They might have to suspend operations or even close their doors. This is precisely what happened to some of the nation's banks in the wave of bank failures over recent years.

When the Federal Reserve was created, paper money issued by the U.S. Treasury was fully redeemable in gold. As we have previously discussed, currency deteriorated from gold backing to silver backing to no backing. Fiat money issued by the Federal Reserve has replaced U.S. Treasury notes.

Incredibly Broad Power

The Fed also establishes interest rates for the entire nation through authority it has been given to set the rates banks must pay to borrow from it. Fed action regarding the "discount rate of interest" triggers the rise and fall of short-term interest rates throughout the nation.

As a result, the Fed has the power to create booms or busts in our nation at will. Each business cycle it creates either eliminates many independently controlled enterprises or paves the way for their absorption into large corporations controlled by Insiders.

Fed power can also be used to influence voters prior to an election. This ability to harm or aid the prospects of presidential candidates was openly discussed by Monroe W. Karmin in the July 25, 1988 issue of *U.S. News & World Report*:

> In short the central bank wants to strike a *pose of neutrality* for the contest between George Bush and Michael Dukakis. The Fed will neither plunge the economy into a recession, as [Fed Chairman] Paul Volcker did in 1980 to sabotage Jimmy Carter's chances for reelection, nor open the money spigots wide, as Arthur Burns did in 1972 to help Richard Nixon win another term. (Emphasis in the original.)[2]

Our nation's founders must be turning over in their graves at the mere mention of such awesome power, let alone the use of it.

Furthermore, foreknowledge of what actions the Fed will undertake gives any possessor the capability of reaping immense profits in the money markets. *New York Times* columnist William Safire confirmed this feature of the central banking process in his *Times* column published on May 16, 1983. During the August 1971 period referred to by Safire, he was a member of President Nixon's White House staff and Paul A. Volcker, a David Rockefeller protégé, held the post of Undersecretary of the Treasury. Here is Safire's revealing commentary:

> The Fed chairman is no stranger to stress-filled meetings. At Camp David on a weekend in August of 1971, when a merry band met to suspend the convertibility of the dollar into gold and impose wage and price controls, we were all impressed with the need for absolute secrecy in our deliberations lest speculators profit. Mr. Volcker, then Treasury Undersecretary, turned to George Shultz,

---

2. "Economic Outlook: Alan Greenspan As King Log," *U.S. News & World Report*, July 25, 1988, p. 49.

then director of the Office of Management and Budget, and asked, "How much is your budget deficit?" Mr. Shultz guessed around $23 billion. "Give me a billion dollars and a free hand on Monday," said Mr. Volcker dreamily, "and I could make up that deficit in the money markets."[3]

Later in this same column, Safire supplied further confirmation of the power of the Fed to manipulate the choice of the American people just prior to an election. When he wrote it, Ronald Reagan was still a year away from having to run for reelection. Here is how the *Times* columnist indicated his own awareness of the Fed's potential political clout:

> Now to the political key: a Presidential candidate wants a Fed chairman who will swing a little. Comes the spring of '84, if interest rates are climbing upward and hurting housing, the incumbent will want a Fed chairman to start shoveling money like mad — even if it upsets conservatives.[4]

Entire books could be written about what was revealed in these admissions. As Safire reported, a few powerfully placed individuals in 1971 planned the hammering of a final nail into the coffin of precious-metal backing for our nation's currency. As a result of those deliberations, action was taken that transformed completely our nation's once-reliable fiduciary currency into absolutely unadulterated fiat money. No one should ever have been given, or allowed to assume, such vast power.

According to Safire, the men at this 1971 gathering also planned the imposition of wage and price controls for our entire nation. A favored maneuver of power seekers throughout many centuries, wage and price controls are the customary response of an inflation creator to the problems caused by his actions.

Then, Paul Volcker, one of the key figures in all that was tak-

---

3. William Safire, "To Pay Paul," *New York Times*, May 16, 1983.
4. Ibid.

ing place, the man who in 1979 would be appointed chairman of the Federal Reserve by Jimmy Carter and reappointed by Ronald Reagan, cavalierly referred to the huge profit-making potential this inside knowledge provided. The illegitimate power possessed by these few is enormous.

Power, Not Necessarily Profit

Let us digress for a moment to point out that the acquisition of personal fortune is not the main goal either of those who created the Federal Reserve or those who have managed it since 1913. Paul Volcker's admission that what he knew could be turned into financial gain does not mean that he used his foreknowledge for that purpose. He may have done so, and others before or after him may have done so as well. A point that must be stressed is that such knowledge should never be at the disposal of anyone.

The main goal motivating those who created the Fed has always been power, not necessarily profit. Conspirators, more interested in control over their fellow man than in piling up personal wealth, have always sought power to control governments, power to compel individuals to abide by their dictates, eventual power through the creation of a world Federal Reserve to do to the entire population of the world exactly what has been and is being done to Americans. In short, the ultimate goal of the power-seekers is the creation of a "new world order."

When the Federal Reserve was established, great care was taken to hide its drive for power. As part of the deception, its chief architects — who were known to be representatives of big banking interests — publicly spoke out against its creation. The system was then deliberately designed with 12 regional banks established across the nation, giving the impression of decentralized control. Privately owned commercial banks were allowed to become shareholders in the Fed and earn dividends for which they paid federal taxes. And the Fed periodically returns the bulk of the profits on its operation to the federal treasury.

Further, each of the Fed's seven-member Board of Governors is appointed by the President and confirmed by the Senate for a 14-

year term. Yet, the Fed is still run independently of the nation's government and has never been publicly audited. [5]

In its *Primer on Money* issued in 1964, the House Banking Committee stated:

> Although a creature of Congress, the Federal Reserve is, in practice, independent of that body in its policy making.... The Federal Reserve neither requires nor seeks the approval of any branch of government for its policies. The system itself decides at what ends its policies are aimed and then takes whatever actions it sees fit to reach those ends.

Counting on a lack of public awareness of the full meaning of the power it has, the Fed itself will occasionally confirm some of its immense centralized clout. In 1963, the Fed's Board of Governors issued a booklet from their Washington, DC headquarters entitled *The Federal Reserve System, Purposes and Functions, Fiftieth Anniversary Edition*. It contained the following statement:

> The Federal Reserve System is the only instrumentality endowed by law with discretionary power to create (or extinguish) the money that serves as bank reserves or as the public's pocket cash. Thus the ultimate capability for expanding or reducing the economy's supply of money rests with the Federal Reserve.

Congressman Wright Patman, the chairman of the House Banking Committee and a foe of the Fed's power, stated in a speech before the House on April 3, 1964:

> The fact is an independent Federal Reserve means something that is not in the framework of our constitutional system, which says that Congress will make the laws and the President will execute them. Those who desire a dictatorship on money matters by a

---

5. Rep. Philip Crane of Illinois introduced H.R. 145 during the 103rd Congress (1993-1995) to have the General Accounting Office audit the Fed and all of its branches and governing components.

"banker's club" — away from the Congress and the President — are in effect advocating a form of government alien to our own.[6]

The Fed is an unconstitutionally established entity that is legally independent of government. But its leaders do not operate independently of the conspiratorial force that brought it into existence. That force, working over several generations to bring about the tyrannical "new world order," can be found in the membership of the Council on Foreign Relations, the Trilateral Commission, the Rhodes Scholar program, the Bilderberg movement, and numerous other organs of the "Establishment." It is a force that dominates government as well as the Fed.

Liaisons amongst the "economists" of the Fed and the movers and shakers in government are carried out regularly in and through memberships in these groups. If George Bush, Bill Clinton, Jimmy Carter, and other presidents are CFR and TC members or alumni, if current Fed chairman Alan Greenspan and his predecessor Paul Volcker have these same credentials, and if Speaker of the House Foley and Senate Majority Leader Mitchell are only two of dozens of House and Senate members who hold CFR and/or TC membership, it is hardly accurate to state that any of these men act independently of the others.[7]

Perhaps our point that power and not personal wealth is the goal can be more easily grasped with the realization that the very idea for the Fed is found in Karl Marx's *Communist Manifesto.* As we have already noted, Marx and Engels outlined in their revolutionary document the steps they felt were necessary for gaining control of nations and peoples. The Fed is the realization of the *Manifesto's* plank number five.

Yet Karl Marx and his followers throughout the past century and a half have always been motivated more by the drive for

---

6. *Congressional Record*, August 3, 1964, p. 17840.
7. Past Fed chairmen Eugene Meyer, Eugene Black, Thomas McCabe, William McChesney Martin, Arthur Burns and G. William Miller have all been members of the CFR, most while they served as Fed chairman. Marriner Eccles is the only Fed chairman from 1930 until the present not to have held membership in this world-government-promoting organization.

power than for personal fortune. Their goals and the goals of those who followed their blueprint and created the Fed were never confined to the acquisition of wealth. The controls over the destiny of our nation and all of mankind were far more important to the schemers who created the Fed than any personal money making. They realized that wealth is power but that absolute power, in human terms, is arrived at politically. And the Fed provided the kind of power they were seeking.

There is no way this conspiratorial monstrosity can be run to the benefit of the American people. Hoping to get the "right man" to run it is like asking the very best driver you can find to steer your auto over a cliff. Giving the kind of authority the Fed possesses to anyone would likely corrupt him. But even more, a free economy is never managed by any single man or group of men. If the economy is managed, it is not free.

No one should have the authority to decide the value, amount, and availability of money. Even well-meaning and incorruptible individuals can never properly and justly countermand the decisions made every day by millions of free individuals in the marketplace.

Also, as explained previously, sound money is a commodity. As such, it is no different from shoes, apples, or automobiles. If there is no need for a national shoe board, or apple board, or automobile board to manage the value, amount, and availability of those commodities, then there is no need to establish a national money board, which is what the Fed actually is.

As to what to replace the Fed with, the answer is absolutely nothing — nothing, that is, except freedom, especially freedom from manipulative and grasping individuals. Abolition of the Fed, repeal of legal tender laws, and return to the gold standard under the auspices of the U.S. Treasury is the only prudent route for Americans.

Who Owns the Fed?

As noted previously, the Fed consists of an appointed Board of Governors and 12 regional banks located across the nation (Boston, New York, Philadelphia, Cleveland, Richmond, Atlanta, Chicago, St. Louis, Dallas, Kansas City, Minneapolis, and San Francisco).

The Fed's real clout resides in its 12-member Federal Open Market Committee, the group that determines most of the Fed's actions. It is made up of the seven members of the Board of Governors and five regional bank presidents, one of whom must always be the president of the Federal Reserve Bank of New York. The other four posts are filled by other regional bank presidents who serve one-year posts on a rotating basis. Many who have examined the Fed's structure have concluded that the president of the New York bank and the Fed Board of Governors, the mainstays of the Federal Open Market Committee, exercise the dominant influence over Fed policy.

The presidents of the 12 regional Federal Reserve banks are chosen by the leaders of commercial banks which are members of the Federal Reserve system. All national banks are required to be part of the Fed; membership of state-chartered banks is optional.

No branch of the U.S. government owns any part of the Fed. Stock in each of the regional Fed banks is owned by the commercial banks within each district. But in "Federal Reserve: The Trillion Dollar Conspiracy," Gary Allen pointed out: "The idea that the Federal Reserve is private because its stock is owned by the commercial banks is very misleading."[8]

Allen quoted the following explanation given by former Congressman Wright Patman:

> Misconceptions about the "ownership" have resulted from the fact that member banks own "stock" in the System. The word "stock" is a misnomer — in reality it is not stock in any generally accepted definition of the word.
>
> Four points about this so-called "stock" clearly differentiate it

---

8. Gary Allen, "Federal Reserve: The Trillion Dollar Conspiracy," *American Opinion*, February 1976.

from the ordinary meaning of the term:

First. It carries no proprietary interest. In this respect, the stock is unlike the stock of any private corporation;

Second. It cannot be sold or pledged for loans. It thus does not represent an ownership claim;

Third. In the event of the dissolution of the Federal Reserve banks, as provided for in the Federal Reserve Act, the net assets after payment of the liabilities and repayment of the stock go to the U.S. Treasury rather than to the private banks; and

Fourth. The stock does not carry the ordinary voting rights of stock. The method of electing officers of the Federal Reserve banks is in no way connected to the amount of stock ownership. Instead, each bank in a district has one vote within its class, regardless of its stock ownership.[9]

Allen then cited an April 18, 1941 letter sent by Marriner S. Eccles, chairman of the Fed Board of Governors, to Patman:

> This so-called stock ownership, however, is more in the nature of an enforced subscription to the capital of the Federal Reserve banks than an ownership in the usual sense. The stock cannot be sold, transferred, or hypothecated, nor can it be voted in accordance with the par value of the shares held. Thus, the smallest member bank has an equal vote with the largest. Member banks have no right to participate in earnings above the six percent statutory dividend, and upon liquidation, any funds remaining after retirement of the stock revert to the government.[10]

Do the member banks own the Fed? No. Their stock is "an enforced subscription to the capital" of the regional bank, not ownership. For providing some of the capital of the regional Fed bank, they receive a proportionate dividend from it.

Who does own the Fed? This pivotal question hasn't been di-

---

9. Ibid.
10. Ibid.

rectly answered by anyone who can do so. If it were an agency of the federal government, however, it would not have been able to withstand inquiries directed its way by members of Congress. All of the secrecy surrounding the Fed is one of many reasons why there is a demand, by Congressman Crane and others, that the organization be audited.

Making Slaves of Free Men

Through the actions of the Federal Reserve and the docile cooperation of Congress, America has seen its honest paper money (the finest the world has ever known, fully and readily redeemable in gold) converted to fiat currency redeemable in nothing. Paralleling this crime, Fed-induced inflation has resulted in a depreciation of the dollar's purchasing power by approximately 90 percent. That lost value, plainly and simply, has been stolen from the American people.

The Federal Reserve, again with the compliance of Congress, has guided the American government into more than $4 trillion dollars of indebtedness, a burden that threatens the very existence of the dollar and the independence of the United States; a burden, also, that is becoming dramatically more oppressive every year.

The American people, generally unaware of the huge amount of interest they pay as a result of government indebtedness, and near totally oblivious to the reason for the shrinking value of their dollars, are in effect working for the Federal Reserve and the banking system it keeps alive.

What has been instituted is a form of slavery, a condition whereby individuals are forced against their will to work for others. The term slavery applies in today's America as rising taxation and the eroding value of the dollar lead to the gobbling up of the property of the American people. As this grand theft proceeds, our nation's middle class — the backbone of any free society — is being destroyed.

When Congress created the Federal Reserve in 1913, it did so with no constitutional authorization whatsoever. As Dr. Edwin

Vieira has stated, "... the Constitution actually settled on one, very specific political formula for money: namely a commodity money of historically proven intrinsic value, the supply of which the political authorities could not manipulate at will."[11] That commodity, specifically noted in the Constitution, was to be either gold or silver, not paper.

By its action in 1913, Congress actually put an official stamp of approval on the replacement of the Constitution as the definer of our nation's monetary policy. The creation of the Fed not only set the stage for the grand theft of the American people's property, it is leading toward a grand theft of the American system of limited government and personal freedom.

Karl Marx would have loved the Fed. As noted in our Introduction, the "unseen guardian angel" of the Fed, Edward Mandell House, wrote in his 1912 book, *Philip Dru: Administrator,* that he wanted "Socialism as dreamed of by Karl Marx."[12] The goals of House, Marx, and their modern-day followers in the CFR, TC, and other elitist organizations are being realized.

All Americans should be outraged at what a few power-hungry individuals have done to our nation and themselves. The Fed must be abolished, but knowing how we got into its grasp is important. In our next chapter, we examine the history of central banking in this nation to show how power-seekers in virtually every generation tried to supplant the Constitution with their own money and banking schemes leading up to the creation of the Fed.

---

11. Vieira, *The Federal Reserve System,* op. cit., p. 5.
12. House, *Philip Dru: Administrator,* op. cit., p. 45.

The Federal Reserve is the realization of the 5th plank in the *Communist Manifesto*, written by Karl Marx and Frederick Engels.

Edward Mandell House called for "Socialism as dreamed of by Karl Marx" in his novel, *Philip Dru: Administrator*.

During the current Congress, Rep. Philip Crane of Illinois introduced H.R. 145 to have the GAO audit the Federal Reserve.

Texas Congressman Wright Patman fought the Federal Reserve as chairman of the House Banking Committee.

Marriner Eccles is the only Fed Chairman since 1930 not to have belonged to the CFR.

Speaker of the House Thomas Foley is a CFR and TC member, and a Bilderberg participant.

CHAPTER 11

The Federal Reserve
and Its Precursors

[A central bank] would be an engine of irresistible power in the hands of any Administration; that it would be in politics and finance what the celebrated proposition of Archimedes was in physics — a place, the fulcrum from which, at the will of the Executive, the whole nation could be hurled to destruction, or managed in any way, at his will and discretion.
— John Randolph of Roanoke[1]

The old Republican from Virginia, John Randolph, could hardly have been more opposed to the idea of a central bank for this nation. He warned that such a bank could hurl the nation to destruction. But he was merely concerned that these powers might be given to "any Administration" or exercised "at the will of the Executive." In other words, he never in his wildest nightmare expected that such power would end up in the hands of a privately run agency such as the Federal Reserve.

Administrations are subject to recall by the voters. A Chief Executive must stand for reelection. The people retain a degree of control over these seats of power. But the people don't elect the officers of the Federal Reserve. And, as we have seen, Fed officials are empowered to act independently of any presidential or congressional direction. They submit to calls for consultation with the President or with congressional leaders. But they retain the power to do as they please.

---

1. As quoted by Murray Rothbard, *The Mystery of Banking* (New York, NY: Richardson and Snyder, 1983), p. 201.

John Randolph would be angry about what 20th Century Americans have allowed to occur. So should anyone who values freedom and all that it entails.

Several Predecessors of the Fed

Our nation had already experienced several periods of central banking prior to 1913 when the Federal Reserve was created. All were nightmarish.

A key feature of a central bank is its possession of a monopoly over the issuance of bank notes or cash. As recounted in Murray Rothbard's excellent study, *The Mystery of Banking*, our nation's first central bank, the privately owned Bank of North America, received its charter in 1781 from the Continental Congress. It was granted monopoly power to issue paper money, and this is exactly what it did.

At first, the paper money the Bank of North America issued was fiduciary money fully redeemable in specie (gold or silver). But, throughout the course of history, the temptation to issue more paper money than can be redeemed by the issuing agency has proven irresistible. The issuance of fully redeemable paper money is customarily followed by issuing irredeemable paper money (fiat money).

Because confidence in paper money was virtually nonexistent in the new nation, and because that is what the 1781 Bank of North America was issuing, it is not surprising that the bank was forced to close its doors after only a few years of operation.

Once the new Constitution had been ratified, another central bank, called the First Bank of the United States, was created in 1791. Rothbard states: "The First Bank of the United States promptly fulfilled its inflationary potential by issuing millions of dollars in paper money and demand deposits...."[2] While doing so, it boldly ignored several sections of the U.S. Constitution as if the document and the warnings of its framers about paper money had never existed.

---

2. Ibid., p. 196.

The First Bank's inflationary policies produced predictable results: the people were defrauded; commerce was slowed; confidence in the credit of the United States suffered; and bankers, merchants, and their allies in politics became wealthy.

When the charter for this First Bank of the United States came up for renewal in 1811, Congress defeated the proposal by a single vote in each House. Powerful interests had not yet become powerful enough to sustain the practice of fraudulent banking. Though defeated, however, the individuals representing those interests licked their wounds and waited for another day.

During the War of 1812, the government encouraged the creation of a large number of local and state banks, each of which issued partially backed paper money. When holders sought redemption of the paper in gold or silver, the government reverted to the age-old practice of allowing the banks to refuse to provide it. Rothbard notes that free banking "didn't work well ... because it wasn't really tried." He explains:

> Remember that a crucial aspect of the free banking model is that the moment a bank cannot pay its notes or deposits in specie, it must declare bankruptcy and close up shop. [3]

Powerful banking interests blamed the failures of banking in the United States on "free banking." Yet, free banking had not been tried. Had it been given a chance, *some* banks undoubtedly would have inflated and defrauded *some* citizens, but competition that always leads to excellence would have shown the public that other banks were sound. Honest banks would have remained in business; fraudulent banks would have failed; and bank customers would have learned a great deal about honest banking, honest bankers, and honest money. The nation would have been spared future agony because of the awareness of the people. But competition in the form of truly free banking simply did not exist.

---

3. Ibid., p. 198.

In 1936, Vera C. Smith gave an excellent definition of free banking. She stated that it constituted

> a regime where note-issuing banks are allowed to set up in the same way as any other type of business enterprise, so long as they comply with general company law. The requirement for their establishment is not special conditional authorization from a government authority, but the ability to raise sufficient capital, and the public confidence, to gain acceptance for their notes and ensure the profitability of the undertaking. Under such a system all banks would not only be allowed the same rights, but would also be subjected to the same responsibilities as other business enterprises. If they failed to meet their obligations they would be declared bankrupt and put into liquidation, and their assets used to meet the claims of the creditors, in which case the shareholders would lose the whole or part of their capital, and the penalty for failure would be paid, at least for the most part, by those responsible for the policy of the bank. Notes issued under this system would be "promises to pay," and such obligations would be met on demand in the generally accepted medium which we will assume to be gold. No bank would have the right to call on the government or on any other institution for special help in time of need.... A general abandonment of the gold standard is inconceivable under these conditions, and with a strict interpretation of the bankruptcy laws any bank suspending payments would at once be put into the hands of a receiver.[4]

Central banking enthusiasts criticized the failed system which had no central bank, claiming that there were too many banks, too little control over them, and too much paper money circulating. Their recommendation for another go at a central bank came as no surprise. Not content with seeing some of the people defrauded some of the time, they wanted authorization to inflate, charge interest, and defraud everyone. *They also wanted author-*

---

4. Vera C. Smith, *The Rationale of Central Banking* (London: King & Son, 1936), pp. 148-149, cited by Paul and Lehrman, op. cit., p. 40.

ity to inflate without having to be compared to any honest bank operating in competition.

The Panic of 1819

The next venture with central banking began when the Second Bank of the United States opened its doors in 1817. In conjunction with various state banks, the Second Bank promptly inaugurated a huge inflationary binge that created a temporary economic boom. Less than two years later, after it had issued a great deal more paper money than it could redeem, the Bank found itself in danger of failing to meet its legal requirement to provide specie for its paper money.

Faced with imminent collapse, the Second Bank called in loans, ceased supplying credit to smaller banks, and even forced banks to repay their loans in specie (precious metal). The Bank had actually flooded the nation with money and then contracted its supply. The predictable result: a full-fledged depression in 1819.[5]

In the short space of two years, the nation had suffered through its first bank-caused and government-sanctioned "boom and bust" cycle. The boom resulted from a dramatic increase in the amount of currency; the bust came on the heels of a contraction in the money supply. Many history books discuss the Panic of 1819, though very few will provide the real reasons for it.

It would be a delight to be able to report that the nation had learned its lesson after 1819, but it hadn't. Even today, we are still suffering the harmful effects of the same kind of artificially created boom and bust cycle that did its damage in 1819.

Jackson to the Rescue

Andrew Jackson campaigned victoriously in 1828 with the following simple pledge:

> The Federal Constitution must be obeyed, states rights preserved, our national debt must be paid, direct taxes and loans avoided, and

---

5. Rothbard, *The Mystery of Banking*, op. cit., pp. 199-206.

the Federal Union preserved. These are the objects I have in view, and regardless of all consequences, will carry into effect.[6]

By 1831, Jackson put his entire political life on the line in a fight over the continuance of the Second Bank of the United States. He won a bruising battle against the bank's partisans in Congress, was reelected in 1832, and presided over the bank's eventual demise. He then proceeded to have the national debt paid off. The nation owes him a great debt of thanks.

But state and local banking practices encouraged by the Second Bank during its existence (1817-1836) continued to plague the nation, leading to more area-wide booms and busts. What the nation needed but did not get was truly free and honest banking.

The Civil War then provided the occasion for the ushering in of another form of money, the issuance of U.S. Treasury notes called "greenbacks." Originally fully redeemable in precious metal, the government created so many greenbacks that redeemability was quickly suspended — not only by the Treasury but by all nationally chartered banks.

Whether practiced by the banks or the Treasury itself, the practice of inflation whereby more paper currency is issued than could ever be redeemed in specie has always led to the cancellation of redeemability. Even if good intentions accompany the initial issuance of redeemable paper money, they are regularly followed by fraud involving the changeover to fiat money.

The experience with Lincoln greenbacks during the very expensive and bloody War Between the States prompted banking interests to get behind passage of a succession of new National Banking Acts. The first, passed in 1863, succeeded in essentially destroying the state banking systems and inserting a centralized system in their place. It created several categories of national banks, none with a complete monopoly, but all chartered by the federal government. Each had the ability to inflate. As could be expected when given such power, inflate they did.

---

6. Cited by William P. Hoar, *Architects of Conspiracy*, op. cit., p. 26.

Subsequent booms and busts were all traceable to the new system. Banking panics plagued the nation in every decade (1873, 1884, 1893, and 1907). Each resulted from a flood of fiat money followed by a period of currency contraction.[7] The American people were being whipsawed on a regular basis by the new banking system. Booms and busts followed one after the other at almost predictable intervals. The failures of this new system, complete with its destructive ups and downs, set the stage for the next try at central banking, the Federal Reserve System. The orchestrators of the failing system were only too willing to create a completely centralized banking system as the solution to the nation's banking woes.

Born in Deep Secrecy

Much has been written elsewhere about the highly secret meeting of a handful of bankers and government officials held in the fall of 1910 at Jekyll Island in South Carolina.[8] Seven individuals whose connections to the world of banking were well-known gathered to lay plans for a new central bank in the United States. Three came from the House of J.P. Morgan, one from a powerful Rockefeller bank, one just happened to be an assistant secretary of the treasury, another was the Rockefeller-connected Senator Nelson Aldrich of Rhode Island, and the final participant was Paul Warburg, a representative of the Rothschild banking empire in Europe and the principal architect of the Federal Reserve.[9]

The extraordinary efforts taken by these men to hide the very fact that they were meeting caused one of the participants many years later to liken himself to a "conspirator." Rockefeller em-

---

7. Rothbard, op. cit., p. 232.
8. See for example: Gary Allen, "The Bankers: Conspiratorial Origins of the Federal Reserve," (Appleton, WI: *American Opinion*, March 1970).
9. The seven at the secret Jekyll Island meeting were Henry P. Davison of the J.P. Morgan Company, Charles D. Norton of the Morgan-controlled First National Bank of New York, Benjamin Strong of the Morgan-controlled Bankers Trust Company, Frank Vanderlip of the Rockefeller-controlled National City Bank of New York, Assistant Secretary of the Treasury A. Piatt Andrew, Rhode Island Senator Nelson W. Aldrich, and Paul Warburg of New York's Kuhn, Loeb & Company.

ployee Frank Vanderlip unabashedly applied that term to himself in an article he wrote for the February 9, 1935 issue of the *Saturday Evening Post*:

> Despite my views about the value to society of greater publicity for the affairs of corporations, there was an occasion, near the close of 1910, when I was as secretive — indeed as furtive — as any conspirator.... I do not feel it any exaggeration to speak of our secret expedition to Jekyll Island as the occasion of the actual conception of what eventually became the Federal Reserve System.
>
> We were told to leave our last names behind us. We were told further, that we should avoid dining together on the night of our departure. We were instructed to come one at a time and as unobtrusively as possible to the railroad terminal on the N.J. littoral of the Hudson, where Sen. Aldrich's private car would be in readiness, attached to the rear end of a train to the South.
>
> ... Once aboard the private car we began to observe the taboo that had been fixed on last names....
>
> The servants and the train crew may have known the identities of one or two of us, but they did not know all, and it was the names of all printed together that would have made our mysterious journey significant in Washington, in Wall Street, even in London. Discovery, we knew, simply must not happen, or else all our time and effort would be wasted.[10]

The plotters produced the plan to have Congress create a privately run central bank with vast monopoly powers including those that had caused so many problems for the nation from its birth. Rothschild agent Paul Warburg supplied particulars based on his experience in Europe.[11]

Previously, inflation practiced by various banks was largely

---

10. Frank Vanderlip, "Farm Boy to Financier," *Saturday Evening Post*, February 9, 1935, p. 25 et seq.
11. The founder of the Rothschild banking dynasty, Meyer Amschel Rothschild, is reputed to have stated, "Let me issue and control a nation's money and I care not who writes the laws." Frederic Morton, *The Rothschilds, A Family Portrait* (New York, NY: Atheneum, 1962).

unregulated with the result that some banks issued more fiat money than others and, in time, defrauded more depositors than others. But the central bank would standardize inflation, steal from the people uniformly, and exercise enormous control over the nation's policies.

Congress Caves In

On December 22, 1913, Congress passed the Federal Reserve Act which established the Federal Reserve with enormous powers and the potential for adding still more in subsequent years. As Gary Allen summarized in *None Dare Call It Conspiracy*,

> The Federal Reserve controls our money supply and interest rates, and thereby manipulates the entire economy — creating inflation or deflation, recession or boom, and sending the stock market up or down at whim. [12]

The cleverly named Federal Reserve, however, is not a federal agency but a privately run corporation that serves as the nation's bank. The Fed will tell anyone that it is owned by its Board of Governors, its 12 regional banks, and its member commercial banks. No branch of the federal government owns any portion of the Fed.

Wright Patman of Texas served for many years as the chairman of the House Banking Committee. He maintained:

> In the United States today, we have in effect two governments.... We have the duly constituted government.... Then we have an independent, uncontrolled and uncoordinated government in the Federal Reserve System, operating the money powers which are reserved to the Congress by the Constitution. [13]

In May 1969, *U.S. News & World Report* published an interview with then-Secretary of the Treasury David M. Kennedy.

---

12. Allen, *None Dare Call It Conspiracy*, op. cit., p. 51.
13. Congressman Wright Patman's Newsletter to Constituents, June 6, 1968.

Kennedy's response to the following simple question must be carefully considered if one wishes to comprehend the power and independence of the Fed:

> Q. Do you approve of the latest credit-tightening moves [of the Federal Reserve Board]?
>
> A. It's not my job to approve or disapprove. It is the action of the Federal Reserve. [14]

Further, Fed Chairman Arthur Burns stated on November 11, 1969, "The responsibility of the Fed is to supervise monetary policy.... The Federal Reserve Board's autonomy was conceived for the purposes of maintaining the integrity of the currency. I think it's quite proper that money authority be independent of political authority." [15]

Warnings Unheeded

Prior to the vote that authorized the creation of the Fed, Massachusetts Senator Henry Cabot Lodge Sr. stated:

> The bill as it stands seems to me to open the way to a vast inflation of the currency.... I do not like to think that any law can be passed which will make it possible to submerge the gold standard in a flood of irredeemable paper currency. [16]

After the vote creating the Fed had been taken, Minnesota Congressman Charles A. Lindbergh Sr. — the father of the future famous aviator — told his colleagues:

> This act establishes the most gigantic trust on earth.... When the President signs this act the invisible government by money power, proven to exist by the Money Trust investigation, will be legalized....

---

14. *U.S. News & World Report*, May 5, 1969.
15. Cited in Gary Allen, *Richard Nixon, The Man Behind the Mask* (Appleton, WI; Western Islands; 1971), p. 361.
16. Cited in *Congressional Record*, June 10, 1932.

The new law will create inflation whenever the trusts want inflation.[17]

Lindbergh would later state, "From now on depressions will be scientifically created."[18] And indeed they have been, including the famous depression that began in 1929.[19]

But the Congress had acted and the Fed was created. The flood of irredeemable paper would soon begin, and the management of the nation's economic life had been centralized and placed at the disposal of a powerful few.

A crucial next step in the conspiracy's master plan is to create an *international* Federal Reserve, have all nations submit to its machinations, and make slaves of all the inhabitants of the planet.

Claiming to Help the Poor

Our nation's Constitution was written to insure that the kind of power possessed by the Fed would never be possessed by anyone or any agency. It was also designed to perpetuate free enterprise and stand as a bulwark against totalitarian government control.

But, with the Fed shoving as fast as it can, the American people are being pushed into economic slavery at the hands of their own government. Created by the people to serve them in a very few clearly specified areas, the U.S. government is fast becoming a fearful master. Much of the growth of government has been accomplished under the guise of helping the poor and downtrodden.

In a June 1981 speech about the lessons of history, Robert Welch discussed how destructive these appeals "to help the poor" have always been:

---

17. *Congressional Record*, December 22, 1913.
18. Charles A. Lindbergh, Sr., *The Economic Pinch* (Philadelphia, PA: Dorrance and Company, 1923).
19. An excellent history of the deliberate creation of the 1929 depression can be found in Murray N. Rothbard, *America's Great Depression* (Kansas City, MO: Sheed and Ward, 1975).

It eventually happened, naturally, in every case throughout all recorded history, that the excessive cost of all these favors to the poor, to persuade them to keep on voting for a continuation and increase of these special favors, so weakened the total economy of the whole principality, province, or empire, that in due course it totally collapsed. And all of its former greatness and prosperity became in a few generations just footnotes in future histories.

One of the most positive and clearcut examples of this development happened to the first Babylonian empire under Hammurabi during the Twentieth Century B.C. And if it has occurred to you that exactly the same thing is happening to the United States during the Twentieth Century A.D., do not pat yourself on the back too hard for having recognized this fact. For it is already extremely well known indeed to scores at least of the very people who are deliberately bringing it about.[20]

Among the "help the poor" schemes building power for socialist conspirators in our nation are numerous programs labelled "entitlements," the subject of our next chapter.

---

20. Robert Welch, "Again, One Man's Opinion," text published in *American Opinion* magazine, September 1981.

John Randolph believed that a central bank would place "irresistible power" in the hands of the government.

Andrew Jackson's efforts led to abolishing a central bank; he then saw to it that the national debt was paid.

Paul Warburg was the chief architect of the Federal Reserve, America's central bank.

Rhode Island Senator Nelson Aldrich was a key player in the founding of the Fed.

Minnesota Congressman Charles Lindbergh Sr. said that the Fed would become "the most gigantic trust on earth."

Frank Vanderlip admitted 25 years later that his activity in helping to found the Fed made him a "conspirator."

As Fed chairman, Arthur Burns held that the Fed should have "autonomy" and should be "independent of political authority."

While Secretary of the Treasury, David Kennedy admitted that our nation's monetary policy was set by the action of the Fed.

CHAPTER 12

Disarming the Entitlements Time Bomb

But how is this legal plunder to be identified? Quite simply. See if the law takes from some persons what belongs to them, and gives it to other persons to whom it does not belong. See if the law benefits one citizen at the expense of another by doing what the citizen himself cannot do without committing a crime.

— Frederic Bastiat[1]

Entitlements are government programs that provide money to anyone who meets congressionally established criteria — age, income, occupation, etc. The term implies that a huge number of citizens have a legal claim on the property of others. The fundamental injustice of the arrangement ought to be obvious.[2] But, even more, it ought to be clear that the mushrooming cost of entitlement programs can steer our ship of state onto a killer reef.

From less than one-third of the federal budget in 1962, federal spending for entitlements has risen to consume over one-half of the budget (see Figure 12-1). This means that more than half of the revenue collected from the American people doesn't pay for government's proper functions, but is earmarked for delivery to recipients and to millions of bureaucrats who administer the programs.

---

1. Frederic Bastiat, *The Law* (Irvington-on-Hudson, NY: The Foundation for Economic Education, 1972 edition), p. 21.
2. It would be perfectly proper for someone to receive payments from a genuine trust fund if one existed. But the government has no trust funds in the real sense, and should not.

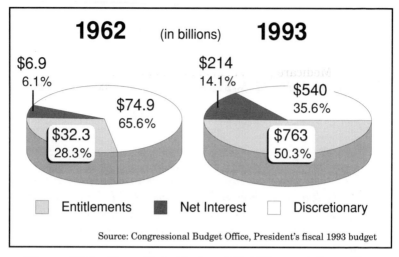

Figure 12-1. Growth in Federal Entitlement Spending

Table 12-1 shows the cost in 1991 of the top 12 entitlement programs. Each year, their total cost rises dramatically.[3]

Ask many members of Congress about this immense drag on America's productive sector and you'll likely be told that nothing can be done about it because these programs are "mandatory." The huge expenditures funding them are termed "non-discretionary," implying that Congress has its hands completely tied and can make cuts only in "discretionary" programs.

Mandatory spending — the total of entitlement programs plus the cost of interest on the national debt — now accounts for approximately two-thirds of federal spending. This leaves one-third for discretionary spending, the portion of the federal budget earmarked for many domestic programs and national defense. Therefore, a cut of 10 percent in discretionary programs would result in a cut of only about three percent of the total federal budget.

---

3. Many Americans who have paid social security taxes for years don't believe that the payments they will eventually receive should be classified as "entitlements" in the same category as direct welfare, medical care, etc. Yet this is the label the U.S. government attaches to social security disbursements. Payments for those who have retired are also considered entitlements by the government but not by recipients .

Program	Actual 1991 Outlays
Social Security	$267 billion
Medicare	114
Deposit Insurance	66
Medicaid	53
Civilian Retirement	37
Unemployment	25
Military Retirement	23
Food Stamps	20
Supplemental Income	15
Family Support	14
Veteran's Benefits	14
Farm Price Supports	10

Table 12-1. Cost of Top 12 Entitlement Programs

Entitlement programs can't be touched? Wait a minute! They weren't handed down from on high by the Almighty; they were created by Congress. What Congress creates, Congress can uncreate. (A very few of these programs, such as military and civil service retirement, are an appropriate expense for government.) No government official should get away with claiming an inability to deal with this situation. If programs can be started, they can be stopped, or converted to private management, or reduced.

The director of the Congressional Budget Office, Robert D. Reischauer, explains why many elected officials won't roll back or kill these programs. "Cutting entitlements sounds painless," he declares. "But when you examine the specifics, you realize this is the third rail of American politics."[4]

Anyone who touches the third rail of an electrified railway, of course, will be seriously injured, maybe even killed. The popular wisdom holds that any elected official who tries to rectify the injustices and dangers inherent in federal entitlement programs

---

4. David E. Rosenbaum, "Answer: Cut Entitlements. Question: But How?" *New York Times,* June 8, 1993.

will be signing his political death warrant. But if this popular notion is correct, then the nation's death warrant has already been signed. Only a bit more time must pass before the United States is officially extinct, done in by its own suicidal policies.

Congress Must Reverse Course

A study of congressional voting records confirms that there are indeed some members of Congress who recognize the perils of big government. Though few in number, they consistently try to stem the socialist tide. But it is also true that many others in Congress are either determined socialists already working to destroy free enterprise in America, or venal politicians who follow the path of least resistance and depend on leftist support.

In 1990, Vermont's voters chose an admitted socialist named Bernard Sanders to represent them as their state's only congressman. Early in 1992, Sander's record for the 102nd Congress (1991-1992) was actually found to be less socialistic than 243 of his House colleagues.[5] That's more than a majority of the House membership. Yet it is an absolute certainty that most of these left-of-Sanders representatives, 225 Democrats and 18 Republicans, aren't socialist conspirators who want America to self-destruct. The great majority are politicians who think — or hope — that America can continue down the socialist path without paying the price other nations travelling that path have paid. That price is the end of liberty.

If they had any assurance they could still be reelected, many representatives would happily vote to undo the federal government's oppressive bureaucratic control. They aren't leaders in the real sense; they are followers who put self above principle and who are willing to sacrifice the future well-being of the nation for the perquisites of power they currently enjoy.

Many elected officials in this nation have a decision to make. They can begin to roll back big government's power and put

---

5. As compiled by *The New American's* "Conservative Index" using the U.S. Constitution as its only measuring rod. See also "Our Socialist Congressmen," *The New American*, February 10, 1992.

America back on the road to greatness, or they can continue appeasing constituents who want something for nothing, hold on to their seat in Congress, and watch as America self-destructs.

If they continue to choose the latter course, the nation will soon be transformed into a carbon copy of thousands of despotisms that have gone before. There is no other choice. Expecting this nation to endure when it is saddled with a multiplicity of programs choking it to death is a patent absurdity.

Only an aroused and informed electorate can help Congress make the right choice. If a majority of voters in the cities and towns of this nation demand less government and a return to economic freedom, hundreds of politicians will respond. Some are even waiting for the voters to force them to do what they know is right.

The Wisdom of Frederic Bastiat

Frederic Bastiat, a member of France's legislature in the mid-19th century, passed away in 1850. But just before he died, he wrote a small book entitled *The Law*, whose timeless message attacked socialist thinking and defined the proper role of government. Of special interest to Americans are Bastiat's words about our nation: "There is no country in the world where the law is kept more within its proper domain: the protection of every person's liberty and property."[6] But Bastiat would hardly say that of America today.

What he wrote for his countrymen in *The Law* in 1850 is needed as much, or even more, by Americans of today. His term for entitlements was "legal plunder." Here is some of what he wrote about it:

> But how is this legal plunder to be identified? Quite simply. See
> if the law takes from some persons what belongs to them, and gives
> it to other persons to whom it does not belong. See if the law ben-
> efits one citizen at the expense of another by doing what the citizen

---

6. Bastiat, op. cit., p. 18.

himself cannot do without committing a crime.

Then abolish this law without delay, for it is not only an evil it-self, but also it is a fertile source for further evils because it invites reprisals. If such a law — which may be an isolated case — is not abolished immediately, it will spread, multiply and develop into a system.[7]

It is this system of wealth distribution — whose modern name is socialism — that sets citizen against citizen, group against group, and faction against faction. Each will succumb to the lure of having the government take from others to supply its wants until such time as the government is invested with so much power that the rights of all to life, liberty, and property are crushed.

Can America recover from the introduction of this system into our midst? Why not? If early Americans could create a nation devoid of socialism's deadly enticements and stifling controls, then current Americans ought to be able to rebuild it. But doing so will require rolling back the entitlement maze that is choking freedom and building an all-powerful government. It will also require a willingness on the part of Americans to expose the conspiratorial forces behind this drain on productive America.

Social Security

At $300 billion per year, social security is the largest of the entitlement programs. Launched in 1937, it initially dispensed cash benefits to retired workers and their dependents, and to survivors of those enrolled in the program. In 1956, disabled workers and their dependents were added as beneficiaries. Then, in 1972, after years of legislating periodic raises for recipients, Congress adopted an automatic increase system tied to increases in the cost of living. An upward cost of living adjustment (COLA) is now made whenever the rise in the consumer price index (erroneously labelled inflation) exceeds 0.1 percent in a year.

Social security checks are now sent to over 40 million recipi-

---

7. Ibid., p. 21.

ents each month. The program has mushroomed into a gigantic mechanism for destroying self-reliance and creating massive dependency on government. Its vaunted "benefits" barely provide a subsistence-level income. Funded by taxes taken from the productive sector, social security in its infancy could claim 16 persons forced to pay into it for every one receiving benefits. That ratio is now down to three to one and will shrink even more in the near future.

When it was begun in 1937, the maximum social security tax was set at $30 per year and an employer was forced to match it, for a total of $60 per year. The maximum tax today is $3,441 which also must be matched by an employer for a total of $6,882 per year.[8] These matching payments constitute a significant portion of an employer's cost of labor, along with salaries and benefits. Because the employer must weigh many factors when determining the cost of doing business, and because he would not likely pay more for labor than the labor is worth to him, the matching payments extracted from the employer are in essence a tax on employment. If these matching payments were eliminated, unemployment would be lessened and the employer would likely be forced by the marketplace to pay higher wages.

Despite widespread belief to the contrary, social security has never been an insurance program, nor should it be, because government is nowhere authorized in the Constitution to be in the insurance business. If social security were an insurance program, each participant would be able to claim the cash value of his policy at any time. Also, no one would be forced to participate, and those who did could decide their own premiums and, therefore, the size of the benefit to be paid.

No matter how much one has been taxed in the name of social security, benefits supplied under the system are not earned by the worker, but are a grant supplied by government. Government can actually alter the amount to be paid, even abolish the entire

---

8. George Hager, "Entitlements: The Untouchable May Become Unavoidable," *Congressional Quarterly*, January 2, 1993, pp. 22-30. Also Gary Allen, "What You Should Know About Social Security," *American Opinion*, March 1981.

program at any time and pay nothing. No insurance program could operate in such a manner.

Nor do the taxes taken from each participant go into any "trust fund."[9] The money paid into social security is considered general revenue just like receipts from taxes on incomes. There is not and never has been any trust fund.

As long as government retains the power to tax, the social security system can continue. But there is always a limit on the amount of taxation the people can or will endure.

While Congress forces Americans into this system that most would never join voluntarily, it exempts itself from the program. Instead of social security, members of Congress are allowed to join a privately run pension program that supplies far greater benefits.[10]

Boiled down to its essence, social security is a transfer-the-wealth, make-the-people-dependent scheme. It has become a huge burden for the young, and its potential for creating a class conflict between young and old is enormous. For dozens of reasons, it ought to be phased out. And the good news is that it can be done away with in a manner that will help the entire nation — if the nation has the guts and good sense to take such a step.

There is a Better Way

Rather than employing government-administered compulsory social security that could bankrupt this nation all by itself, America ought to try free enterprise. Chile has shown that it can be done.

By 1973, Chile had endured nine years of socialistic control (under U.S.-backed social democrat Eduardo Frei from 1964 to 1970

---

9. See discussion of *Helvering v. Davis* Supreme Court decision in Chapter 5.
10. Congress has exempted itself from the following: Americans With Disabilities Act; Age Discrimination Act; Civil Rights Act of 1964; Ethics in Government Act of 1978; Family and Medical Leave Act; Freedom of Information Act; Independent Counsel Act; National Labor Relations Act; National Labor Standards Act; Privacy Act; Occupational Safety and Health Act; Rehabilitation Act; Social Security Act; Title IX of the Higher Education Act. See "Make Congress Obey Itself," *New York Times* editorial, April 12, 1993.

and under communist Salvador Allende from 1970 until late 1973). In 1973 alone the nation's wholesale price index had climbed 1,147 percent, the budget deficit was 25 percent of national income, debt service (taxation to pay interest) was stifling all economic activity, and the country was surviving on expensive imports, even of food.

In addition, government-imposed price controls on over 3,000 items had spawned a huge black market and the inevitable police powers to combat it; the banking, steel, electric, telephone, and manufacturing industries had been nationalized; and farms that had been under family ownership for generations were being seized by government for "redistribution" to the poor.

Everything about Chile in 1973 spelled totalitarianism when a coup d'etat led by military leaders rescued the nation from socialist tyranny.[11] In just a few years, the turn to free market practices resulted in stable prices, a favorable export/import ratio, a balanced budget, low interest rates, and rising employment. By 1980, Chile had risen from a chaotic economic calamity to become one of the world's most envied nations.

Then in 1981, government leaders turned their attention to their own "third rail" when they began to dismantle the social security system. (Chile's social security system also included health care, unemployment insurance, and family income supplements.) Begun in 1925, the program had been collecting 29 percent of each worker's salary with an additional 20 percent paid by each employer. It had become a costly, bankrupt, and inequitable drag on hiring and productivity, and an open door to tax evasion and a police-state bureaucracy to catch evaders.

Chilean leaders arranged to get the government out of the so-

---

11. A great deal of unfavorable propaganda has been spread about the military government led by Augusto Pinochet from 1973 until he submitted to a plebiscite and stepped down in 1990. For an honest survey of Chile's plight leading up to the 1973 takeover, including the years of Pinochet's rule and the numerous attempts by new world order forces in the United States to undermine Chile's dramatic move to free enterprise and national prosperity, see Jane Ingraham, "Chile After Augusto Pinochet," *The New American*, July 30, 1990.

cial security mess by turning it over to private enterprise. Under a plan begun in 1981, employers paid nothing and employees who wanted out of the government program were required to choose from a number of privately owned, for-profit investment firms offering sound pension programs, medical plans, and unemployment insurance. As it launched this free market approach to social security, the government announced that it would phase out the old system in five years. [12]

Workers who joined the new program immediately saw larger take-home pay. Employers, relieved of enormous tax burdens, began a hiring spree. The money paid to the various privately run pension companies was speedily reinvested in the Chilean economy. The nation, already the envy of neighboring Latin American countries, became known as the site of "El Boom." [13]

Why Not Here?

Chile's plunge into socialistic control was even deeper than our own nation's has become. But she pulled out of it and is thriving. If Chile's leaders dared to attack "the third rail," why can't ours? Might it be that many of our nation's leaders don't want to end socialism? Could it be that they want government controls to bring America down economically on the way to a planned transition to world government?

Think about it. If Americans were given the option of enrolling in a private pension plan, wouldn't millions do so? Wouldn't there

---

12. Kenneth Freed, "Chile Dismantling Social Security System," *San Francisco Chronicle*, April 15, 1981; Jean A. Briggs, "A Political Miracle," *Forbes*, May 11, 1992; Warren Brookes, "Chile Leads the Way on Social Security," *Boston Herald*, June 24, 1989.
13. Malcolm MacPherson, "Back From the Brink," *Reader's Digest*, June 1993. The economic boom in Chile developed not only from the phasing out of the nation's compulsory social security system but also from the widespread privatization of businesses and industries once held — and poorly managed — by the government. Privately owned firms have been created in the fields of mining, electricity production and distribution, telephone service, air transportation, housing, and many other industries previously under total government control. In addition, many firms and properties nationalized during the reign of the socialists have been returned to their rightful owners.

be hordes of salesmen showing working men and women the advantages of protecting their own future? Wouldn't the huge amounts of money everyone is now forced to give to non-productive government end up in privately run plans where the funds would be reinvested in business enterprises? Wouldn't this enormous influx of money quickly translate to more jobs, more businesses, and greater productivity?

How about young people starting a lifetime of employment today? They will have tremendous sums of money extracted from their wages for a program the vast majority would never join if given the choice. Even if the social security tax remains at its present level — which is unlikely — average working people will be forced to send tens of thousands of dollars into the program. Their return when they retire will amount to bare subsistence, or less. And not a dime of their money will be invested in the free enterprise system.

If young Americans were free to steer their money into non-government programs, they would earn a very comfortable retirement even as they were helping their nation and their fellow citizens prosper. What ever happened to freedom of choice in the land of the free?

As currently administered, the social security system even refuses to provide full payments to citizens whose earnings exceed a federally established ceiling. Also, should a recipient's earnings top another government-established level, his social security benefits themselves are taxed. Just imagine a private pension fund telling a longtime investor that he can't continue working if he expects to receive his full pension. Or that his income is such that payments will not be forthcoming. Or that he must give back a portion of his benefits because he earns too much from other sources. Yet, this is the way social security operates.

An American Answer

Here is an American answer to the social security swindle:

1. Government should announce that the program will be phased out with no new participants allowed into it.

2. All who are currently receiving payments should continue to receive them according to existing schedules.

3. Those who wish to quit the program immediately and never receive any benefits should be allowed to do so. However, some arrangement might be made for repayment of whatever amount has been taken from each participant. These payments need not be a lump sum, but could be spread out over an agreed-upon time period.

4. Those nearing retirement age who wish to continue paying into the program should be allowed to do so, and benefits paid to them upon retirement should be made according to existing schedules.

5. Young people entering the work force should be encouraged — but never forced — to begin an investment/pension plan of their own. Without doubt, the end of compulsory participation in the social security program would trigger the creation of numerous privately run companies offering pension, investment, health care, and unemployment plans.

6. The money needed to carry the system while it is being phased out can be realized through the sale of vast federally owned lands. (See the map in Figure 12-2 showing the extensiveness of federal holdings in the western United States.) In addition, all businesses owned unconstitutionally by the federal government should be sold or abolished.

The market value of federally owned land, practically all of which should never have been purchased or seized by the federal government in the first place, easily exceeds $10 trillion dollars. Any purchases of federally owned land must, of course, meet with the approval of the state government in which it lies. [14]

---

14. Article I, Section 8 of the Constitution authorizes the federal government to own the land on which sits "the seat of the Government of the United States," and to own other parcels "purchased by the consent of the legislature of the State in which the same shall be, for the erection of forts, magazines, arsenals, dock-yards, and other needful buildings...." Ownership by the federal government of all other properties — including enormous tracts in each of the 13 western states — has never been constitutionally authorized.

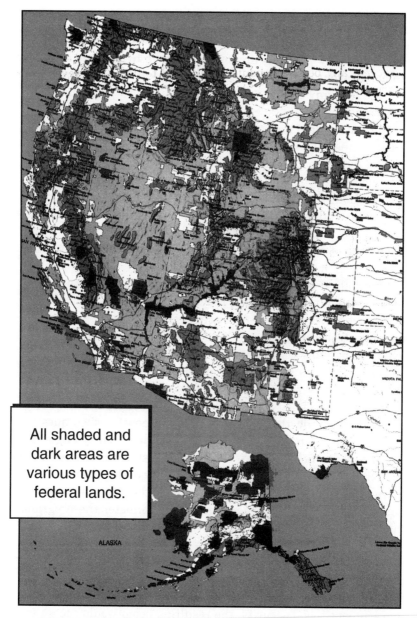

All shaded and dark areas are various types of federal lands.

Figure 12-2. Federal Holdings in the Western States

Why Not Freedom?

Any discussion of the inequities and downright dangers in the social security program invites a challenge by persons claiming to be paragons of compassion. The customary claim by such persons is that any change in the present system will produce a social catastrophe.

But not only did the scrapping of the system fail to produce any catastrophe in Chile, it helped spur a national boom. Chile's adoption of free enterprise led to better wages, less unemployment, a decline in taxation, and a reduction in government indebtedness. In addition, the Chilean people are more self-reliant, more responsible, and less prone to class consciousness. And they are not only responsive to the need for charity for those who really can't take care of themselves, but their improved financial condition leaves them better able to help the truly needy.

Our nation would likewise enjoy similar and perhaps even greater benefits if freedom to provide for one's own security were introduced. Each year in America, even as taxation and government controls continue to cut into personal wealth, the amount of charitable giving rises. Mushrooming government power, on the other hand, owns no monopoly on compassion and will become a promoter of misery for all.

Will private charity be sufficient to provide for all who are in need? First of all, the answer to that frequently asked question has to begin with the realization that the mere entry of government into the field of charity inevitably results in an immediate swelling of the number of "needy." Not only does welfare of every variety became a "right" (which it is not!), the overwhelming majority of government workers hired to administer the programs hardly work to get their "clients" off the rolls. If they did, they'd do themselves out of jobs. Human nature being what it is, government welfare programs, always create an ever-expanding number of applicants and bureaucrats.

Secondly, if our nation were to adopt a Chilean-type solution to government social security, the resulting boom would see an immediate reduction in unemployment. Millions of Americans who would rather work but are unable to find decent jobs are being victimized by too much government. Reduce the government's stifling influence — taxation, regulations, controls, bureaucracy — and jobs will begin to develop along with a corresponding increase in self-reliance and personal pride. And, of great importance, as America turns away from socialism, it will become impossible for the enemies of freedom to sweep this nation into their new world order.

Wouldn't it be wonderful if all those "pro-choice" bumper stickers seen throughout America were actually calling for freedom of choice in social security and other government-mandated programs!

If only freedom were given a chance!

Health Care Entitlements

The Chilean success story isn't confined to social security alone. It also encompasses health care and unemployment insurance. So, too, an American system based on free choice could provide for all these needs — if such a system were allowed to exist. Instead, American health care, the finest in the world in spite of the negative effects government has already caused it, is under attack by government planners who want to take it over completely. Anyone who surveys what several decades of federal aid to education have done to America's schools ought to shrink in horror at the thought of allowing government to get its hands on medicine.

But government already has a sizable presence in the medical field. The cost of the Medicare entitlement, at $114 billion per year and rising, is second only to social security. Medicare, too, is now being financed by a payroll tax similar to the social security tax.

Add to Medicare the $53 billion cost of the federal Medicaid system and the enormous amount of government involvement becomes obvious. *One-quarter of the rising cost of hospital and physician care goes for paperwork forced on health-care providers by government.*[15]

---

15. William P. Hoar, "Bandaged With Red Tape," *The New American*, May 17, 1993.

What government finances it will control. In fact, it would be dereliction of duty for the government to finance something and not control it. The problem is that government, spurred on by conspirators seeking total power, has invaded numerous fields where it never should have become involved.[16]

Americans are repeatedly being told that our nation should copy the Canadian government (socialized) medical system. But Canada's supposedly magnificent system is imploding, as have the fabled British system of socialized medicine and others before it. Canadian patients are already being forced to pay for services they thought were free, even while their taxes have skyrocketed.

As is the case with any product or service, making medical care available at no charge results in more seeking it, so that the system becomes glutted. In addition, many Canadian doctors are paid based on the number of patients they see — which translates to more than a few doctors actually giving less attention to some patients, or supplying services to others that aren't needed.

For a quick assessment of the worth of Canada's medical system, consider that Americans don't go to Canada for care and never did. But Canadians have come here in the past and still do. Early in 1993, it was reported that there are lengthy waiting lists in Canada for various types of surgery: 18 months for hip replacement; 12 months for cataract removal; and three to six months for elective coronary bypass. In Western Canada, a government-run medical bureau sent 200 patients to Seattle for treatment its overburdened staff could not supply.[17]

On March 23, 1993, the *Wall Street Journal* noted that Canadians can now purchase an insurance policy that will pay the cost of travel to the United States, plus food and lodging, for an ailing

---

16. In 1942, the Supreme Court handed down a ruling in a case involving the Agricultural Adjustment Act. It contained the following terse statement issued by Justice Robert H. Jackson: "It is hardly lack of due process for the government to regulate that which it subsidizes." *Wickard v. Filburn*, 311 U.S. 111.
17. Clyde H. Farnsworth, "Patients Footing the Bill Amid Canadian Cutbacks," *New York Times*, March 7, 1993.

person and a loved one if the treatment sought in Canada is not available in 45 days.[18] Still, the Clinton Administration is working hard to establish socialized medicine here in the United States.

In Sweden, a socialized medicine system that is also lionized by American socialists is proving costly and inefficient. The Swedish people, already taxed more than anyone else in the Western world, have seen spending for an array of social programs rise to 70 percent of their nation's economic output. Sweden is now piling up huge deficits, productivity is down, and unemployment is up dramatically. Swedes are reluctantly concluding that paternalistic government has destroyed their incentive to work. The dream promised by socialist planners has become a nightmare.[19]

The solution to health care concerns in America is to get the government out of the medical field, not more deeply into it. We already have the best medical system in the world — built by private enterprise and caring medical providers. That system has supplied better health care to more people than any other system on earth. As government continues to move in, it is certain that the quality and availability of the care will go down. Socialized medical programs in Canada, Britain, Sweden, and elsewhere confirm that the route to better health care is not with more government but with less.

Yet America isn't following the sensible course in the fields of medical care and a great many others. Evidence showing failure in foreign government-run medical care is readily available. But this information is rarely cited and acted upon. Instead, a socialist agenda covering all fields is being implemented, and Americans are being lured into the condition of economic control by government, part of the new world order.

Food Stamps

The entitlement drag on America also includes a $24 billion per year food stamp program. Begun in 1961 as a pilot program in

---

18. "Health Bubble," *Wall Street Journal* editorial, March 23, 1993.
19. Paul Klebnikov, "The Swedish Disease," *Forbes*, May 24, 1993.

John F. Kennedy's New Frontier, it was expanded in 1964 as part of Lyndon Johnson's Great Society.

When the program was in its infancy, only one out of every 439 Americans received food stamps. By 1970, one out of 50 were receiving this form of welfare. At first, recipients had to pay a fee for their stamps (a sliding scale based on income resulted in a cost of $72 for $178 worth of stamps). That practice was abandoned in 1978. Once payments were no longer required, the program grew explosively. By March 1993, 27.4 million individuals in this nation — more than one out of 10 — were receiving food stamps.[20]

As costly as the program is, terminating it overnight would be inhumane. But something has to be done, and federal officials are making no effort whatsoever to phase out the program. Instead, proposals are being made to ease the eligibility criteria so that more Americans can be brought into dependency. If a program is a failure but backed by a conspiratorial drive for power, it is likely to be increased instead of abolished.

Supporters of the food stamp program insist that it is absolutely necessary to help the needy. Are there really 27.4 million Americans who need the federal government to feed them? Are there no private charities to care for those truly in need? Or is the food stamp program another of many federal monstrosities designed to buy votes with taxpayers' money and tear America down — morally, economically, and spiritually — in order to pave the way for the new world order?

It Can Be Done!

Any insistence that nothing can be done about entitlements should be immediately challenged and disputed by informed Americans. If nothing can be done about these programs, America is doomed to consume itself and drown in a flood of federal

---

20. Fox Butterfield, "Record Number in U.S. Relying On Food Stamps," *New York Times*, October 31, 1991; Carole Sugarman, "27.4 Million Receiving Food Stamps," *Washington Post*, May 29, 1993.

programs.[21] Those who contend that entitlements are untouchable also maintain that restoring the free enterprise system and "turning the clock back" to limited government can't be done either. They are wrong.

Look what Germany and Japan did in the aftermath of World War II. From ashes, each built a thriving economy largely free of socialism.[22] Does America have to experience some sort of similar economic devastation before socialism's deadly consequences are recognized? Do we have to hit rock bottom before steps are taken to climb to newer heights? Do we have to commit national suicide — or have it committed for us by our leaders — forcing future inhabitants of this land to rebuild on the ashes of former greatness?

The "it can't be done" crowd ought to look at South Korea, Singapore, Taiwan, and Hong Kong for examples of what can be done when governments get out of the way and let the people produce. None of these modern examples of economic progress is perfect, but each is growing and prospering while America's economic vitality is shrinking and dying.

19th Century Britain Showed the Way

Nor are we required to rely only on modern instances of a nation successfully climbing out of the morass of too much government. In the January 6, 1992 issue of *Forbes* magazine, Peter Brimelow reviews Alvin Rabushka's book, *From Adam Smith to the Wealth of America*.[23] Brimelow notes that, according to Rabushka, the beginning of the 19th century saw the British gov-

---

21. Other entitlement programs not discussed in these pages include bank deposit insurance, unemployment compensation, supplemental security income, family support, and farm price supports. See George Hager, op. cit.
22. The sad element in any discussion about the miraculous recoveries in these two nations is that both are currently plunging headlong into socialism (committing economic suicide) today. But the fact that each did rebuild from devastation cannot be denied.
23. Peter Brimelow, "It Can Be Done," *Forbes*, January 6, 1992; Alvin Rabushka, *From Adam Smith to the Wealth of America* (New Brunswick, NJ: Transaction Books, 1985.)

ernment consuming 27 percent of the nation's gross national product. (This figure is even less than the percentage of GNP being spent by the U.S. government today.)

Rabushka reveals that Britain's private sector in the early 1800s was overwhelmed by massive regulations, price controls, crushing taxation, and huge costs for interest on government debt. By the end of the century, however, government spending had shrunk to 7.3 percent of GNP, the nation was enjoying unparalleled economic growth, and the standard of living had more than doubled.

The British didn't accomplish this turnaround with smoke and mirrors. They instituted a welfare reform system chock full of harsh disincentives to be on the dole. They scaled down the national debt and removed much of the burden of interest payments. When the government budget was balanced, they reduced taxes. But most of all, they repealed an enormous tangle of regulations (collectively known as "corn laws") that had been stifling the productivity of the people and their ability to market their products.

Let's repeat this success story in a very few words: The British made welfare less available and downright unappealing, sharply lowered the national debt, reduced taxation, and abolished the regulatory maze. The result: A sick England became the world's leader — until burgeoning free enterprise in America and growing socialism in England saw America rise to world leadership and England decline.

There's nothing mysterious about the formula; it calls for lowering taxation through less government. If it worked in England more than 100 years ago, it will work in America today.

A Chilling Opinion from Sweden

In today's Sweden, newly elected conservative leaders are working hard to pull their nation out of decades of socialism. Prime Minister Carl Bildt has cut taxes and reduced welfare, but he still faces huge problems associated with debt and entrenched socialist opposition. Nonetheless, Ian Wachmeister, the leader of Sweden's new free enterprise-promoting New Democracy Party, remains optimistic about his nation's future. He recognizes the difficulty of repealing deeply rooted socialism. But he also believes it will be easier for his nation to reverse course than it will be for America. He told *Forbes* magazine's Paul Klebnikov:

> Right now, I'd rather be in Sweden than in the U.S. because we have seen the problems and are moving away from the welfare state. On your side [of the Atlantic], you are moving right into it, and you risk destroying your country.[24]

Wachmeister is certainly correct about America "moving right into" the welfare state. And if this former industrialist and new political leader in Sweden can see what our leaders are doing to America, is it possible that our leaders can't see it themselves? Hardly.

The problem in America is not that our leaders are trying to eliminate debt, deficits, and government control. Many follow an agenda calling for the exact opposite. They are determined to use debt, deficits, and government control to destroy America's might and ease us into their new world order.

How do we extricate ourselves from too much government? Even if other nations can do it, or try to do it, can America reverse course and start climbing back toward freedom?

The answer is an absolute and emphatic yes — but only if America's best are willing to expend the effort. It will not be easy, and it must start with the realization that our nation's woes have been deliberately inflicted by internal enemies bent on building their new world order. But it can be done.

Our next chapter shows the way.

---

24. Klebnikov, *Forbes*, op. cit.

Frederic Bastiat's warnings in *The Law* apply just as much today as they did in 1850.

According to *The New American's* February 1992 Conservative Index, admitted socialist Bernard Sanders had a less socialistic voting record than 243 of his colleagues in the U.S. House of Representatives.

While leading Chile, Communist Salvador Allende brought the nation to economic collapse with socialism.

Augusto Pinochet rescued Chile from communist/socialist rule, established free enterprise, and stepped down in 1990.

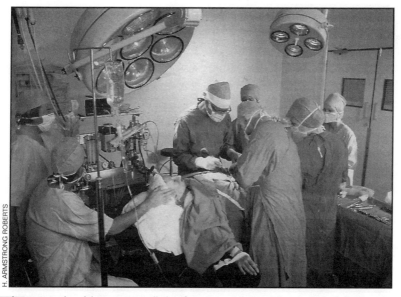

American health care is still the finest in the world in spite of the negative effects government has already caused it.

Begun as a pilot program in John F. Kennedy's New Frontier, more than one out of 10 Americans now receive food stamps.

Private charity would be able to do a much better job helping the truly needy if government were limited to its proper functions.

CHAPTER 13

TRIM: A Way Out of the Mess

Opportunity is missed by most people because it is dressed in overalls and looks like work.

— Thomas Edison

If the American people who pay the bills fully understood what their own government was doing to them, they wouldn't stand for it for ten seconds.

Fellow Americans, here's the condition of our beleaguered nation: monstrous debt, stifling bureaucracy, growing dependency, declining productivity, jobs flowing to other countries, corrupted currency, leaders steering our nation into world government, and a huge voting bloc delightedly using government power to live off the labors of others.

It doesn't take a genius to conclude that America is sick — and getting sicker. But we've already examined the patient and diagnosed her ailments. Now it's time to prescribe the medicine; it's time to start climbing out of the mess we're in; it's time to put America back on the course that made her what she became, and can become once again.

How have all these ailments developed? Simply stated, too much government. And how did too much government occur? A conspiracy and its legions of self-serving followers created, fostered, nurtured, and promoted it according to a plan.

If an enemy has a plan and is succeeding, there had better be another plan to stop him. And it need be neither complex nor devious. The essence of brilliance has always been simplicity. And where others have operated in conspiracy-created shadows, freedom loving opponents should operate in full view. Where there is darkness, freedom's champions must bring light. Where there are

213

lies and subterfuge, they must counter with truth and honor. Our nation has had enough of the tactics of plotters.

Happily, the plan to restore America is already written. It needs only an aroused and determined citizenry to put it to work. It is the same plan that unleashed our nation's greatness in the first place. It is the Constitution of the United States of America.

The Constitution Still Stands

Despite intense efforts on the part of a variety of destroyers to change it or scrap it entirely, the U.S. Constitution still stands. Sure it has been ignored. Yes, it has been circumvented. And you're correct if you've noticed that it has been contravened by the courts, tortured by the Congress, abused by educators, given lip-service by politicians, and discounted by the media.

But it's still there. And if a majority of America's voters demand that it be obeyed, its government-limiting strictures can be put to work to reshackle our runaway government and restore our nation's fading independence.

Americans must begin to realize the power they still possess in *their* Constitution. What's needed is a second War for Independence. Not against the abusive power of a king as in the epic battle more than 200 years ago, but a non-shooting war to get government off our backs and out of our pockets. Success in waging this modern-day War for Independence would mean the end of many forms of oppression rising from the would-be imperialists in our own nation's capital.

In Chapter 9, we emphasized that the federal government may not legally exercise any power or assume any authority not explicitly granted in the Constitution. And we noted that the founders spelled out that elementary principle in the Constitution itself with the Tenth Amendment.

With the Constitution to back them up, here's the message citizens can and must deliver to elected and appointed leaders: *If we (the people) did not specifically give you (the federal government) power in any area whatsoever, you do not have it. And if we over-*

looked specifically prohibiting some power you crave, you do not have it either.

The reality in present-day America is that government has broken away from its constitutional restraints and gone wild. Congress has passed a multiplicity of laws that have no constitutional basis. The executive branch's gigantic bureaucracy is bludgeoning the people with programs whose legitimacy can nowhere be found in the Constitution. And the Supreme Court has joined in the assault on freedom by putting its stamp of approval on much of this oppression, regularly adding more outrages that hadn't yet been created, and refusing to declare unconstitutional an array of attacks on liberty and property.

So where do we start? How do we get the American people to understand that *their* Constitution doesn't permit what's being done to them? How do we gain their attention long enough to show them that freedom is in jeopardy? How can we organize those who still yearn to be free? How do we corral the government of the United States before it becomes another of history's fearful masters?

The answer begins by focussing attention on the pocketbook. No other topic interests Americans more than "pocketbook" issues. It certainly was the key concern in the 1992 election, and it was successfully exploited by Bill Clinton with his focus on "the economy, stupid!" during his run for the presidency.

If the gigantic federal octopus squeezing the life out of this nation is to be restrained, addressing pocketbook issues and returning to the Constitution are essential.

Congress Is the Key

According to the Constitution, only Congress can make the laws; the President's job is to execute them faithfully. Congress is indeed the key. And, within the Congress, the House of Representatives enjoys more legislative power than does the Senate.

A careful reading of the Constitution will enable anyone to discover the little-known but extremely important stipulation appearing in Article I, Section 7 of the document:

All bills for raising revenues shall originate in the House of Representatives; but the Senate may propose or concur with amendments as on other bills.

That's pretty clear, and it still governs the conduct of the Congress. If a majority of the House of Representatives refuses to "originate" a bill to fund foreign aid, OSHA, EPA, the Department of Education, the Department of Energy, and a host of other extra-constitutional programs and agencies, there's nothing either the President or the Senate can do about it. Note that the Senate may propose amendments to a revenue bill originated by the House, but it can't very well propose an amendment to a bill the House never originated.

Without funding, these government programs and agencies will die. With no more taxpayers' money sustaining them, they will be out of business and no longer able to stifle our nation's producers. In short order, there will be far less taxation and control. And when there's no funding for all of this imperial power, government will cease being the distributor of wealth and the controller of the people.

Article I, Section 7 of the Constitution makes clear that the most threatening power of government, the power of the purse, was deliberately placed in the House of Representatives, the body closest to and most responsive to the people. Unlike the President who must go before the voters for reelection after four years in office, or members of the Senate whose term of office is six years, each member of the House must stand for reelection every second year.

If a representative fails to use his or her voting power to keep government within constitutional boundaries, or to roll back illegally acquired oppressive power, then the people have the opportunity — every 24 months — to choose someone else. Moreover, there are 435 House members compared to only 100 senators and one President. Political manipulators will always find it more difficult to influence the electorate in 435 congressional contests than they will in senate and presidential races.

The American system was created by farseeing individuals who carefully retained for themselves the ultimate authority of governing. They had no intention of allowing government to become dominant. All of history, as well as their own experience, showed them that government and governors must be legally restrained and carefully watched. They did not want any repeat of the royal-style government from which they separated. It is a stunning indictment of contemporary Americans to know that our nation's founders put their lives and fortunes on the line to combat far less tyranny from King George's governors than is currently flowing from Washington, DC.[1]

TRIM Has the Answer

If today's Americans will use the weapons at their disposal, they can put government on a diet. One specific power available stems from citizen awareness, and the way to unleash it is through an already existing program called TRIM, Tax Reform IMmediately. TRIM can gain and keep the attention of citizens who, in turn, can gain and keep the attention of the local U.S. representative.

TRIM distributes the voting record of every U.S. representative on pocketbook issues. Published for all 435 representatives on three separate occasions each year, each of TRIM's four-page Bulletins contains general information about government's spending excesses and also a report on exactly how the local representative voted on as many as eight separate measures.

All TRIM Bulletins describe the votes being reported, note the cost of the measure to each household, and indicate whether the local representative cast his vote for "Lower Taxes and Less Government" or for "High Taxes and Big Government." (See samples of TRIM Bulletins pictured on the following pages.)

TRIM is a nonprofit, nonpartisan, educational movement organized and directed by the John Birch Society. It never advocates

---

1. For just one indication of how much less government oppression existed in colonial America, King George's government imposed no income tax.

TRIM Bulletins are published three times per year

the reelection or defeat of any elected official. It simply provides a service to the voters, informing them about the way their representative voted in Congress.

Over the years, TRIM has been wrongfully blamed by numerous ex-representatives for their defeat at the polls. The truth is that their voting records caused their defeats; all TRIM did was place those records before the public.

In 1978, four unhappy representatives decided to challenge TRIM after large numbers of voters learned of their big spending habits via TRIM Bulletin distribution.[2] They prevailed on the Federal Election Commission (FEC) to investigate the activities of local TRIM committees to determine if TRIM had violated any federal election laws.

The FEC eventually claimed that TRIM had "expressly advo-

---

2. The four were Les AuCoin (D-OR), Helen Meyner (D-NJ), Jerome Ambro (D-NY) and Leon Panetta (D-CA).

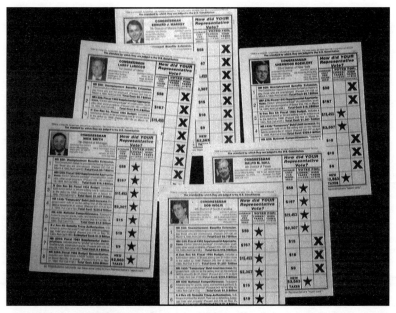

Back page of TRIM Bulletin is tailored to local representative

cated the defeat of a clearly identified Federal candidate," was conducting "political" activity, and must therefore submit to FEC monitoring.[3]

Claiming freedom of speech and insisting that it was not involved in endorsing, financing, or advocating the election or defeat of any candidate (the definition of political activity), TRIM refused to submit to the FEC's demands and was subsequently hauled into federal court by the agency. The case became a celebrated test of First Amendment guarantees. In February 1980, a nine-judge federal panel in New York City dismissed FEC's contentions, ruling that TRIM's activities cannot be covered by federal law because its widely distributed Bulletins "did not advocate the election or defeat of any candidate."[4]

---

3. Peter Kihss, "U.S. Says L.I. Group Broke Election Law," *New York Times*, February 19, 1978.
4. *Federal Election Commission v. Central Long Island TRIM etc.*, 616 F.2d 45 (1980).

In his written opinion buttressing the decision, Chief Judge Irving Kaufman termed the FEC's action against TRIM "somewhat perverse."[5] He added that he found it "disturbing, because citizens of this nation should not be required to account to this court for engaging in debate of political issues."

The TRIM Plan

Most voters have little knowledge about the performance of their representative in Congress. Over and over again, TRIM Committee members have found that fellow citizens appreciate receiving a TRIM Bulletin and are eager to digest the information it provides. Once in possession of their representative's actual record, voters become armed with the information they need to help House members stand by the Constitution. Citizens who examine a number of TRIM Bulletins are better able to judge whether they ought to contact their representative. And any representative can then heed the urging of his constituents or ignore them and run the risk of rejection on a future election day.

Until recently, TRIM's activities were limited by the number and energy of local committees that alone were supplied with camera-ready materials enabling them to print the Bulletins. In 1991, TRIM headquarters began printing individualized Bulletins for all 435 representatives and made them available to anyone. As a result, TRIM's citizen education efforts have reached a far larger portion of the population.

TRIM's leaders envision a surge of activity and interest that will attract the close attention of all who serve in Congress. There will likely be attacks directed at its efforts — which TRIM leaders believe will only heighten their program's effectiveness. But they are convinced that big spending representatives whose constituents are regularly being handed TRIM Bulletins will begin to have second thoughts about how they vote in Congress.

As rising taxes, mushrooming controls over the private sector,

---

5. E.J. Dionne, Jr., "Court Upholds Campaign Funds," *New York Times*, February 8, 1980.

horrendous debt, mounting costs for interest, and the heavy hand of bureaucracy continue to ravage America, more concerned citizens will seek out TRIM. Americans in great numbers will begin to realize that virtually any government program can be stopped if a simple majority in the U.S. House of Representatives — 218 is all that's needed — will stop it.

Newly awakened citizens will also begin to realize that they must become better informed about a whole range of issues, including all phases of the planned new world order, especially who is promoting it and why. For many, TRIM will stimulate a desire to gain answers to questions about government and current events they heretofore couldn't even begin to ask. TRIM has the potential of developing a much-needed new cadre of well-informed opponents of the conspiracy gripping our nation.

TRIM leaders have always maintained that members of Congress are generally not well-schooled about the Constitution. Most, they say, have only demonstrated their ability to get elected. According to TRIM, many elected officials actually rely on voter unawareness and apathy. Their main concern is saying and doing whatever it takes to stay in office.

While there is indeed a conspiracy working to destroy freedom and establish a "new world order," few elected officials are unwaveringly tied to it. Most who hold office are politicians who bend with the wind and operate almost entirely to satisfy their own self-interests. If it becomes politically advantageous for them to stand firmly for the Constitution, that's precisely what they'll do. It's up to the people, therefore, to force their hand. In the final analysis, the American people will get the kind of government they work for and deserve.

When TRIM grows and reaches many more millions of citizens, voters will often determine that there isn't a need for a replacement; some big spenders will become ardent penny-pinchers once they realize that this is exactly how they must perform in order to hold on to the job they love.

TRIM's efforts will reinforce the importance of the Constitution. Once aware of the people's determined intention to hold them to their oath of office, representatives will begin to realize that government is taxing the people into the poorhouse; that unconstitutional regulatory agencies are destroying America's productive might; that the Marxist Federal Reserve is destroying our currency; and that leaders in government have been chipping away at the freedom they have verbally championed and are supposed to protect.

When a rising number of voters "back home" let it be known that they want less government, no-nonsense national sovereignty, and removal of bureaucratic tyranny, many politicians will adopt and even champion a completely new agenda.

TRIM can indeed lead to a restoration of limited government. Properly and widely employed, it can reverse America's downward trend and start the climb back up to the economic health she once enjoyed. But TRIM has to be put to work by many determined citizens. The opportunity to restore America is waiting for willing hands to seize it. It should not be missed "because it is dressed in overalls and looks like work."[6]

Endorsements

As we have noted, TRIM's activities have prompted some members of the House of Representatives to complain bitterly about the wide distribution of their own voting record. TRIM maintains that these politicians should be proud of their stands, but they obviously aren't. Many big spenders would prefer continuing to masquerade before constituents as frugal guardians of the public purse. Their complaints to TRIM's growing army of constitutionalists amount to clumsy endorsements of TRIM's effectiveness.

But TRIM also receives plaudits from House members who are trying hard to make government fiscally responsible and constitutionally correct. These endorsements, too, supply grand testimony to TRIM's enormous potential. Consider:

• In 1977, Congressman James Collins of Texas wrote to a con-

---

6. TRIM can be contacted via P.O. Box 8040, Appleton, WI 54913. A supply of TRIM Bulletins for any member of the U.S. House of Representatives may be purchased for a modest charge by calling 1-800-SPL-TRIM.

stituent: "Those who are active on the TRIM Committee have performed a great community service. It is very good to keep all the community residents informed on how we have voted here in Congress.... You are leading the way in sharing the story of sound common sense economics."

• In May 1979, Congressman Larry McDonald of Georgia, a member of the John Birch Society, commented about TRIM's effectiveness in a speech he delivered in Midland, Texas. He stated:

> Barry Goldwater, Jr., a sort of semi-conservative from California, called the leader of the TRIM Committee in his district and said, "You TRIM people are the talk of Capitol Hill."
>
> A representative from South Carolina who was getting away with murder suddenly started voting conservative.... Some of his colleagues began asking him, "Why in the world are you voting that way?" He responded, "I have to! I've got a TRIM Committee back in my district that's eating me alive!"
>
> Congressman Bill Goodling of Pennsylvania, another fairly good man, told the TRIM chairman back in his district that the TRIM program can be the making or breaking of any member of Congress.

• In 1982, Congressman Ken Kramer of Colorado wrote to a constituent: "All of my votes which you have listed in the bulletin are indeed correctly recorded. I was certainly pleased to receive such a score. You and the other members of the TRIM Committee may be assured that I will continue to work for less government spending, reduced taxes and less federal interference in the lives of American citizens."

• In 1990, California Congressman Wally Herger stated in a letter to a voter: "Thank you for letting me know of your opposition to runaway federal spending. As you know from Tax Reform IMmediately's (TRIM) recent bulletin, we are in complete agreement on the issue."

• In 1991, a voter sent her own congressman's TRIM Bulletin indicating his big spending proclivities to neighboring Congressman Mel Hancock of Missouri. Mr. Hancock replied: "Thank you for sending to my attention a copy of the TRIM Bulletin containing your Congressman's voting index. I hope he does better in the 1992 session. Yours for *better* — but *less — government*."

• In 1993, Congressman Jack Kingston of Georgia wrote to a constituent: "Thank you very much for sending the TRIM Bulletin Report Card.... I will continue to vote against wasteful government spending. Thank you again for the kind words and I hope that you will continue to stay in touch."

Our Responsibility to the Future

Too many Americans have taken freedom for granted. As a result of the courageous efforts of the principled individuals who peopled this land and formed this nation, the average U.S. citizen enjoys more freedom than any other person in all history.

It is also true that we who live in these United States didn't earn our good fortune. Simply by being born here, or choosing to live here, we have inherited what others won for us long ago. What shall we pass on to those who come next? Will our labors insure that they, too, will be free? Or will we, in the midst of plenty, forget that freedom isn't free and allow internal enemies to destroy it? Will the next generation thank us for being vigilant? Or will it condemn us for laziness and monstrous folly?

America is dying — but she isn't dead. Her ailments can be cured if her people will recognize and treat them. The prescription for national good health is a solid dose of time, effort, and courage from her sons and daughters.

How about it Americans? Will you seize the opportunity to restore America's greatness? It won't always be available. A time could come — and soon — when the forces of the new world order will have blocked all opportunities to return to limited government. We can all hope that such a situation will never occur in America. But we all know that most if not all of our hopes are realized because of hard work, the kind that too few Americans are exerting at present.

Will we turn over to our sons and daughters the America we inherited? The decision is yours.

Leon Panetta, who tried to block TRIM activity as a congressman, now serves as the Clinton Administration's budget director.

In 1977, Texas Congressman James Collins praised TRIM activists for performing "a great community service."

Former Congressman Larry McDonald authored a superb book about the Constitution and strongly promoted the TRIM program.

Congressman Bill Goodling felt that the TRIM program could make or break any member of Congress.

While serving in the House in 1982, Ken Kramer, now a senator, acknowledged TRIM's good work.

Congressman Jack Kingston thanked a constituent for sending him a copy of the TRIM bulletin showing his voting record.

Congressman Wally Herger expressed his "complete agreement" with TRIM's opposition to "runaway federal spending."

CHAPTER 14

Much More Than Tinkering Needed

For as in the days before the flood, they were eating and drinking, marrying and giving in marriage, even till that day when Noah entered into the ark, and they knew not till the flood came and took them all away....

— Matthew 24: 38-39

Tens of millions of Americans are concerned about our nation's rush to fiscal suicide. But most do nothing about their concerns. They lack an energizing realization of the peril they face. They have avoided or never been introduced to the hard reality: Debt, deficits, monetary control, socialism, and looming world government are the products of a conspiratorial drive for power.

Without an awareness that our nation is being deliberately destroyed, the ordinary citizen offers little or no response to appeals for action. From coast to coast, decent and honorable individuals, all of whom are slowly and steadily being victimized, continue to go about their daily business, "eating and drinking" as did everyone but Noah and his family in the days leading up to the flood recounted in Genesis. Many comfort themselves with the belief that their concerns have also been detected by our nation's leaders who will, therefore, take proper steps to correct problems. Others have actually given up, believing that nothing they do will make any difference.

Yet the condition of our nation continues to deteriorate, not because our leaders are doing all they can to make things better, but because the hidden agenda followed by many actually calls for making things worse.

Since most Americans remain unaware of this duplicity at the top, it is not surprising that confusion reigns. Compounding the confusion, a host of single-issue partisans readily offer quick-fix solutions often amounting to mere tinkering with government but sometimes calling for fundamental change. Such misdirected remedies, however, cannot correct deep-seated, suicidal policies. Like those who failed to react to storm clouds in the biblical account of Noah's experiences, Americans today are vulnerable to being swept away — this time in a flood of debt and government control.

Warnings Galore

Several years into President Franklin Delano Roosevelt's revolutionary turn to the left, former New York governor Alfred E. Smith, the Democratic Party's nominee for President in 1928, stated in 1936, "foreign isms have invaded our way of life." The chief of those "isms" was and still is conspiracy-fostered socialism. America's limited government is being superseded by socialism's economic control: taxation, regulation, bureaucracy and Big Brother government.

Al Smith wasn't the only well-known American to recognize that government control of the economy had taken firm root in the land of the free and the home of the brave. Socialist Party leader Norman Thomas had offered himself as a candidate in six presidential elections (1928-1948). His best showing in any of those contests saw him capture a mere 190,000 votes.

Thomas eventually concluded that the American people would always reject socialism whenever it was honestly labelled. But he also learned that calling it something else would lure many to vote for it.

In his 1953 pamphlet entitled *Democratic Socialism*, Thomas stated: "... here in America more measures once praised or denounced as socialist have been adopted than once I should have thought possible, short of a socialist victory at the polls."[1]

Later, the *Congressional Record* for April 17, 1958 recorded his

---

1. Cited by W. Cleon Skousen, *The Naked Capitalist* (Salt Lake City, UT: Published by Mr. Skousen, 1970), p. 130.

increasing joy: "The United States is making greater strides toward socialism under Eisenhower than even under Roosevelt, particularly in the fields of federal spending and welfare legislation."[2] Sad to say, these were not unfounded boasts.

Others who opposed socialism warned of its destructive consequences. Congressman Samuel Pettengill lamented government's obvious turn to the left in his book entitled *Smokescreen*.[3] Journalist John T. Flynn's magnificent *The Road Ahead* deplored socialism's progress.[4] Another famous writer of his day, Garet Garrett, told of socialism's growing dominance in his classic series of essays entitled *The People's Pottage*.[5] And Notre Dame University Law School Dean Clarence Manion issued another warning with his *Let's Face It!*.[6]

These and other volumes capably analyzed what was happening. But America continued on her slide into totalitarian socialism. Obviously, there was a need for more than the warnings contained in these books. Awareness that the treachery had been planned was also required. And there was a further need for some vehicle to organize the American people into action to expose the conspirators and their plans.

So Let's Do Something

In December 1958, at the founding meeting of the John Birch Society, Robert Welch carefully presented evidence leading to the conclusion that our nation was indeed falling victim to a powerfully entrenched conspiracy. He claimed that its final goal included totalitarian socialism and world government. Along the way, he took the opportunity to look ahead and offer predictions about what was in store for our nation — if the American people

---

2. Ibid.
3. Samuel Pettengill, *Smokescreen* (Kingsport, TN: Southern Publishers, Inc., 1940).
4. John T. Flynn, *The Road Ahead* (New York, NY: Devin-Adair Company, 1949, 1961).
5. Garet Garrett, *The People's Pottage* (Caldwell, ID: Caxton Printers, Inc., 1953).
6. Clarence Manion, *Let's Face It!* (South Bend, IN: The Manion Forum, 1956).

weren't awakened and motivated to put a stop to the plans of a diabolically driven few.

Many have been alerted through the efforts of the group he founded. And a considerable number were motivated to join with him in the organized effort to expose the monster plot and restore sound government. While the movement he launched has not yet succeeded, competent observers of the American scene both here and abroad have expressed their conviction that the John Birch Society has slowed the conspirators down, forced them to alter some of their tactics, and bought time for effective resistance to build.

Any freedom-loving American surveying the current condition of our nation today would easily concur with the major predictions Robert Welch gave in 1958. But he issued them 35 years ago! As you will see, he was worth listening to — then and now. Of his ten forecasts for the future, seven dealt with the economic treachery destroying our nation. They were:

1. Greatly expanded government spending, for missiles, for so-called defense generally, for foreign aid, for every conceivable means of getting rid of ever larger sums of American money — as wastefully as possible.

2. Higher and then much higher taxes.

3. An increasingly unbalanced budget, despite the higher taxes....

4. Wild inflation of our currency, leading rapidly towards its ultimate repudiation.

5. Government control of prices, wages and materials, supposedly to fight inflation.

6. Greatly increased socialistic controls over every operation of our economy and every activity of our daily lives. This is to be accompanied, naturally and automatically, by a correspondingly huge increase in the size of our bureaucracy, and in both the cost and reach of our domestic government.

7. Far more centralization of power in Washington, and the practical elimination of our state lines....[7]

---

7. Robert Welch, *The Blue Book of The John Birch Society* (Appleton, WI: Western Islands, 1992, 24th Printing), p. 23.

Robert Welch has been called virtually every nasty adjective imaginable by political adversaries and the Establishment media. But after listing these predictions in his August 26, 1971 column, journalist and editor Mike Culbert commented: "Call him all those things — but also call him 'correct.'"[8]

With the single exception of wage and price controls — imposed by the Nixon Administration in 1971 and later removed — everything Robert Welch predicted in 1958 is reality today. Were he still alive, he would now be telling Americans that the Clinton agenda seeks to finalize the far-advanced transformation of government from servant to master.

But he would also insist that stopping the socialist, world government juggernaut won't be accomplished by anyone who refuses to recognize its conspiratorial origins. He would further maintain, of course, that realistically combatting debt, deficits, and bureaucratic control can't be done with mere legislative tinkering.

Ignoring the Constitution

Totalitarian socialism could never be built in America without circumventing the U.S. Constitution. Why? Because the Constitution contains no authorization for the federal government to impose government's controls over the American people. It's as simple as that.

If the Constitution were respected and obeyed, there wouldn't be any socialism-promoting Federal Reserve, and no debt-accumulating foreign aid, agriculture subsidies, government health insurance, food stamps, etc. If the Constitution were adhered to faithfully, there would be no wild spending binges, fiat money, crushing taxation, or gigantic bureaucracy. Nor would there be any astronomical national debt necessitating astronomical interest payments.

The cure for America's descent into the new world order is right before the American people: the Constitution. Our leaders must

---

8. Mike Culbert, "Whatever Else, Call Him 'Correct,'" *Berkeley (CA) Daily Gazette*, August 26, 1971.

be forced to submit to the limitations placed on them by this "supreme law of the land." The President and all members of Congress swear an oath to abide by the Constitution. Each must be made to honor that solemn pledge.

There really isn't any other way. Insurrection isn't the answer. Wishful thinking will get us nowhere. Accepting what has been done and demanding no further increases in government power is absurd. And while prayer is always a good idea, those who pray ought to be asking for courage and strength to do what they are able to do before ever asking God to intervene. "God helps those who help themselves," still applies.

Restoring the Constitution can be accomplished with a three-pronged strategy: Supply needed information to the American people through a broad-based educational crusade; organize the resistance generated by the information; and expose the conspiracy. Once this plan is carried out, an increasing number of our nation's leaders will adhere to their oath of office, put a stop to the rush into totalitarian socialism, and begin to undo the damage already done to America.

Education is the key. Awareness of conspiracy will both motivate the people and provide needed perspective enabling them to see through and reject false solutions, soothing rhetoric, and contrived tangents. And organization is essential in the face of a highly organized enemy. When the effects of this activity permeate the cities and towns of America, either the elected officials will respond or the people will find replacements. The battle must be fought first in the cities and towns of America. Then, it can be successfully waged in the halls of government.

Gimmicks, Quick Fixes, Blind Alleys, and Busywork

For some, creating sufficient understanding so that voters will demand that government officials adhere to the Constitution isn't a quick enough answer to debt, deficits, controls, and destruction. But no quick and easy way to cure such ills exists.

In and around the nation's capital, groups promising overnight solutions, individuals touting various gimmicks, and an array of single issue fund-raising or candidacy-promoting schemes continue to proliferate. Most add up to blind alleys easily distinguished by their calls for meaningless busywork and constant requests for money.

There are even clever schemes designed to lead angry and frustrated citizens into working against their own purposes. The most prominent of these call for amendments to the Constitution — even for exposing it to fundamental change during a constitutional convention.

Amend the Constitution? Why? There's nothing wrong with the Constitution (except for the need to remove a few amendments already attached to it). The problem facing Americans is the refusal of elected officials to honor it and abide by its limitations. The Congress, the President, and the Supreme Court should be amended, not the Constitution.

The Concord Coalition

For a good example of a well-publicized non-solution to the problems brought on by debt and deficits, consider an organization known as the Concord Coalition. Begun in September 1992, its three leaders are former Massachusetts Democratic senator Paul Tsongas, former New Hampshire Republican senator Warren Rudman, and New York investment banker Peter G. Peterson.

Newspaper accounts publicizing the launching of this group reported its claim that it would work to save America by reducing the debt and rebuilding the economy.[9] But there was no mention of Peter G. Peterson's chairmanship of the world-government-promoting Council on Foreign Relations. Nor was Warren Rudman's membership in the CFR noted.[10] Also missing was any mention of the debt-creating voting records of these two former senators.

Paul Tsongas stepped down from the Senate in 1984 for health

---

9. Associated Press account, "Tsongas, Rudman Form Coalition," *Manchester (NH) Union Leader*, September 15, 1992.
10. See *CFR Annual Report 1992*, New York, NY: Council on Foreign Relations.

reasons. Before he left office, he voted for increases in the debt ceiling in 1981, 1982, and 1983. Had he and his colleagues refused to raise this limit, the debt spiral would have ceased because Congress would have been forced either to cut back and abolish some programs, or close the government down. Tsongas voted against an amendment calling for a cut of $285 billion from federal spending totals. He voted consistently for foreign aid, tax increases, and federal funding of virtually every socialist program imaginable. [11] Now he presents himself as a crusader for debt relief.

Warren Rudman declined to run for reelection to the Senate in 1992. In 1991, he voted for a $24 billion foreign aid bailout package for Russia, a separate $14.1 billion foreign aid measure, and an appropriation of $87.8 billion for unconstitutional agencies such as the Department of Housing and Urban Development and the Environmental Protection Agency. [12] What kind of leadership in the fight against deficit spending and big government can he be expected to provide?

While in office, both of these former senators regularly avoided making any reference to the Constitution as the test of legitimacy for government spending programs. But they now loudly complain about the flood of government red ink they helped to create.

Their Concord Coalition partner, Peter G. Peterson, has never spoken out against the stream of recommendations for world government and socialism regularly flowing out of the CFR he chairs. In October 1987, *The Atlantic Monthly* featured his personal urging for a gasoline tax of 25 cents per gallon and a broad-based value added tax (VAT) on manufactured products. [13] Is this the

---

11. Beginning in 1971, *The Review Of The News* magazine published the voting records of all House and Senate members on scores of issues each year. The listings are called "The Conservative Index." In 1985, *The Review Of The News* was superseded by *The New American* which has continued to publish "The Conservative Index." The votes recorded by Tsongas are gleaned from these reports which are compiled from the *Congressional Record*.
12. Recorded votes for Rudman gleaned from the same source as those of Tsongas. See immediately preceding footnote.
13. Peter G. Peterson, "The Morning After," *The Atlantic Monthly*, October 1987.

way Americans want to fight deficits?

On December 1, 1992, the *New York Times* published Peterson's column calling for a "consumption tax" on gasoline, a "progressive value-added tax," and a "consumed income tax."[14] He obviously wants to balance the budget by raising taxes. He never seems to have heard of cutting or eliminating programs and reducing the power of government.

During 1977-1980, this supposed crusader against America's fiscal profligacy was one of only two U.S. citizens to participate in the Socialist International's 18-member Brandt Commission, named in honor of the group's leader, lifelong socialist Willy Brandt of Germany. (The other U.S. participant with Peterson was Katharine Graham, chairman of the *Washington Post* and *Newsweek*.)[15]

Organized in 1864, the Socialist International originally claimed Karl Marx as its honorary secretary. Its goal throughout several reorganizations has always been one-world socialism.[16] The recommendations of its Brandt Commission, presented in 1980 with appropriate fanfare at UN headquarters in New York City, called for: the transfer of resources to developing nations; supranational authority to regulate the world's industry; international supervision of the world's oil production and consumption; an international currency; and a "new international economic order."[17] Anyone whose name appears on such recommendations is an obvious enemy of economic freedom and hardly a legitimate spokesman for Americans who want to rein in their government.

Yet, Peterson, Tsongas, and Rudman now pose as saviors of the American people from the ravages of Big Government. While announcing the formation of the Concord Coalition, they told the

---

14. Peter G. Peterson, "Hard Truths for Better Days," *New York Times*, December 1, 1992.
15. John Nielsen, "Brandt Unveils His Plan," *Newsweek*, February 18, 1980, p. 63.
16. Rose L. Martin, *Fabian Freeway*, op. cit.
17. *Newsweek*, op. cit.

press in a joint statement, "We are here because we believe the time has come for citizens of this country to have another voice."[18]

In a lengthy article in the February 7, 1993 *Washington Post*, these Concord Coalition officials spelled out their desire to "broaden the tax base by a strict cap on the home mortgage deduction and the exclusion for employer-paid health care," and to "institute a general-purpose consumption levy, either by setting up a broad-based energy tax or value-added tax." They are far more interested in raising taxes than in cutting programs. The only worthwhile portion of their article was its title, "False Choices." Posing as leaders of America's resistance to deficits and big government, they are indeed false choices.[19]

The most infuriating aspect of this performance is that, while they served in the Senate, Tsongas and Rudman were never crusaders for what they now claim is essential. Even though no longer in office, each still possesses the kind of notoriety and ability that could help in a truly determined campaign to cut the deficits, hold back tax increases, and rescue America from its suicidal path. But expecting them to do so is a bit like expecting shrimps to whistle. The very fact that they teamed up with CFR Chairman and Brandt Commission member Peter G. Peterson indicates that this Concord Coalition is far from the answer America needs.

Empower America

On January 12, 1993, Vin Weber, Jack Kemp, William Bennett, and Jeane Kirkpatrick announced the formation of Empower America, their version of America's response to deficits. This organization is a thinly disguised launching pad for the presidential aspirations of Kemp and Bennett, even while each uses the notoriety it provides to undermine the other long before virtually anyone else is even thinking about the 1996 race.

Empower America claims that it "defines the Reagan coalition

---

18. *Manchester (NH) Union Leader*, op. cit.
19. Warren P. Rudman, Paul E. Tsongas, Peter G. Peterson and John P. White, "False Choices," *Washington Post*, February 7, 1993.

projected into the 1990s."[20] The leaders of this group want to be known as Reagan conservatives. They would have the nation forget that Ronald Reagan presided over an explosive growth of the national debt — from less than $1 trillion when he took office in 1981 to approximately $3 trillion after his eight years at the nation's helm. They also don't want to remind anyone that Reagan never intended to cut taxes and spending, only to reduce "the rate of increase in taxing and spending."[21]

As a congressman from Minnesota, Weber compiled an undistinguished middle-of-the-road record. In his last term, he voted for $178 million for the pornography- and blasphemy-promoting National Endowment for the Arts, $52.6 billion for domestic food programs (including food stamps), $23.8 billion for the Department of Housing and Urban Development, and $800 million for a National Police Corps.[22] Never a crusading enemy of the federal government's big spending steamroller, he managed in many cases to be an ally. As a leader of a supposed anti-spending group, he will pose little real threat to the nation's debt and deficit promoters.

Jack Kemp spent 18 years as a congressman from New York and then served as the Bush Administration's Secretary of Housing and Urban Development. During his last two terms in Congress, he supported legislation calling for $10.5 billion for educational grants, $169.2 billion for agriculture price supports and food stamps, $5 billion for the Commodity Credit Corporation that sends taxpayers' money to foreign nations, $15 billion for federal housing programs, $45.2 billion for more agriculture programs, and $14.36 billion for bilateral foreign aid.[23] These are

---

20. Thomas B. Edsall, "Conservative Republicans Join to Redefine Party," *Washington Post*, January 13, 1993.
21. On February 18, 1981, in one of his first speeches as President, Mr. Reagan said: "It is important to note that we are reducing the rate of increase in taxing and spending. We are not attempting to cut either spending or taxing to a level below that which we presently have." Speech text published, February 19, 1981, *New York Times*.
22. See footnote 11.
23. Ibid.

the types of programs that have caused our nation's bloated deficits.

Immediately after accepting George Bush's invitation to head HUD, Kemp told the U.S. Conference of Mayors that he wanted henceforth to be known as "a big-L liberal" on race and policy issues. Asking to be described as a "bleeding heart conservative," and "progressive conservative," he said: "I'm going to throw the labels out. We're going to throw out ideology."[24] Expecting this man to lead America out of a suicidal plunge into debt and deficits is like expecting the sun to rise in the west and set in the east.

William J. Bennett never served in Congress but has served in various federal posts, the first of which found him director of a National Humanities Center in North Carolina. In 1981, Bennett became the director of the National Endowment for the Humanities. Under his leadership, NEH provided grants to the University of Southern California for college teachers to study Karl Marx; to Dickinson College for secondary school teachers to study Marx; to the University of Maryland to commemorate Marx; and to the University of Illinois and Louisiana State University to reinterpret and publish Marx's works.[25]

In March 1982, the *Raleigh (NC) Spectator* quoted Bennett as follows: "I was once identified as a liberal Democrat. I must be honest and tell you I don't think my position has changed that much." In 1984, the Bennett-led NEH joined with the Democratic Socialists of America and *Socialist Review* as co-sponsors of a conference in Berkeley, California to study socialism.[26] Early in 1985, Bennett accepted appointment as the Secretary of Education, a post no believer in the Constitution would ever take unless he intended to abolish both the department and the post. He is another whose actions and past beliefs have contributed to the problems

---

24. Associated Press, "Kemp Promises to Throw Out Ideology," *Houston (TX) Chronicle*, January 19, 1989.
25. National Endowment for the Humanities "Grant Information" releases, August 1983, copies in author's files.
26. *Organization Trends*, Capital Research Center, Washington, DC, January 1985.

sensible Americans are realistically trying to solve.

Jeane J. Kirkpatrick once described herself as a Hubert Humphrey Democrat. She came to national attention as U.S. Ambassador to the United Nations. Critical only of the way the organization was performing, she remains an advocate of UN-style globalism. As a member of the board of directors of the CFR, her pro-UN stance is hardly surprising. What continues to amaze, however, is the characterization of this promoter of the new world order as a conservative.

Empower America is not the answer to America's debt and deficit problems.

Balanced Budget Amendment

The first thing that has to be stated about any proposal to amend the U.S. Constitution in the interests of a balanced budget is that it's aimed at the wrong target. The Constitution isn't deficient and in need of amendments; the members of the legislative and executive branches are at fault.

Next, consider that every proposal for a balanced budget amendment contains a loophole allowing Congress to add to the deficit if 60 percent of both Houses approve. Then, consider that the present attitude of many in Congress ensures that they would, if forced, balance the budget by raising taxes rather than cutting programs. The nation does not need more taxes; it needs less government.

But the real key to understanding the phoniness of the drive for adding a balanced budget amendment to the Constitution comes with a realization that an amendment to the Constitution initiated by Congress must be approved by two-thirds of both Houses of Congress before being sent to the states for ratification. This means that 67 senators and 290 representatives would have to approve a formal measure.

In 1989, the U.S. Senate voted 66 to 34 for a balanced budget amendment, one vote short of the two-thirds needed but well over a majority. In the House, 238 members (again, less than two-thirds but more than a majority) had already co-sponsored a balanced budget measure.[27] So the drive for a congressionally-initiated amendment failed. But, if our lawmakers really meant to balance the budget, only 51 of those senators and 218 of those representatives could have balanced the budget with their votes — with no amendment required!

The same revealing deceit occurred in July 1992 when 280 representatives voted for a balanced budget amendment (10 fewer than needed for passage in the House).[28] But, at the very same time, the House couldn't muster 218 votes needed to balance the budget through the ordinary legislative process.

Representatives and senators repeatedly engage in this type of slight-of-hand. They vote for a constitutional amendment, yet they refuse to take the easier — and always available — route of simply voting against any measure that will produce an unbalanced budget. They play this game in order to be able to assure many voters that they are doing everything in their power to balance the budget. They most certainly are not.

But the worst feature of the drive to require a balanced budget is its use to stimulate state calls for a constitutional convention. Many of the best state legislators, motivated by a sincere desire to rein in the federal government, have been persuaded that a con-con is their only recourse. They are told that such a convention could be limited to a single issue such as balancing the budget. But a constitutional convention cannot be limited; once convened, it would open the way for a complete rewriting of the Constitution.

New world order promoters would dearly love to use a con-con to rewrite the entire Constitution. If it could be compromised or destroyed, speeding the nation into world government would become a great deal easier for them.

---

27. Letter from Utah Senator Orrin Hatch, cited in *Birch Log* column "O.K. Congress, Balance It!" by this author (Appleton, WI: The John Birch Society Features, January 18, 1990).
28. H.J. Res. 290, Balanced-Budget Constitutional Amendment, defeated 280-153, *Congressional Record*, June 11, 1992, pp. H4670-71.

Line Item Veto

Too often, Congress presents the President with a piece of legislation containing hundreds or even thousands of pages. The President is supposed to pore over all of those pages before exercising his privilege either to sign or veto it. In addition to the sheer size of these measures, recent Presidents have complained that they are restricted by the prevailing procedure which forces them to accept or reject the entire bill. Hence the call for presidential line item veto power that will enable the chief executive to strike out portions of the bill but not the entire measure.

Proponents point to the use of line item veto power by the governors of 42 states. If governors have this power, they maintain, surely the President should have it as well. But their assumption that state budgets are reduced through the use of this procedure is not borne out by the facts. Professors Burton A. Abrams of the University of Delaware and William R. Dougan of Dartmouth College have shown that the spending records of governors who have line item veto authority are indistinguishable from those who do not. Line item veto power does not lead to less spending, these professors claim, only to spending on different programs. [29]

In effect, the line item veto gives the chief executive (either the president or a governor) much greater power to determine how funds are spent. This added clout comes at the expense of the legislature. Is this what Americans want?

The CFR-laden Committee on the Constitutional System (CCS), formed to "reform" the American system, published a number of proposals to make government more efficient, mainly calling for the enhancement of the President's power at the expense of the legislative branch. James Sundquist, a CCS board member, stated his enthusiasm for line item veto power as a way to weaken the separation of powers that inhibits the executive branch. In his view, a line item veto would help to concentrate power in the office of President, something our founding fathers

---

29. Burton A. Abrams and William R. Dougan, "The Effect of Constitutional Restraints on Governmental Spending," *Public Choice*, Issue #2, 1986.

carefully guarded against.[30]

A President wielding a line item veto would be able to use it to exert pressure on a congressman or senator who wants passage of some pork barrel measure favoring his district. For refusal to veto the measure, the President would then expect support for some proposal he favors — maybe even one with a huge price tag — that the congressman or senator might otherwise oppose. There is no assurance whatsoever that line item veto power would result in less spending by government; it could actually trigger additional spending.

The problem even the most honorable proponents of the line item veto seek to address is far more fundamental than this or that federal spending project. It is that government has become too large, too involved in areas it has no authority to enter, and too open to political deal-making. Since government has become for many the ultimate guarantor of income, health, housing, pensions, etc., budgets should be expected to balloon, taxes should be expected to rise, and the Treasury should be expected to be either empty or running in the red.

The presidential line item veto is another form of tinkering with the Constitution. While some proponents favor it in the belief that it would reduce government spending, they are avoiding the fundamental problem of too much government, ignoring conspiratorial forces working to build totalitarian socialism, and opening the way for the concentration of power in the executive branch.

Term Limitations

Another favored stratagem of the quick-fix brigade is to limit the number of terms any politician may serve. Those who favor it claim that replacing older big spenders with new individuals will result in better government. But there is no evidence whatsoever to back up their claim. Limiting the term of the President has not resulted in better chief executives, only more of them.

---

30. Donald L. Robinson, Editor, *Reforming American Government: The Bicentennial Papers of the Committee on the Constitutional System*, (Boulder, CO: Westview Press, 1985).

The problem with the quality of those in office is the quality of understanding amongst the electorate voting for them. If the people have little knowledge of what constitutes good government, they will send newer big spenders to replace those presently serving. They will treat the symptom, not the problem.

There is little sense in passing legislation to limit the number of terms (and especially none in amending the Constitution for such a purpose) when voters can limit the time in office of any House member every 24 months, and any senator every six years. If someone in office isn't adhering to the solemn oath to stand by the Constitution, he or she can be ousted on election day.

The founding fathers expected the people to keep themselves well-informed and to reward good performance by reelecting deserving officeholders and retiring others. But enacting term limitations will force out good elected officials as well as bad. Alexander Hamilton addressed this very issue while deploring the idea of term limitations because it would force out of office any number of capable and experienced legislators. He said:

> Can it be wise to put this desirable and essential quality under the ban of the Constitution, and to declare that the moment [experience] is acquired, its possessor shall be compelled to abandon the station in which it was acquired and to which it is adapted?[31]

Moreover, limiting terms strikes a blow at accountability. With a more rapid turnover of elected officials, voters would increasingly be forced to make their choices based on candidate rhetoric and promises rather than performance. Fewer office holders would have to stand before the electorate and defend their records.

Term limits aren't the answer, and will even do more harm than good. There is no substitute for an informed electorate. Which is why we are so enthusiastic about the TRIM program discussed in Chapter 13.

---

31. Hamilton, Madison and Jay, *The Federalist Papers*, op. cit., Essay #72. See also Don Fotheringham, "Revolving Socialists," (Appleton, WI: TRIM, 1990).

H. Ross Perot

Where H. Ross Perot will be positioned when you read this is anyone's guess. His meteoric rise to political prominence in 1992 saw him taking stands that placed him all over the political spectrum. But one of his more disturbing stands has been given little publicity. Simply stated: Ross Perot has given up on America's system of government.

Several months before jumping into the 1992 presidential race, Perot told a Florida audience that the Constitution was outmoded and "Our system of government is the problem.... You've got to change the system."[32] On January 28, 1993, he stated during an appearance on the CBS *This Morning* program: "Only two more states as I understand it are needed to force a constitutional convention. I am certain that the members of United We Stand America in their sleep can get those other two states." He ignored the actions of three states (Alabama, Florida, and Louisiana) that have withdrawn earlier calls for a constitutional convention. Because of these withdrawals, con-con proponents need formal convention calls in at least five more states.

Perot may insist that the system isn't working, but the real problem is that the system is being ignored by all branches of government. It doesn't need fixing, it needs enforcement. A man as bright as Perot should be aware that a constitutional convention would allow determined enemies to scrap the document completely. He should also know that there is no such thing as a "limited" constitutional convention. Those who claim that it can be held to only one topic are wrong. A constitutional convention is a sovereign body with the power to discard the entire Constitution that has been in place since its ratification in 1789.[33]

---

32. Speech before the Coalition for Better Government, Tampa, Florida, November 2, 1991, excerpts published in *The New American*, May 4, 1992.
33. For perspective about the threat of a constitutional convention, see Don Fotheringham "Silent Crisis," Appleton, WI: The John Birch Society, February 1, 1990; Fotheringham, "The Con-Con Network," Appleton, WI: *The New American*, February 10, 1992, pp. 19-26; and Fotheringham, "Testimony Before Louisiana Legislature, House and Government Affairs Committee," May 12, 1993, *JBS Bulletin*, July 1993, pp. 15-18.

Beyond his attitude about the Constitution, his many pronouncements on other topics lead to the conclusion that he's not for less government; he's for efficient government. He called for "strategic plans on an industry-by-industry basis" in an August 30, 1992 column he wrote for the *New York Times*. He even wants a government-created national energy policy when leaving producers alone is the answer to America's energy dependency.[34] These ideas are chillingly reminiscent of Benito Mussolini's socialist plans for Italy.

Perot enthusiasts ought to be asking why a man who claims to be on the side of the ordinary taxpayer would donate $3,000 to the Democratic Senatorial Campaign Committee, which works constantly to elect or reelect liberal big spenders such as Ted Kennedy, Joe Biden, and Paul Simon. Or why he would send the maximum allowable contribution of $1,000 to tax-spend-deficit legislators like Representative Dan Rostenkowski, Senator Frank Lautenberg, and Representative Martin Frost.[35] Or why, if Perot were such an opponent of the way government was being run, President George Bush would write a letter seconding the man's candidacy for membership in the Council on Foreign Relations.[36]

On March 21, 1993, Perot purchased 30 minutes of prime television time to draw attention to mounting federal debt and deficits but also to introduce his "National Referendum." One of its questions asked if the President should present a statement of his overall plan to the people *before* taxes are raised. Mr. Perot is obviously committed to having the American people pay more taxes. Other questions subtly promoted a balanced budget amendment and term limitations for Congress, more tinkering with the Constitution that avoids the fundamental problems plaguing this nation.

Perot's critics frequently chide him for having the attitude that

---

34. Ross Perot, "How Stupid Do They Think We Are?" *New York Times*, August 30, 1992.
35. William F. Jasper, "Who Is Henry Ross Perot?", *The New American*, May 4, 1992.
36. "Washington Wire," *Wall Street Journal*, May 29, 1992.

money can buy anything. One such critic is retired Marine Lieutenant Colonel Oliver North. In his book *Under Fire*, North told
of receiving intense pressure to "absolve" President Reagan of any
knowledge of the Iran-Contra transactions. He mentioned receiving visits and communications from numerous individuals in and
out of government, all for the purpose of convincing him to do
what he could to exonerate the President. One such individual
was Ross Perot.

Under Fire tells of Perot's protestations to North's lawyer,
Brendan Sullivan. The book recounts Perot's request to Sullivan
followed by North's comments:

> "... why doesn't Ollie just end this thing and explain to the FBI
> that the President didn't know. If he goes to jail, I'll take care of his
> family. And I'll be happy to give him a job when he gets out."
>
> That's just like Ross, I thought when I heard his offer. He thinks
> money can buy everything.
>
> Six days later, Perot was back. This time he met with Brendan
> and me together, but the message was the same: I should forfeit my
> Fifth Amendment rights and make a statement that "cleared" the
> President.
>
> I find it hard to believe that Ross Perot was acting on his own.
> But if anyone sent him, they left no fingerprints. [37]

Perot's strong opposition to the North American Free Trade
Agreement (NAFTA) had him on the right side of an issue but he
blamed congressional enthusiasm for it on the power of "lobby-
ists for foreign interests," not on the power of new world order
enthusiasts within our own government. NAFTA has little to do
with free trade but everything to do with creating economic union
among several nations, including the United States. Economic
union, of course, precedes political union, the ultimate goal of new
world order supporters. Gathering several unions of nations into
a world government would be a great deal easier for the conspira-

---

37. Oliver North, *Under Fire*, (New York, NY: Harper Collins, 1991), pp. 15-16.

tors than luring nearly 200 independent nations into their web one at a time.

Our nation desperately needs elected officials who are fiscal conservatives, defenders of the Constitution, and champions of less government. Ross Perot simply doesn't qualify.

Bankruptcy 1995

One of the most talked-about books in recent years hit hard at the threat to America posed by the soaring national debt. Written by industrialist Harry Figgie Jr. with help from Arizona University professor Gerald J. Swanson, the book predicts that in only a few more years, the U.S. government will have to spend all of its income tax receipts just for interest on the nation's debt, and will be bankrupt.[38]

The book's projections are realistic, and forecasting bankruptcy for America by 1995 is not terribly far-fetched. Figgie, who has been crusading in his own way against deficits for years, then concludes that hyperinflation is inevitable. He convincingly reports on the horrifying consequences of such a development as it occurred in Argentina, Brazil and elsewhere.

But Figgie's book, like many others, completely avoids the conspiratorial design guiding America's descent into debt. Conspirators don't want the chaos of hyperinflation here, only the threat of it. Far more likely is the continued steady erosion of the nation's financial well-being accompanied by reasonable-sounding proposals that will propel America into the new world order. More taxation, inflation, deficits, controls, regulations, and bureaucracy are paving the way for entry into economic unions, and then the establishment of an iron-fisted world monetary system as part of a world government.

Presenting solutions that are naive at best and misleading at worst, *Bankruptcy 1995* leaves a lot to be desired. For instance, its authors accept all of the nation's socialistic programs as if they

---

38. Harry E. Figgie, Jr. and Gerald J. Swanson, Ph.D., *Bankruptcy 1995* (Boston, MA: Little, Brown and Company, 1992).

are carved in stone, complaining only that they are run poorly. "We can reduce costs simply by doing the same jobs more efficiently," they maintain.[39] Can federal welfare, housing, transportation, energy and foreign aid programs really be run efficiently? Can any federal bureaucracy? But even if all of the government's existing bureaucracies were run efficiently, their stifling effect will still drive this nation toward bankruptcy.

Nor do we harbor any enthusiasm for *Bankruptcy 1995's* heavy emphasis on the President's Private Sector Survey on Cost Control, the Grace Commission (on which Figgie served), as the way out of red ink. While everyone should be desirous of putting an end to government waste, expecting a huge bureaucracy to run without it is ludicrous. And expecting to balance the budget and then pay off the enormous national debt merely by attacking waste is even more absurd.

The authors of this best seller point out that entitlement programs are already consuming a huge portion of the federal budget and then proceed to praise their origin, Lyndon Johnson's Great Society program, as "a noble cause, to be sure, but the timing was disastrous."[40]

Noble cause? Timing the only problem? On January 15, 1964, President Johnson stated his overall intention regarding the Great Society in a White House speech he delivered to leaders of several organizations of senior citizens. He said:

> We are going to take all the money we think is unnecessarily being spent and take it from the "haves" and give it to the "have-nots" that need it so much.[41]

Florida Congressman William Cramer correctly characterized that statement as "a direct attack on free enterprise, on individual initiative, and on constitutional government as we know and enjoy it." He considered it to be "one of the most radical state-

---

39. Ibid., p. 141.
40. Ibid., p. 27.
41. *Congressional Record*, February 6, 1964, p. 2227.

ments ever made by a Chief Executive of the United States." And he added: "It goes beyond the wildest pronouncements of former liberal administrations. It is an affront to Americans everywhere."[42] He could have added that such a statement contains the thinking of every socialist.

But the worst part of President Johnson's revolutionary intention is that, with the help of Congress, he succeeded in gaining passage of a number of his Great Society programs. Harry Figgie says a great deal about his own perception of the American system and the proper role of government when he calls the Johnson program "a noble cause" that was only deficient because of its "timing." Great Society programs have led inexorably to America's monstrous debt and to our nation's plunge toward totalitarian socialism.

The Figgie book's definition of inflation, "more money chasing the same amount of goods and services," is also deficient. It leaves the door open for blaming the nation's producers for higher prices because they didn't produce enough. And it fails totally to expose the thievery and destruction that inflation accomplishes.

Figgie proposes appointing a Constitution-skirting "general" who would lead an army "numbering perhaps 1,000 to 1,500 souls" in an effort "to attack and defeat the deficit."[43] In other words, forget the Constitution, give Congress and the President a breather from their responsibility and the public's wrath, and turn the nation's well-being over to efficiency experts. *Nowhere in this book are there any calls for demanding that Congress obey the Constitution and abolish unauthorized programs.*

To write the Foreword for their book, Figgie selected retired Senator Warren Rudman, the CFR member who never distinguished himself as a serious opponent of debt.

The Impact of Talk Shows

One of the best remaining examples of a free press in America is the radio (and television) talk show. While the popularity of

---

42. Ibid.
43. Figgie and Swanson, op. cit., p. 140.

these shows can hardly be denied, their value in restoring sanity to our nation has frequently been overblown. For providing a mere introduction to views regularly suppressed by the Establishment and its conspiratorial allies, some of these shows do a fine job. Many others, however, supply credibility to views that range from "off the wall" to downright false.

Perhaps the most popular talkshow host in the history of this industry is Rush Limbaugh, now being heard on over 600 stations every weekday. He also has a television show, a newsletter, and two best-selling books. Limbaugh holds many views shared by conservative Americans although he is fiercely opposed to the mere mention of conspiracy. He bashes Democrats unmercifully and regularly suggests that Republicans have the answers for America. The truth, of course, is that each party is dominated by bad influences and that party labels in America have meant little or nothing for decades.

It's Limbaugh's show, of course, and he certainly has the right to accept or reject the opinions of some of his listeners. While Limbaugh partisans have elevated the man to unwarranted heights as a national political leader, others are finding out that he is far more superficial in his thinking than he would have listeners believe. His strong support for foreign aid disqualifies him as a principled conservative.

But, as he himself has insisted, Limbaugh is primarily an entertainer. If ratings and public popularity are any indication of his talent, he is a good one. Entertainment, however, is not going to solve America's problems.

The May/June 1993 issue of *The Saturday Evening Post* featured an article about this man. Author John McCollister quotes him as saying, "First and foremost I want to be an entertainer." The article then adds Limbaugh's conviction that people "listen to radio for three reasons: 1) to be entertained, 2) to be entertained, 3) to be entertained."[44] So he's an entertainer whom liber-

---

44. John McCollister, "The Rush Is On," *Saturday Evening Post*, May/June 1993, p. 54 et seq.

als generally find outrageous and whom many middle-of-the-road and conservative Americans enjoy.

It's sad but true that to be successful in the radio talkshow business at Limbaugh's level, one has to knuckle under to the conspiracy's party line. He can go only so far, promote none but silently sanctioned notions, dignify only some ideas and groups. He must submit to an iron-clad form of political correctness. Limbaugh knows this better than anyone. But at least he's honest about his main intention — to be an entertainer.

Truth-starved Americans aren't going to get the full story from Rush Limbaugh.

No Easy Way Out

There are numerous other books, organizations, and quick-fix gimmicks regularly paraded before the American people. Some are the efforts of honorable patriots with whom we merely find ourselves in disagreement about tactics. But, as we stated previously, the problems of too much government (taxation, control, bureaucracy, regulations) cannot be solved overnight.

What America needs is a sharp increase in citizen awareness undergirded with a solid understanding of conspiratorial tactics designed to keep good citizens placated with empty promises, meaningless busywork, and false alternatives.

Many more citizens of this great land have to be brought to understand what freedom is, and what it is not. They must realize that it is being deliberately stolen from them by their own government leaders, and that they have the power to force change: They can force their elected officials to obey the Constitution.

There is no short cut. There is no overnight solution. There is, instead, a need for the hard work of educating, organizing, and motivating many fellow citizens.

Longtime Socialist Party leader Norman Thomas was delighted to see his program adopted by Republicans and Democrats.

A congressman during the 1930s, Samuel Pettengill warned about government's turn to the Left in his book, *Smoke-Screen*.

Warren Rudman, who voted for numerous big-spending proposals as a senator, is now a leader of the Concord Coalition.

CFR Chairman Peter G. Peterson went from the Nixon Cabinet to the Socialist International to leadership in the Establishment.

Katharine Graham, the top official at *Newsweek* and the *Washington Post*, participated in the Brandt Commission.

William Bennett helped to fund studies about Marxism and led the unconstitutional Department of Education.

Former congressman Jack Kemp wants to be known as a conservative but once told the press to consider him a "big-L liberal."

H. Ross Perot supports government planning "on an industry-by-industry basis," an idea once proposed by Benito Mussolini.

Liberal Chicago-area Congressman Dan Rostenkowski has
received campaign financial assistance from H. Ross Perot.

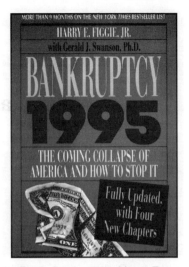

In *Bankruptcy 1995*, Harry Figgie
shows how deeply in debt the nation has become, but fails to point
to the Constitution as the solution.

Lyndon Johnson's Great Society
programs were praised by Figgie
as "a noble cause" the "timing"
of which wasn't right.

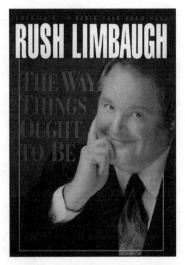

Popular talk-show host Rush
Limbaugh, author of a best-
seller, insists that he is mainly an
"entertainer."

CHAPTER 15

Which Way America?

The battle, sir, is not to the strong alone; it is to the vigilant, the active, the brave.

— Patrick Henry
March 23, 1775

Americans, here's where we are. Our leaders are working overtime to lead us right up to the door of national bankruptcy — right up to it but not through it. They have long sought to have the American people *choose* to become enslaved. They want us to *vote* ourselves into the new world order.

When we're softened up by a declining living standard, fear of bankruptcy, and years of propaganda telling us how hard government officials have worked to ward off imminent collapse, we will be told that there's no other alternative but a world monetary system and a world government. Of course, it will also be a world tyranny, but that will be kept quiet for a time.

This nation is staggering when it used to sprint. Soon it will be unable even to stagger. And the attitude of those in charge is that there is no alternative to their leadership while they continue to do more of what got us into the mess in the first place.

Consider: The Clinton medicine for an over-taxed citizenry, horrendous indebtedness, and escalating entitlement programs is more taxes, more debt, and more entitlements. Over the first five years of the President's highly touted "deficit reduction package" (whose "reduction" is merely a lowering of a previously issued projected deficit), there will be $247 billion more in taxes (the largest single tax increase in U.S. history), $313 billion more in government spending, and $1.1 trillion added to the national debt.[1] And adding national health care to the list of entitlements will only rocket federal expenditures skyward.

Yes, they're trying. But they aren't trying to do what their rhetoric conveys. They aren't trying to put America's fiscal house in order; they're doing just the opposite.

Throughout this book, we have suggested what government could do to stop the bleeding. But the bleeding continues. As we stated above, plans exist to bring the nation to the brink of bankruptcy — so that the new world order will be seen as the only plausible alternative.

Therefore, America is at a crossroads. Continuing down our present road will have tragic consequences similar to those experienced by the Hart family in the scenario we painted in Chapter 1. In the real world of today, *your* job is at stake and *your* home is threatened. Those who want a new age and a new world order even want your children. In fact, everything's on the line. Individual freedom, national sovereignty, personal assets, even life itself. The kind of future being planned for Americans is unthinkable, yet it looms on the horizon.

Make no mistake about the goals of the those who would rule us. They want our property; they intend to enslave us; they mean to convert the United States into a mere province in a UN-led world tyranny; they will use their ill-gotten power to eliminate anyone who gets in the way. And they are winning.

Over 50 years ago, famed British playwright George Bernard Shaw, a determined leader of the British Fabian Society, bared the totalitarian fangs lurking behind all socialist rhetoric. In his *The Intelligent Woman's Guide to Socialism and Capitalism*, he indicated the kind of future he had in mind. Here's what he wrote:

You would be forcibly fed, clothed, lodged, taught, and employed

---

1. In August 1993, Senator Richard Shelby (D-AL) refused to vote for the "deficit reduction package" offered by his fellow Democrat. He said: "The first year has nine dollars of tax increases for every dollar of spending cuts. The second year has seven dollars in tax increases for every two dollars of cuts, and so forth. The great majority of the spending cuts are in the out years. And I doubt that they will ever happen."

whether you liked it or not. If it were discovered that you had not character and industry enough to be worth all this trouble, you might possibly be executed in a kindly manner;..."[2]

The truth is that there's no future worth living if Shaw and others like him aren't stopped. Don't for a moment think that life in their world will be anything but hell on earth.

Such a fate is not inevitable, however. Our future does not have to resemble "a boot stamping on a human face forever." We don't have to fall victim to totalitarian government. We don't have to lose our freedom.

To stop what's being designed for our future, we must first get out of our minds any hope that current leaders will abandon their plans of their own volition. Their agenda is clear. It has to be blocked by aroused and determined Americans who will spend the time, energy, and resources to take their country back.

The Battleground Isn't in Washington

Next, we have to realize that there's a war going on. It's not the usual kind of war against a clearly visible enemy who declares his intention, aims his weapons, and stations his troops at our doorstep. This is a war from within, a war against the American people waged by smooth-talking but deceitful leaders, a war whose very existence remains hidden to most.

Ultimately, who wins and who loses in this epic struggle will be decided by what happens in the cities and towns of this nation, not in the nation's capital. The decision will be made in the highest court in the land — which isn't the Supreme Court but the court of public opinion. If the sleeping giant of public awareness is stirred to action, it can tell those we send to Washington: *We've had enough of economic and political betrayal; either cease destroying this nation and start working to break the back of the conspiracy threatening our future, or we'll get someone else to do the job.*

---

2. George Bernard Shaw, *The Intelligent Woman's Guide to Socialism and Capitalism* (NY: Brentano's Inc., 1928), p. 470.

You know what needs to be done. Don't wait for some day in the hazy future to get started doing it. The threat to life, liberty and property continues to increase as more debt, more controls, and more moves toward UN control are added almost daily. If we do nothing, or if we get caught up in the conspiracy's web, the cost will be immense.

Nor should anyone consider fleeing to some other land to get away from tightening government domination. The conspirators haven't overlooked building their power and influence elsewhere. Ask yourself: Where would one go to escape their grasp?

Thirty years ago, a refugee from Castro's totalitarianism fled to the United States only to discover that what he risked his life to get away from was being duplicated here. When it was suggested to him that Americans were very fortunate to be living in a free country, he shot back: "You're not as fortunate as I was; I had somewhere else to go. You can't escape; you must stand and fight if you want to be free."

It's Decision Time!

Here's are the choices before us:

1. **Get Busy and Take Our Country Back.** The result: A return to constitutionally limited government, freedom in the market place, the productive sector unshackled, undiluted national sovereignty, less taxation, more productivity, more jobs, and honest money. Also, national prosperity, a surge in responsible citizenship, and the promise of a brighter future.

2. **Do Nothing and Allow the Conspiracy to Succeed.** The result: A sharp reduction in the standard of living accompanied by the suppression of God-given rights to speak, publish, worship, assemble, bear arms, own property, etc. Also, a world order brutally administered by agents of the world government — some of whom would be the children of once complacent Americans — in the same manner that enforcers of the Twentieth Century's most oppressive regimes carried out the will of their masters. That's not the kind of world anyone should ever have to tolerate, and certainly not the kind a parent wants to leave for a child.

Having read this book, you have seen a portion of the evidence showing that deeply entrenched enemies are remaking our nation according to their diabolical designs. They are succeeding because too many of us have ceased being vigilant. Too many have enjoyed freedom and forgotten that it must always be guarded and fought for. What most Americans believed could never happen is happening right before their eyes. This isn't the way anyone proud of the label "American" should behave.

So, it's decision time. You know the problem and you have a real, workable solution. Because no problem ever goes away of its own accord, you and others like you all across this land have to address it and solve it. Not with half-hearted efforts and punch-pulling timidity, but with courage and determination. The enemy has great strength but, as Patrick Henry stated, the battle indeed is to the vigilant, the active, the brave.

Wage it for yourself, for your loved ones, for generations yet to come. But wage it — now!

Patrick Henry said that the battle was to "the vigilant, the active, the brave."

Socialist Bernard Shaw wrote that under socialism those who were not worth the trouble might "be executed in a kindly manner."

America is at a crossroads. What responsible citizens do now will determine whether our legacy of freedom is passed on to future generations or allowed to be stolen from us.

Appendix

There is a power somewhere so organized, so subtle, so watchful, so interlocked, so pervasive that they better not speak above their breath when they speak in condemnation of it.

— President Woodrow Wilson[1]

President Bill Clinton is a Rhodes Scholar, holds membership in the Council on Foreign Relations, is now listed by the Trilateral Commission as a "former member in public service," and attended the 1991 Bilderberger Conference held in Baden-Baden, Germany. He admitted none of this during his presidential campaign and, instead, presented himself as merely the hard-working governor of a small state. He is another in a long line of international socialists whose commitment to the new world order's world government and economic control makes his swearing an oath to "preserve, protect and defend" the U.S. Constitution a complete mockery.

*   *   *

The **Council on Foreign Relations** (CFR) was founded during the period 1919-1921 by President Woodrow Wilson's close confidant, Edward Mandell House. In his 1912 book, *Philip Dru, Administrator*, House stated that was seeking "Socialism as dreamed of by Karl Marx." From its outset, the Council has sought to lead the United States into Marxian socialism, and then into world government.

The December 1922 issue of the CFR's *Foreign Affairs* contained a lament about the existence of "fifty or sixty independent states" and a call for "world government." This CFR objective appears throughout succeeding decades, though perhaps never so explicitly stated as when CFR member Richard N. Gardner ex-

---

1. Woodrow Wilson, *The New Freedom* (New York, NY: Doubleday, Page, 1914), p. 13.

plained in "The Hard Road To World Order" (*Foreign Affairs*, Fall 1974) that "an end run around national sovereignty, eroding it piece by piece, will accomplish much more than the old-fashioned frontal assault."

Chaired for many years by banker David Rockefeller, the current CFR leader is Peter G. Peterson, a cabinet official from the Nixon Administration. Members of the organization have dominated the U.S. government and the mass media for decades. As of June 1992, the organization listed 2,905 members, 387 of whom were "U.S. government officials," and 327 of whom were "journalists, correspondents and communications executives" (leaders of the mass media). Most of the Clinton cabinet officers are CFR members. The CFR seeks to arrive at the goal of world government through the political/foreign policy arena. The organization strongly supports the United Nations.

*　　*　　*

The **Trilateral Commission** (TC) was the brainchild of CFR member Zbigniew Brzezinski, whose 1970 book *Between Two Ages* outlined his thinking. In the book, the future director of national security for the Carter Administration claimed that the United States was becoming obsolete and called for central planning on a worldwide scale. After suggesting that three areas of the industrialized world (U.S., Western Europe, and Japan) become linked, the book proposed world government.

In 1973, David Rockefeller formed the TC according to the Brzezinski outline. He then hired the former Columbia University professor to lead the organization. The two men enlisted TC members, never more than 300 total. One of the first U.S. members was Jimmy Carter, who campaigned deceitfully as an "outsider" with no ties to the Establishment, was a TC member at the time, and later filled his administration with TC/CFR members.

Among many Clinton Administration cabinet officers who are TC members can be found Secretary of State Warren Christopher, Secretary of the Interior Bruce Babbitt, Secretary of Health and Human Services Donna Shalala, and Secretary of Housing and Urban Development Henry Cisneros. The TC works for world government primarily in the sphere of economics. Like the CFR, the organization is strongly supportive of the United Nations.

* * *

The **Rhodes Scholar Program** grew out of the desires and financial backing of Cecil J. Rhodes. Bill Clinton's mentor at Georgetown University, Carroll Quigley, wrote that "the scholarships were merely a facade to conceal the secret society" founded by Rhodes and others that led to the formation of the CFR. [2]

According to Quigley, Rhodes directed in his will that the purpose of the scholarships and the secret society of which he was a leading figure was "the ultimate recovery of the United States of America as an integral part of the British Empire." [3] That goal is completely incompatible with the oath of office taken by any U.S. official.

The overall Rhodes goal, according to Quigley, was "nothing less than to create a world system of financial control in private hands able to dominate the political system of each country and the economy of the world as a whole." [4]

In addition to Mr. Clinton, prominent Rhodes scholars — not all of whom are necessarily in sympathy with the entire Rhodes program — include Secretary of Labor Robert Reich, CIA Director James Woolsey, Assistant Secretary of State Strobe Talbott, New Jersey Senator Bill Bradley, Oklahoma Senator David Boren, Indiana Senator Richard Lugar, Maryland Senator Paul Sarbanes, South Dakota Senator Larry Pressler, presidential adviser George Stephanopoulos, and Supreme Court Justice David Souter.

* * *

The **Bilderberg Conference** is an annual three-day gathering of approximately 100 of the western world's leaders in the fields of finance, government, business, labor, and education. Launched by David Rockefeller and Holland's Prince Bernhard

---

2. Carroll Quigley, *The Anglo-American Establishment* (New York, NY: Books In Focus, 1981) p. 33.

3. Ibid., p. 33.

4. Carroll Quigley, *Tragedy and Hope*, op. cit., p. 324.

in 1954 at the Hotel de Bilderberg (hence the name of the group) in Oosterbeek, Holland, each conference is held in deep secrecy at one of the world's plushest resorts. No reporters are allowed, and no information is made public about topics discussed or conclusions reached.

Prince Bernhard was forced out of Bilderberg leadership in 1976 as a consequence of his participation in a bribery scandal. But before his departure, he admitted against interest that a topic of Bilderberg discussion was "a change in the world-role of the United States."[5] In keeping with the world-government designs of the group, he told his own biographer, Alden Hatch, of the difficulty of leading "people who have been brought up on the idea of nationalism to the idea of relinquishing part of their sovereignty to a supranational body."[6] Bilderberg attendees can be counted on to support the United Nations.

Bilderberg veterans from the United States include David Rockefeller, Henry Kissinger, Robert McNamara, Gerald Ford, Zbigniew Brzezinski, George Ball, Robert L. Bartley, Peter G. Peterson, Paul Nitze, Cyrus Vance, Vernon Jordan, Walter Mondale and many others.

---

5. *Rutland (VT) Herald*, April 20, 1971. The report in this newspaper followed the April 1971 meeting of the Bilderbergers at Laurance Rockefeller's Woodstock Inn in Woodstock, Vermont.

6. Alden Hatch, *Bernhard, Prince of the Netherlands* (New York, NY: Doubleday, 1962).

Bibliography

Allen, Gary. *Richard Nixon: The Man Behind the Mask*. Appleton, WI: Western Islands, 1971.

———. *Say "No!" To the New World Order*. Seal Beach, CA: Concord Press, 1987.

——— with Larry Abraham. *None Dare Call It Conspiracy*. Seal Beach, CA: Concord Press, 1971.

American Institute For Economic Research. *Why Gold?*. Great Barrington, MA: American Institute For Economic Research, 1965.

Anderson, Benjamin J. *Economics and the Public Welfare*. New York, NY: D. Van Nostrand Company, 1949.

Bastiat, Frederic. *The Law*. Irvington-On Hudson, NY: The Foundation for Economic Education, 1972.

Batten, Samuel Zane. *The New World Order*. Philadelphia, PA: American Baptist Publication Society, 1919.

Bergsten, C. Fred. *Reforming the Dollar: An International Monetary Policy For the United States*. New York, NY: Council on Foreign Relations, 1972.

Brzezinski, Zbigniew. *Between Two Ages: America's Role In the Technetronic Era*. New York, NY: Viking Press, 1970.

Budget of the United States Government, Fiscal Year 1993. Washington, DC: U.S. Government Printing Office, 1992.

Budget of the United States Government, Fiscal Year 1994. Washington, DC: U.S. Government Printing Office, 1993.

Carson, Clarence B. *Basic Economics*. Wadley, AL: American Textbook Committee, 1988.

Carter, Jimmy. *Why Not the Best?*. Nashville, TN: Boardman Press, 1975.

Constitution of the United States of America. Appleton, WI: American Opinion.

Corti, Count Egon Caesar. *The Rise of the House of Rothschild*. Appleton, WI: Western Islands edition, 1972.

Cuddy, Dennis L. *The New World Order: A Critique and a Chronology*. Milford, PA: America's Future, 1992.

Figgie, Harry E. Jr. *Bankruptcy 1995*. Boston, MA: Little, Brown and Company, 1992.

Flynn, John T. *The Road Ahead*. New York, NY: Devin-Adair Company, 1949, 1961.

Garrett, Garet. *The People's Pottage*. Caldwell, Idaho: Caxton Printers, Inc., 1953.

Goldwater, Barry M. *With No Apologies*. New York, NY: William Morrow and Company, 1979.

Greaves, Percy L. *Understanding the Dollar Crisis*. Appleton, WI: Western Islands, 1973.

———. *Mises Made Easier*. Dobbs Ferry, NY: Free Market Books, 1974

Griffin, G. Edward. *The Fearful Master*. Appleton, WI: Western Islands, 1964.

———. *A Survival Course On Money*. Westlake Village, CA: American Media, 1985.

Hazlitt, Henry. *Economics In One Lesson*. New York, NY: Crown Publishers, Inc., 1979.

———. *What You Should Know About Inflation*. New York, NY: Funk and Wagnalls, 1968.

Hicks, Frederick Charles. *The New World Order*. Garden City, NY: Doubleday, Page and Company, 1920.

Hoar, William P. *Architects of Conspiracy*. Appleton, WI: Western Islands, 1984.

Jasper, William F. *Global Tyranny ... Step By Step*. Appleton, WI: Western Islands, 1992.

Kelly, Rev. Clarence. *Conspiracy Against God and Man*. Appleton, WI: Western Islands, 1974.

Lee, Robert W. *The United Nations Conspiracy*. Appleton, WI: Western Islands, 1981.

Lindbergh, Charles A. Sr. *The Economic Pinch*. Philadelphia. PA: Dorrance and Company, 1923.

Manion, Clarence. *Let's Face It!* South Bend, IN: The Manion Forum, 1956.

Martin, Rose L. *Fabian Freeway*. Appleton, WI: Western Islands, 1966.

Marx, Karl and Engels, Frederick. *The Communist Manifesto*. Appleton, WI: The John Birch Society, 1990.

McDonald, Lawrence P. *We Hold These Truths*. Marietta, GA: Larry McDonald Memorial Foundation, 1976, 1992.

McManus, John F. *The Insiders, Architects of the New World Order*. Appleton, WI: The John Birch Society, 1992.

Morton, Frederic. *The Rothschilds, A Family Portrait*. New York, NY: Atheneum, 1962.

North, Oliver. *Under Fire*. New York, NY: Harper Collins, 1991.

Orwell, George. *Animal Farm*. New York, NY: Signet Classics, The New American Library Edition, 1946.

———. *Nineteen Eighty-Four*. New York, NY: Harcourt Brace Jovanovich, 1949.

Paul, Ron. *Ten Myths About Paper Money*. Lake Jackson, TX: Foundation for Rational Economics and Education, 1983.

——— and Lewis Lehrman. *The Case For Gold*. Washington, DC: Cato Institute, 1982.

Perloff, James. *The Shadows of Power*. Appleton, WI: Western Islands, 1988.

Pettengill, Samuel. *Smokescreen*. Kingsport, TN: Southern Publishers, Inc., 1940.

Quigley, Carroll. *Tragedy and Hope: A History of the World in Our Time*. New York, NY: Macmillan, 1966.

———. *The Anglo-American Establishment*. New York, NY: Books In Focus, 1981.

Rabushka, Alvin. *From Adam Smith To the Wealth of America*. New Brunswick, NJ: Transaction Books, 1985.

Ricardo, David. *The Principles Of Political Economy and Taxation*. New York, NY: E.P. Dutton, 1911.

Rothbard, Murray N. *What Has Government Done To Our Money?*. Novato, CA: Libertarian Publishers, 1981.

———. *The Mystery of Banking*. New York, NY: Richardson and Snyder, 1983.

Schlafly, Phyllis with Chester Ward. *Kissinger On the Couch*.

New Rochelle, NY: Arlington House, 1975.

Sennholz, Hans F. *Age of Inflation*. Appleton, WI: Western Islands, 1979.

Shaw, George Bernard. *The Intelligent Woman's Guide to Socialism and Capitalism*. NY: Brentano's, Inc., 1928.

Shirer, William L. *The Rise and Fall Of the Third Reich*. New York, NY: Simon and Schuster, 1960.

Sklar, Holly. *Trilateralism*. Boston, MA: South End Press, 1980.

Skousen, W. Cleon. *The Naked Capitalist*. Salt Lake City, UT: Skousen, 1970.

Smith, Adam. *The Wealth of Nations*. New York, NY: Penguin Books, 1970.

Smoot, Dan. *The Invisible Government*. Dallas, TX: Dan Smoot Report, Inc., 1962.

Soddy, Frederick. *Wealth, Virtual Wealth and Debt*. London, George Allen & Unwin, 1926.

Sundquist, James. *Reforming American Government*: The Bicentennial Papers of the Committee on the Constitutional System. Edited by Donald L. Robinson. Boulder CO: Westview Press, 1985.

Turk, James. *Social Security: Lies, Myths and Reality*. Greenwich, CT: Greenfield Books, 1992.

Vieira, Edwin Jr. *Pieces Of Eight*. Fort Lee, NJ: Sound Dollar Committee, 1983.

von Mises, Ludwig. *Human Action*. New Haven, CT: Yale University Press, 1949.

———. *The Theory of Money and Credit*. Irvington-on Hudson, NY: The Foundation For Economic Education, 1971.

Webster, Nesta. *World Revolution: The Plot Against Civilization*. London: Constable and Company, 1921.

Welch, Robert. *The Blue Book of The John Birch Society*. Appleton, WI: Western Islands, 1959,1992.

Wells, H.G. *The New World Order*. New York, NY: A.A. Knopf, 1940.

White, Andrew Dickson. *Fiat Money Inflation in France*. New York, NY: D. Appleton-Century Company, 1933.

Index

About the Author

John F. McManus graduated in 1957 with a Bachelor of Science degree in Physics from Holy Cross College in Worcester, Massachusetts. At graduation he received a commission as a Lieutenant, United States Marine Corps, and served on active duty for three years. For six years, he was employed as an electronics engineer in New England.

Mr. McManus joined the staff of the John Birch Society in 1966. In 1973, he became the organization's director of public relations and its chief media representative throughout the United States. He has appeared on hundreds of radio and television programs, including C-SPAN and the Larry King Show.

Also in 1973, Mr. McManus began writing and syndicating a weekly newspaper column entitled *The Birch Log*. He has authored and produced numerous audiovisual programs and written extensively for JBS-affiliated publications. His book *The Insiders* has gone through three editions. He is in wide demand as a speaker.

Mr. McManus is the publisher of *The New American* magazine, a biweekly journal of news and commentary. In June 1991, he was named President of the John Birch Society.

Recommended Reading

Global Tyranny ... Step By Step . . . . **pb $12.95**
WILLIAM F. JASPER — A counterpart to *Financial Terrorism*. Thoroughly documents the plan to build the United Nations into a world tyranny. Extremely compelling. (1992 ed., 350 pp.)

The Shadows Of Power . . . . **pb $10.95**
JAMES PERLOFF — An exposé of the Council on Foreign Relations and its tragic impact on American foreign policy. Compiled from the group's own documents. Highly recommended. (1988 ed., 266 pp.)

The Insiders . . . . **pb $3.00**
JOHN F. MCMANUS — A look at the powerful few who really dictate America's policies. Spotlights the Council on Foreign Relations and Trilateral Commission. (1992 ed., 144 pp.)

The Law . . . . **pb $3.95**
FREDERIC BASTIAT — Arguably the best essay ever written on the proper role of government. Bastiat, a French statesman and economist, confronted socialist tyranny in the middle 1800s. (75 pp.)

The Blue Book Of The John Birch Society . . . . **pb $5.95**
ROBERT WELCH — The transcript of the entire two-day presentation that launched this organization in 1958. (1992 ed., 202 pp.)

John Birch Society Introductory Packet **$5.00**
Numerous pamphlets analyzing current events, a sample *JBS Bulletin*, and a sample of *The New American* magazine.

The New American . . . . **(see below)**
The New American magazine, a biweekly publication affiliated with The John Birch Society, is must reading for those who would be truly informed about the plans and programs of the Insiders.

- **Six-months subscription** **$22.00**
- **One-year subscription** **$39.00**
  (Please contact *The New American* for foreign rates.)

Except for subscriptions to *The New American*, please add 15 percent for postage and handling ($2.00 minimum).

American Opinion Book Services
P.O. Box 8040 • Appleton, WI 54913
(Credit card orders accepted at 414–749–3783.)